Praise for Freedom and Accountability at Work

"This book deepens the ongoing economic and social dialogue about balancing wealth creation with core human values. The authors' words offer encouragement to people in organizations who choose to elevate their work by using it as a vehicle to discover and strengthen the links between identity and industry, passion and prosperity, meaning and marketability, service and success."

—Joseph A. Braidish, director, Kelley Executive Partners, Indiana University Kelley School of Business

"Peter Koestenbaum brings the full force of his intellectual prowess to bear on the major questions of human existence. His insights are priceless, even as they challenge some of our most deeply held assumptions about organizational life."

—Camden C. Danielson, executive director, Kelley Executive Partners, Indiana University

"This work is one of those rare business book breaks from the 'how to' . . . to the 'what if?'. Block and Koestenbaum provide the foundation for a philosophy of hope for the workplace for life, adding meaning to both."

—Howard Schultz, co-founder, The Learning Consortium

"This book is for the curious and the courageous. The curious will learn from a master philosopher and be intellectually challenged. The courageous will be asked to choose freedom and accountability. Be forewarned!"

—Charlotte Roberts, author, *Fifth Discipline Fieldbook,
The Dance of Change*

"Tired of being held—and holding others—accountable? Disappointed that your time management system didn't reduce your stress? Think freedom in the workplace is an oxymoron? Then get ready to go deep, and immerse yourself in the wisdom of Koestenbaum according to Block."

—Paul Anderson, dean, Northern California School for Managing and Leading Change

"I've taught Peter Koestenbaum's leadership philosophy all over the world . . . and it works! Its broad and all-encompassing . . . and brings a powerful message of hope to us in the workplace."

—**George I. Fitzpatrick,** The Authentic Leader, teacher and practitioner

"This is an important book by two important management thinkers. Peter Koestenbaum and Peter Block offer an alternative, if not an antidote, to the shallowness of 'speed, simplicity, and (unwarranted) self-confidence' by challenging managers to think about freedom and accountability."

—**Robert M. Fulmer,** co-author, *The Leadership Investment,*
Distinguished Visiting Professor, Graziadio School of Business,
Pepperdine University

Freedom and
Accountability at Work

ALSO BY PETER KOESTENBAUM

The Language of the Leadership Diamond® (videotape with Peter Block)

Leadership: The Inner Side of Greatness—A Philosophy for Leaders

The Heart of Business: Ethics, Power, and Philosophy

Is There an Answer to Death?

Managing Anxiety: The Power of Knowing Who You Are

The New Image of the Person: The Theory and Practice of Clinical Philosophy

Existential Sexuality: Choosing to Love

The Vitality of Death: Essays in Existential Psychology and Philosophy

ALSO BY PETER BLOCK

The Answer to How Is Yes: Acting on What Matters

Flawless Consulting: A Guide to Getting Your Expertise Used

The Empowered Manager: Positive Political Skills at Work

Stewardship: Choosing Service over Self-Interest

The Flawless Consulting Fieldbook and Companion: A Guide to Understanding Your Expertise

Freedom and Accountability at Work

APPLYING
PHILOSOPHIC INSIGHT
TO THE
REAL WORLD

PETER KOESTENBAUM
PETER BLOCK

JOSSEY-BASS/PFEIFFER
A Wiley Company
San Francisco

Published by

JOSSEY-BASS/PFEIFFER
A Wiley Company

350 Sansome St.
San Francisco, CA 94104-1342
415.433.1740; Fax 415.433.0499
800. 274.4434; Fax 800.569.0443

www.pfeiffer.com

Jossey-Bass/Pfeiffer is a registered trademark of Jossey-Bass Inc., A Wiley Company.

ISBN: 0-7879-5594-9

Library of Congress Cataloging-in-Publication Data

Koestenbaum, Peter, 1928—
    Freedom and accountability at work: applying philosophic insight to the real world /
Peter Koestenbaum, Peter Block.
      p. cm.
    Includes bibliographical references and index.
    ISBN 0-7879-5594-9 (alk. paper)
    1. Management—Philosophy. 2. Liberty. 3. Responsibility. I. Block, Peter. II. Title.
    HD31 .K5983 2001
    128—dc21

                                      2001002026

Printed in the United States of America

We at Jossey-Bass strive to use the most environmentally sensitive paper stocks available to us. Our pub-
lications are printed on acid-free recycled stock whenever possible, and our paper always meets or exceeds
minimum GPO and EPA requirements.

Acquiring Editor: Matthew Holt
Director of Development: Kathleen Dolan Davies
Developmental Editor: Leslie Stephen
Editor: Rebecca Taff
Senior Production Editor: Dawn Kilgore
Manufacturing Supervisor: Becky Carreño
Interior and Cover Design: Bruce Lundquist
Cover Art: Audrey Heard
Illustrations: Lotus Art

Printing   10   9 8 7 6 5 4 3 2 1

In memory of Jim and Jean

—*P. K.*

In memory of Ira Block

—*P. B.*

Contents

Note to the Reader

THIS BOOK IS WRITTEN in two voices. The heart of the book is the philosophy, research, and understanding of Peter Koestenbaum. What appears here is a restatement of selected chapters from two seminal books he wrote more than thirty years ago: *The Vitality of Death* (Greenwood Publishing, 1971) and *The New Image of the Person* (Greenwood Press, 1978). Originally addressed to the world of clinical philosophy and psychotherapy, these ideas are the foundational core of his current work with the Leadership Diamond® and his seminars and consultation with leaders from around the world. Koestenbaum has added to the insights of this seminal work by providing a summary and reflections on his experience in his Afterword and by explaining key terms and concepts in his final piece, A Short Glossary.

The second voice belongs to Peter Block, who selected the excerpts from the two books and revised them by both updating and redirecting much of the text to make it more meaningful to readers working in business and industry, education, government, health care, and other service organizations at the beginning of the twenty-first century.

The commentary that surrounds the philosophic discussion is also from Peter Block. Through his Prologue, Introduction, and introductions to the four parts, Block shares his thoughts about why philosophy is important for modern organizations. In his Implications following each major section, he outlines what would be different in our institutions if we took Koestenbaum's philosophy to heart. When the text refers to "Peter," it is referring to Peter Koestenbaum, spoken by Block.

Prologue:
The Time Is Right

THE INTENT OF THIS BOOK is to bring the depth and inward values of philosophy into the practical world. The book had its beginning twenty years ago. There have been very few times in my life when I knew at that instant that something in me was going to change. This moment was in 1980 during a lecture by a San Jose State professor named Peter Koestenbaum. Up to that moment in my life, I was focused on questions of how to make life work, how to make relationships work, how to make family work, how to make a business work. Questions of destiny, courage, and freedom were vague and off my field of vision. The experiences of aloneness, anxiety, and my woundedness I treated as problems to be endured or solved.

My belief was that a person could overcome these problems, and I was working hard to do just that. I had been in therapy, participated in personal development groups (even conducted them), worked hard on difficult relationships, and thought that at some point in life I would leave anxiety behind and in essence have it together. I was like a male Sleeping Beauty, waiting to be kissed by the prince of self-awareness, perhaps then only a short journey to living happily ever after.

I thought that my personal history essentially explained who I was and that the key to relationships was honest and timely feedback (I gave lectures on this). I believed in problem solving and was good at it. On the work front, I thought organizations existed to make money, serve customers, and meet their objectives. Work, for me, was a place to build self-esteem, pursue ambition, and make a living as best I could with as little stress as possible.

In the course of this one-hour lecture, all of these beliefs were seriously undermined. This professor took the position that my anxiety, isolation, feeling out of control, helplessness, and inner and outer conflicts were not so much my own unresolved psychological inadequacies, but were permanent qualities of the human condition. In other words, they were philosophical, not psychological, concerns. I understood him to say that no amount of treatment, no list of accomplishments, no amount of sincere effort would resolve these experiences. What we experience as personal and individual is really universal and collective. We are each "wounded at the moment of birth" and, rather than treat this as a problem to be solved, it is what makes us human and binds us together.

I found those ideas deeply disturbing and compelling, and when the lecture was over, I went right to the front of the hall, found Peter, and asked him if I could come to see him in California. He said "yes," and told me how to find him—and that began what is at this point a twenty-year effort to reframe much of what I had been taught and had chosen to believe.

My relationship with Peter evolved from being a client of his to becoming a friend and colleague. In the early 1980s I began to invite Peter into the consulting world where I lived and introduced him to all my clients. This supported a direction he had already started to take, and he soon left the academic world where he had lived for thirty-five years to commit himself full time to bringing philosophy into the world of business.

This book is another step to widen the audience for Peter's ideas. It is an adaptation of foundational writings contained in two books he wrote in the 1970s. One was titled *The Vitality of Death,* the other called *The New Image of the Person.* Peter's ideas and work have moved far beyond these earlier books; he has written many others since then, the most recent ones aimed directly at leadership in the world of business. Yet as much as I continue to learn from Peter, to this day, I still find myself drawn to the more fundamental ideas of philosophy that these early books defined.

Now is the time to reach back and bring the essence of philosophical insight into our contemporary thinking about what it means to live and work in today's world. The conventional wisdom most of us now operate from is based on a belief system articulated by the economist, engineer, and psychologist. The problem is that we have spent and consumed much of the value these disciplines have to offer us, and much of what we call "new" is really a recycling through ground we have been walking on for at least one hundred years.

Philosophy offers the possibility of providing new ground to explore. While the discipline of philosophy has been developing for much of the last century, it has not found its way into practical life or into organizational life, and we need a deeper and more profound way of thinking about what we are doing.

A gentle warning: This is not an easy exploration for many of us. Philosophy brings us into a realm of constructs and language that many of us are less familiar with. The language of philosophy is an example of its own content, its own point of view. It is not the language of the engineer and economist. It places meaning and experience first, and utility and practical commerce second. As you read Peter's writing, suspend your need for precise definition; the ideas are meant to be absorbed and felt. As you continue to read, they will work on you; you do not have to work on them.

The writing works on you by continually circling the ideas about freedom, anxiety, death, and suffering—much as we circumambulate an ancient cathedral, or labyrinth, or temple. Each time we walk around or, in this case, read the words, we gain a deeper understanding of their implications and their value. My experience with Peter over these twenty years is one of occasional frustration—I have no idea what he is talking about. Then, just as I am about to give up, I hear or read a sentence that is golden. It stays with me; it changes my way of thinking about something that matters. It is patience rewarded, a form of alchemy where the lead of my confusion is turned into the gold of my heightened consciousness.

Philosophy is something you wake up to, not something you quickly get and use. In this world of speed and freeze-dried food, this is a significant shift. The willingness to engage these ideas fully, with some fragile trust and faith, is, in itself, the experience of our freedom. Freedom, in its deepest sense, means that we are writing the book that we are reading; and to decide to understand what we read, despite our feelings at the moment, is to decide to understand ourselves and to have the courage to live with all the implications and hope and futility that this entails.

Our current world view of the marketplace and its organizations has for a hundred years been dominated by the thinking of engineering and economics, psychology, and even religion. The hope for this book is to take a small, but clarifying step in changing that and to begin to see the real world through the lens of philosophy. We hope to make this shift through you, the reader. We invite you to join in this conversation about freedom and accountability, to find interest in a discussion about the value of anxiety, the life-giving force of death, and the motivating inevitability of evil and guilt. These subjects are our friends and are potential gifts, not burdensome liabilities. They help us see more clearly our own face, bring what we thought was peripheral into the center of our awareness, and help us bring light into a dark room.

—Peter Block
May 2001

THE PHILOSOPHIC INSIGHT

Peter Block

W̲HAT WE ARE ABOUT to explore is a realm of ideas that are as elusive as they are important. They deal with our way of experiencing our lives, something that is so ingrained and foundational that most of us are unaware of the nature of this experiencing. It is like trying to look at your face without a mirror. You go through the day, knowing your face is there, visible to the world, but you alone cannot see it. These ideas can also be thought of as being like peripheral vision: you look at something, say a picture on the wall, and on the edges of your field of vision are images that are definitely there, but difficult to see definitively and clearly. No matter where you look, there are always images on the periphery that you cannot quite tie down. The classic description of the elusiveness of these ideas is that they are so much a part of us that to see them clearly is to be a blind man searching in a dark room for a black cat that is not there.

This is the realm of philosophy. Philosophy not only has to deal with that aspect of life that is difficult to grasp, but it is a discipline that has created its own language—so much so that, if you study philosophy, you spend much of your time on the definition of words you will never use again, all the time wondering why these words and what they are trying to describe even matter.

Our purpose in this book is to bring a set of ideas—namely philosophy, or more specifically existential philosophy—into the real world, especially the world of work. To simply understand this philosophy, let alone make use of these ideas, we are required to understand what is meant by "phenomenology," "existentialism," "consciousness," "being," and more. These are difficult concepts to grasp, made more so by the fact that much of what philosophers have written has been written for other philosophers or for students in a philosophy class who are required by the power of a grade to take the time to understand the terms.

CONVERSATIONS ON FREEDOM AND ACCOUNTABLITY

Our goal is to make the ideas of existential philosophy more easily accessible to us all. This book is written for those of us who traditionally care more about living well and productively in the world than about understanding the nature of being alive. It is written for those who typically care about actions, not the bases that underlie our actions. This book takes us into conversations about ideas such as freedom, anxiety, death, and guilt—ideas that we may talk about in moments of reflection, or often in times of crisis—but usually try to avoid or approach with great caution. In fact, we spend more energy trying not to think or talk about these questions than we do trying to figure them out. We typically get interested in these ideas and questions only late in life when we are trying to make sense of it all.

It is exactly these conversations, which we have lumped under the title of "Freedom and Accountability," that we need to talk more about, know more about, and take seriously earlier in life, while we are in the midst of creating the drama of our life, rather than looking back on it. We have focused this book on freedom and accountability because our most common ways of thinking about them do not serve us well. We think that freedom is associated with doing what we want, feeling happy much of the time, and in general living an unburdened existence. A vivid example of this is that we think winning the lottery will help set us free. We believe that if we had a different boss or labored in a more enlightened workplace, we could more fully experience our freedom. This version of freedom is too narrow, and it is based more on a marketing illusion than on our experience of the real difficulty of life.

We also have a small way of thinking about accountability. We think that people want to escape from being accountable. We believe that accountability is something that must be imposed. We have to hold people accountable, and we devise reward and punishment schemes to do this.

These beliefs are so dominant in our culture that they are difficult to question, yet they are the very beliefs that keep us from experiencing what we long for. As long as we believe that our freedom and well-being are dependent on an absence of problems, on our economic situation, and on the actions of those we work for and live with, we are in trouble.

And as long as we think accountability is to be avoided and it thereby requires force to bring it into being, we are unintentionally creating a breeding ground for entitlement. When others try to hold me accountable, I double my efforts to claim what is mine and to be given special treatment.

THE VIEW FROM WHERE WE ARE

Many of our beliefs are driven by the generators of modern culture, the marketplace, the modern organization, and our ways of thinking about leadership. Philosophy is really about a universal form of leadership and the possibility open to each person to shape or create an environment that supports the pursuit of meaning and purpose, rather than our current obsession with financial security and material wealth.

The Culture

It is by looking briefly at modern life that we begin the dialogue about how to sustain ourselves in the face of the dominant culture and to bring philosophy into the foreground of a practical life.

The more immersed we become in a changing culture, the more we need to be reminded of what is timeless and fundamental. We live in a culture that measures progress by scientific and technological improvement and economics. Today's science or technology progress is about the electronic possibilities of the computer. With this electronic revolution, our notions of time, space, and distance shift. My distance from anywhere in the world is now measured by the inches between me and my computer screen. Time has become a scarcity, and the on-call notion of 24/7 rules our consciousness. Speed has become a value in and of itself; waiting one minute for a program to download seems an eternity.

Relationships are becoming more automated. I email letters that I used to write by hand; I sustain relationships by writing what I used to speak; I have an address book where with the touch of a key I broadcast a message to everyone I know. This modernism, as always, is being driven by commerce. The person is transformed from a human being to a consumer, a target market, and the business world now knows more about my taste and preferences than I do. As this electronic connection continues to grow, it is accompanied by scientific achievements. We are on the verge of being able to synthetically replace ourselves, and a computer will soon outperform my brain and match what makes me human—my consciousness and capacity to reflect on my own thinking.

All of this is the reality of our culture; it will not fade away and carries with it many benefits for us all. In the face of all of this, however, there is an increased need to be reminded of all that is still true about being human. At the moment when science and the computer are able to replace and even exceed all of what I am able to do, my determination to deepen my uniqueness and humanity will grow stronger. The more control we develop over the material world, the more urgent the question "What does it matter?"

The Individual

In addition to finding ways to balance the power of the culture, we also need to interpret what constitutes a meaningful life in the face of our passion for the practical and engineering question of "What works?"

For the last century, our understanding of what it means to be human has been dominated by a focus on our behavior, our needs, our wish to be more effective—in other words by the study and application of psychology and the "social sciences." Our bookshelves are filled with advice and wisdom about "how to" do about anything: sustain a relationship, raise children, manage people, live forever, develop habits of effective people, pack our parachute, navigate the shoals of midlife crises, and basically get what we want out of life.

This focus on what works—our instrumental nature—creates a vacuum for the question of "What is the point," which rises from our human nature. These are very different questions. "What works" is born of a problem-solving orientation. It is an engineer's version of our experience that we bring into our own inner world. In his *Interpretation of Dreams,* Freud said, "The dreams of young children are pure wish-fulfillment and are for that reason quite uninteresting compared with the dreams of adults. They raise no problems for solutions." The attention to what works is an expression of our problem-solving approach to life—as if life were a problem to be solved. Even relationships are approached on the basis of how they are "working." We want to know what is the use-value or utility of relationships. No wonder we begin to believe that technology can improve relationships, make them more efficient and effective.

This is where psychology has made its contribution. It has taught us how to condition and modify our behavior for the sake of effectiveness. We have one hundred years of practice in this. The dominance of the question of "What works" becomes a form of psychic materialism where we measure ourselves on our results, on our effect. It becomes an instrumental view of ourselves. This is deeply reflected in how we have constructed our organizations and workplaces.

We have defined management as the cause of the workplace and employees as the effect. It is an instrumental transaction.

Our model of leadership is constructed in this engineering, cause-and-effect vein. We have urged leaders to be role models, have vision, be situational in their treatment of subordinates, and take responsibility for the well-being of those they lead. Our training of managers reflects this. We invest freely in techniques and skills that improve supervision, that train them to motivate and reward employees in order to achieve organizational outcomes. Employees have been defined as the problem and management as the solution.

Philosophy takes a different stance. It proposes that the day-to-day problems facing us are universal and inevitable. Plus, they are better viewed as symbolic examples of the larger question facing us. This allows them to become the doorways to our transformation and opportunities to experience our freedom, our strength, and our humanity. And we need this kind of perspective. We have become so schooled in the perspective of psychology that we are losing faith in the popular belief that there are simple answers or seven steps to effectiveness. All the how-to-do-it books have been written. What is needed is a book on *why* we are doing it and ways we can experience our freedom, regardless of the particulars of our workplace.

The Organization

The philosophic insight re-frames the job of a manager. Instead of overseeing, creating vision, becoming a role model for the sake of subordinates, and, in essence, taking personal responsibility for the well-being of subordinates, a key task of management would be to confront subordinates with their freedom. We would treat those who work for and around us as people who are free and who are creating the world within which they live. In contrast to this, we now treat employees as children. No wonder our organizations evoke feelings of helplessness and entitlement.

Treating people as a freedom balances the conventional belief that people in organizations are resources, products, or effects of the culture and leadership in which they operate. For example, I read some research that tried to attribute the causes of a child's behavior to about 30 percent genetics, 35 percent parental influence, and 35 percent the culture in which they live. (Don't hold me to the exact numbers.) When I mentioned this finding to Peter, he responded, "Why is there no acknowledgement of free will?" What we have come to believe about child rearing, we have transferred to our thinking about leadership and the workplace. We continue to explain employee behavior by examining the management. We hold managers responsible for the morale and productivity of their subordinates. We hold top management responsible for the culture and values they create for others to live in. Management and culture are cause and employees are effect. Management and culture are subjects and employees are objects.

If we began to believe that employees are "walking freedoms," accountable for creating the world in which they live, it would change many of our ways of dealing with them. For one thing, it would take the monkey off the back of the manager to develop, nurture, grow, and guide their subordinates. If people want mentors, let them find them. If people want to learn and grow, let them organize their own apprenticeship and find their own teachers. The organization could support these efforts, but not initiate and institutionalize them, as it now does.

This belief would also reduce the coerce and seduce strategies that now dominate our thinking about how organizations should recruit and keep good people, and how organizations change and adapt. We would stop the mentality of buying and releasing employees, as if they were just another asset or commodity. Employees would become true partners, instead of in name only. We would acknowledge that employees are freely choosing to create this institution, freely choosing to perform well or poorly, freely choosing to blame management or the culture for their suffering. This might lead us to the insight that the employees we most want to keep are the ones who will not stay for the money.

We would not stop caring about employees, but we would speak to them in a different voice. We would place aside our paternalistic instinct to take care of them, which includes feeling guilty for not having taken care of them. Our voice would be one of a partner, not a parent. Managers would free themselves to be themselves, and the role model yoke would be taken from their shoulders. Managers would have room for the range of human responses and in that way affirm their own freedom.

SHIFTING THE CONTEXT

Philosophy asks us to shift the framework of how we understand our experience, to essentially place us in the first-person perspective in relation to our experience. This shift requires some patience in discovering what is useful and practical in the book. If we too quickly demand practical solutions and quick applications, we will be destined to continually solve problems in the same context in which we always have operated. In this way, the future will continue to be like the past, even more so—like the joke, "What is the difference between the future and the past?" "Nothing, only the future is much longer."

The ideas here, which we are calling "philosophic insight," are intended to shift our context. For example, my parents grew up in the great depression, and my children are now young adults in a period of the great progression. Growth, materialism, and wealth are growing in value. This is taking place at a time when individuals are increasingly on their own, with no loyalty to the organizations where they work. It is a time when organizations, in turn, exist primarily for stockholders, whereas a short time ago their focus was on customers and employees. We also have lost our trust in government, education, and even the idea of public service.

All of this creates great volatility and, like every time of change, carries great possibilities—the price of which is great anxiety. If we can change the context in which we view anxiety, and even the way we view our mortality or evil in the world, then we are better equipped to manage ourselves when all around "melts into air." In the end, our freedom and our experience of accountability may be all we have to hold on to, and in the context of existential philosophy, that is more than enough.

To capture in a nutshell the philosophic insights that will aid this shift:

1. Freedom is a fact of our existing in the world,

2. Accountability cannot be imposed or demanded; it occurs as an inevitable outgrowth of that freedom, for we account for what we choose and what we claim as our own, and

3. As inevitably as the existence of our freedom, we are forced to experience and confront:

   - *Anxiety* over the choices we have made as a result of our freedom

   - *Guilt* from having said no to either ourselves (existential guilt) or others (neurotic guilt)

   - *Death* of others, first, and the anticipation of our own, next

   - *Evil,* which exists because all persons are free, and it will not go away; it is not solvable.

4. And most important—and this is the unique insight of philosophy—these experiences are what give meaning, character, and texture to our lives; they are not negatives or failures that a healthy person should move beyond.

5. Finally, when we can accept the above, we realize we constitute the world in which we live, which is to fulfill the promise of being created in God's image.

From Philosophic Insight to the Real World

To understand how these insights might be translated from abstractions to facts in our own lives, there are two phrases in the title of this book that we want to turn to:

- We are interested in freedom and accountability "*at work*"

- We want to apply philosophic insights to the "*real world.*"

These intentions are not only about this book; they are the work of each of us. We each have to answer questions about how an in-depth understanding of our freedom changes the way we function. Also, these are questions for the collective as well as the individual. Where much of traditional philosophy is aimed at what it means to be an individual human being, we want to widen this to explore how a belief in the primacy of our freedom would impact our institutions.

Real World

As Robin Williams once said, "Reality! What a concept!" Yet it is often more elusive than we admit. If we want to address the real world, then we have to consider what is real and who decides it. When we typically talk about facing reality, it is a call for getting practical, temporizing our idealism, and accepting the world as it is, not as we wish it to be. Reality has, in a way, gotten a tough reputation. When we are told to face reality, it is generally to prepare for bad news.

We call this the "hard stuff" and include science, engineering, the world of numbers, and the drumbeat of the marketplace under this umbrella. The arena of our humanity, relationships, feelings, vision, and meaning is commonly relegated to the "soft stuff." Hence we have bought the notion that reality is hard-nosed, an invitation to despair, and in general a negative energy field that we all are forced to endure.

Perhaps we have it backwards. Facing our freedom, and the consequences of this, is really the hard work. Confronting those parts of organizational life that offer numerical certainty or the ability to predict an outcome accurately is really the softer aspect of our workplaces. We allow others to define reality for us when we accept the engineers' and economists' definition of what is real.

What is most real in our lives is not so much the truth about the way the world is, but actually what we know to be true, which is a world defined around our own experience. It is the existence of our consciousness that is most enduring and permanent and therefore real to us. All that happens around us, which we call "objective," is open to our interpretation. The same events will be seen uniquely by each person who observes them. The engineering or scientific viewpoint, which relies on data and predictability, at best only pays attention to part of the story. For after applying all of our analytical tools and collecting all the data we can, in every case a choice will have to be made in the face of an uncertain world. It is in making these choices, which are the moments when our freedom is revealed, that the world becomes real.

We use the term "real world" also to acknowledge that something is at risk, and the stakes are high. The marketplace symbolizes this for organizations, for it operates without personal preference for who it rewards or punishes. It is a test for our actions and can dictate the survival or death of our institutions. The risk of the marketplace, rather than a problem, can be seen as a gift. It gives our life meaning, it is a testing ground for our deepest beliefs, it is an arena where we answer basic questions about our survival, our value, our capacity to do something useful. This reality of the marketplace animates our freedom and gives us a canvas on which to display our accountability.

Despite the fact that most organizations have evolved into a collection of boundaries, defined roles, and limitations, freedom is not a stranger to the marketplace. The language we have used for freedom in the marketplace is the term "entrepreneur." This word captures the act of creating something out of nothing. We talk about the entrepreneurial spirit, which is the institutional counterpart of our individual freedom. A startup operation is a good model for an institutional form that operates with a tolerance for freedom and benefits from a generally shared sense of accountability. And this often succeeds in the real world.

If we are willing to accept that beginning a venture requires this freedom, we should ask why, once it is established, our faith in freedom dwindles and we think that controls are needed, that professionalism must be installed, and that rules and regulations must be defined. We believe that we must sacrifice freedom for the sake of scale.

We operate as if freedom is fine for a short while, under special circumstances, but cannot endure. It seems to be acceptable for a small group around us, but when it comes to numbers of others, it becomes less trustworthy. And so our workplaces are soon well-structured, roles are defined, behavior is prescribed, and what was a startup now becomes a place we call "work." Even when, as in a startup, freedom passes the test of a marketplace reality, we are still quite ready to surrender it.

At Work

For the most part, we have not organized our institutions around the existential viewpoint that freedom is a fact of our existence or that accountability stems from the acknowledgement of that freedom. We are more organized along determinist lines that believe that we are the result or product of our history and our culture and that our behavior is open to modification by those around us. How would organizations be different if they fully accepted that each person is, in fact, a freedom and that the recognition of anxiety, guilt, death, and evil is essential to creating organizations that work and are real?

If you look at most management theory, you will find a set of techniques designed to influence and control other people's behavior. Current management theory gives us a series of admonitions about the importance of management role modeling, walking talk, walking around, reinforcing desired behaviors, articulating visions, defining strong cultures, and more. This all sustains management as the subject and employees as the object.

One implication of this thinking is that behavior is ripe for barter—that good management is a set of actions undertaken for their effect, not for their own sake. Role modeling, walking the talk, articulating a vision, and the rest are all good qualities, but when we care about them for their effect on employees, we are bringing an engineering materialism of the marketplace into the human relationships of the workplace. It is this link that denies the factual existence of employee freedom and depends on a theory of accountability that requires a lot of handholding and a generous amount of oversight.

Or think about our passion for high control systems. One way to understand them is to view them as a socially condoned defense against our freedom and the anxiety it imposes. We create high control environments and justify them with the belief that, without controls, collective effort toward a common goal would not be possible. We then seal this stance by naming it reality. Much of this would shift in a freedom-based leadership, which would encourage a culture of deeper accountability.

The main intent is not to argue with the existing thinking about management, for many of these strategies have their advantages. It is just that the more self-centered, prescriptive, and parental management becomes, the more this reinforces employees as objects or effects we think resist change and need more and more atten-tion. As we explore both how cautious we are about allowing the institutional exercise of our freedom and what the alternative might look like, notice that there is nothing in the ideas about freedom that argues against the need for structure or the need for controls. The questions are where do the controls come from and how do we create and use structure?

If we long to triumph in the struggle for our own freedom, as so much of this book describes, then why not look for ways for our freedom to be institutionalized in our construction of the workplace? We take on this task knowing that, up to this moment, much of how we construct our collective efforts is based on the projection that not only are restraints and controls necessary, but that people want it that way. Our institutions have become places where we are sup-ported in our escape from freedom. And if we can escape from free-dom, then we have lifted the burden of accountability.

There is a cost to an organization committed to the freedom of its members, and that is the anxiety and seeming unpredictability that this carries. Managers would lose some of the hunting rights that par-enting carries with it. We would have to confront our own need for control at a deeper level and, more important, confront our own lack of faith in the possibilities of the people around us. We are each afraid of our freedom, and thus we are afraid of the freedom of those around us. Especially when we are in a workplace that has goals, deadlines, boundaries, and an infinite number of restraints.

It is in this paradox—freedom in the midst of restraints, faith in the accountability of others in the face of a history of disappointment—that the search begins. The question these pages pursue is whether there is a way of creating a life and a culture of accountability based on freedom and its possibilities, as opposed to the current strategies of creating accountability through inducement and coercion, with all of their inherent costs.

Part I

THE POWER AND STRUCTURE OF FREEDOM

WE BEGIN with a discussion of the nature of human free-dom—freedom for our own lives and the place of freedom in our institutions. For individuals, the ideas are compelling and in some ways overwhelming. If we bring these ideas into an organizational setting, however, they appear even more radical. As dear as freedom might be to us personally, it is a subject rarely discussed in our institutions.

You might think that, in a democracy, we might be concerned with protecting our freedoms in the workplace. There is little, however, in our theories about management or the psychology of human behavior that celebrates our freedom or helps us to understand its existence and nature. In fact the opposite is true. We are more likely to focus on ways that management needs to control and channel behavior, as if people's exercising their freedom were a problem to be solved. This is true in our institutions and in the society at large.

The belief that behavior needs to be channeled is ingrained in more than our organizations' management. For a hundred years since Freud, the behavioral sciences have led us to believe that behavior is determined not by free choice, but by the family, culture, and organizational context into which we were born or find ourselves. Given this belief, it is a logical step to act as if the organization has the responsibility to guide its members toward a useful existence.

We believe that management is the driver and cause of employee behavior, performance, and satisfaction. We conduct attitude surveys to determine employee satisfaction and then—with the enthusiastic agreement of the employees—we expect management to do something about it if it is too low. If we want high performing, satisfied employees, we train managers on how to motivate, inspire, and guide their people.

Our belief in the behavior-modification responsibility of management reaches its zenith in the enormous emphasis we place in the power of reward systems to drive employee behavior. We have a long-term love affair with reward systems and their ally, punishment systems, so much so that the belief that behavior is driven by rewards is held with near-religious fervor. You hear as gospel the belief that people will only do what they are rewarded for, and the corollary that you will never achieve actions that you cannot or do not measure.

FREEDOM, REALITY, CHOICE, AND WILL

In the following four chapters on free will, freedom, choice, and their philosophical underpinnings, these beliefs are challenged and the philosophical option of the primacy and pain of free will is explored. Peter argues the possibility that each of us, even in a highly controlled workplace, is fundamentally a freedom and, in essence, at every moment, we are cause, not effect. This is both a liberating and disturbing thought.

Some of the difficulty we have with talking about freedom stems from confusing it with liberty. Liberty is the absence of oppression. It is a political term, embodied by a democratic system, where each citizen has the opportunity to eventually replace its leaders. Liberty is about the lessening of external constraints on our actions. Our modern electronic, virtual, and instrumental culture may, in fact, give us more liberty and reduce constraints. We may have no boss or many bosses, we work more at home, we dress casually, we have portable pensions, we take no loyalty oaths, and we soon might manage our own social security accounts.

Our increasing free agency and independence may increase our liberties, but this is a neutral force with respect to how we think about and experience our freedom. Much of our thinking about leadership and how to structure organizations is based on our basic questions about freedom: how people will use it, whether people want more or less of it, how to achieve common goals and still acknowledge the reality that people always have a choice.

The philosophical insight that Peter lays out here is important: If we were to take seriously the existentialist view about the human condition, it would shift not only how we organize human effort, but also how we relate to the organizations of which we are a part.

ACCEPTING OUR FREEDOM

Is there no one—regardless of cultural differences or personal beliefs—who does not in some way long for freedom? Yet we often act as though we doubt its existence. We are cautious of exercising our free will in our everyday lives. We demand proof or assurance that we are free, or we retreat into the security of "rationality."

Our organizations are full expressions of our belief in rationality. We often treat the workplace, which is a human system, as if it were a mechanical system—or most recently, an information system.

We put great organizational effort into constructing a world of control, consistency, and predictability. We engage in planning that attempts to predict the future, we believe that structure and rewards drive behavior, and we trust that for every problem there is a solution.

We hold this set of beliefs together by focusing on measurement with deep and abiding resolve. This is most clearly expressed in the statement, "What does not get measured does not get done." We act on the belief that if we cannot measure something, it does not exist. The corollary is that if we want to bring something into existence, it has to be defined in concrete, measurable terms.

This set of beliefs is the engineering mind in action. It leaves little room for valuing the element of surprise, discovery, and creativity. Our holding onto our belief in the rational, explainable nature of existence is a major reason organizations have such a difficult time changing and adapting. We often feel that if we want innovation or agility, we are better off starting from scratch, a green field, than to try to change the system we already have.

Reason interferes with change because of its need to predict and control itself. Our change efforts are filled with the language of prediction. We talk about "driving change" as if it were a car. We "cascade change down through the organization" or "drill down" a new business strategy. The first question in a shift in direction is defining the "metrics" we will use in determining the success of the shift. Next, we decide what new behaviors will be required and then add them to our people-evaluation system. Finally we reward the new behaviors. Rewards and measurements are intimate companions and become cornerstones in the engineer's view of how change happens.

The cause-and-effect version of reality constrains us into a utilitarian quality to our thinking. We begin to believe that all our actions have meaning and value only according to their effect, or their results. It leads us away from doing things for their own sake. We even mold our behavior into tactics that work. The emphasis for the person is away from self-expression and toward instrumentality. If something does not show a result—for example, expressing feelings—then we think it is the wrong, or unwise, thing to do. This is why so many of us come to believe that we cannot be ourselves and be successful.

This is not to argue against reason and measurement, only to question its pervasiveness. As Peter argues throughout—and most directly in Chapter 3, "Determinism and the Case Against Freedom"— our belief in reason is a choice, not an immutable fact of nature and existence. If we keep our need for control and measurement in perspective—considering this different viewpoint we might hold—it opens us to more possibilities for what organizational life can become. It honors the complexity and creativity of a human system and might nourish this, rather than treat it as a problem.

THE FUNDAMENTAL INSIGHT

In the world of action and results, thinking is often viewed as lost production. In many of the training workshops we conduct, participants are sometimes asked to reflect on their own beliefs, to voice their own theory of how things work, or to analyze some action that has taken place in the room. When this is done, they often comment that it was fun to have to really think for a change, that it has been a while since they were forced to do that. Some even comment that they have not really had to explore new ideas since they were in school.

The practical world does not usually require in-depth reflection; in fact it is often hostile to it. The claim is made that we do not have time to question and reflect—as if wonder or plain curiosity might harm productivity or were a sign of uncertainty, perhaps even a weakness. This alienation from thought carries a cost. It forces us to keep repeating the way of thinking and acting that brought us here.

Chapter 4, "The Existential Understanding," goes into existentialism in more depth to identify the basic assumptions about being human that define our freedom. One radical premise of this book is that we have choice over how we view every aspect of our experience and our lives. This goes against most people's experience in organizations. Most of us are keenly conscious of the constraints that surround us. We spend a significant part of our conversations filing complaints about who is to blame, how others need to change, how it was not our fault. I have always felt that if we really wanted short meetings, we would live by the rule that no one can talk about anyone not in the room.

According to existential thinking, our blame and judgment of others is merely a symptom, as are our feelings of vulnerability. A root cause of the blame, judgment, and complaining is our denial of our freedom. We institutionally deny the fact that each of us—through our actions and our view of the world—is creating the organization and the leadership we are so fond of complaining about. Deciding that I have created the world around me—and therefore I am the one to fix it—is the ultimate act of accountability.

Most managers see the cost of all the blaming and avoidance of responsibility, but their efforts to evoke more accountability tend to reinforce the illness. We think we can bring accountability into being through rewards, reinforcement, punishment, and even role modeling. These strategies increase the constraints on people, as if accountability were an unnatural act that needed to be taught or induced.

The philosophic stance gives clues to an alternative strategy, one that confronts people with their freedom and treats accountability as an inherent quality that needs more understanding than instruction or inducement.

Chapter 1

THE EXPERIENCE
OF FREEDOM

To feel responsibility for our actions is above all
the recognition of a fact of human existence,
a fact that follows directly from understanding our freedom.

THE STARTING POINT for understanding how philosophic insights can change our lives is to explore the meaning of freedom. This chapter introduces us to a perspective on freedom and what it means to be a human being. We are introduced to existentialism, a philosophy that has had a significant influence on literature, art, and political thought in the last half of the twentieth century. It is a way of thinking that provides a profound statement of the crucial characteristics of our being-in-the-world.

Adapted from Peter Koestenbaum, "The Power of Freedom," in *The Vitality of Death: Essays in Existential Psychology and Philosophy,* Westport, CT: Greenwood Publishing Co., 1971 (originally reprinted with permission from *International Forum for Existential Psychiatry* 1, no. 2 (Summer 1966): 208–218 and 1, no. 3 (Fall 1966: 323–337)).

TO ESCAPE OR EMBRACE
OUR FREEDOM

The central tenet of existential philosophy is the unequivocal conviction that every person's will is free. Our freedom, within certain areas, to be sure, is boundless. In this respect, the stance expressed in this book, which is commonly called *existentialism,* stands in stark opposition to the prevailing winds of doctrine.[1] The belief that currently dominates western thinking is that we are not completely free, but are a product of our culture, our upbringing, and our genetic composition. If our will is completely free, then that truth must override these other powerful influences. The absoluteness of our freedom is not all blessing, however. We do not rejoice over the total freedom that we possess, but, on the contrary, make great efforts to hide it from ourselves. For with freedom comes accountability, with accountability comes guilt, and with guilt comes anxiety. Since our freedom leads to anxiety, it is easier to repress it than to bear it proudly.

We find evidence of this "escape from freedom," as Erich Fromm has called it, in the trend toward conformity, in the disregard and disrespect for individual differences, in the rise of dominating regimes and high control institutions, and in the impersonality of modern man and woman in the vast states and populations of the twenty-first century. We see our escape from freedom in the advanced technology of our means of production and ways of communicating with each other. At work, we find it difficult to identify ourselves with the products we make or the organizations we work for. The constant threat of violence, local and global, makes us at times feel singularly insignificant and helpless, and as a result, if we can afford it, we have security systems in our homes, and gates around our neighborhood.

Finally, the mushrooming of science has given us a magnificent excuse and a sophisticated rationalization to abrogate the dreadful sense of personal freedom and the painful anxiety of personal responsibility. Environmental forces and unconscious motivations are presumed to exonerate us of responsibility—of being accountable for the world around us—and drain us of all real power and direction over our lives. We now can say to ourselves—buttressed by the best minds of the last century—that we are not responsible for the vast problems facing us and our world. We can feel justified, exonerated, relaxed, and at peace—at least for the moment. We choose to deceive ourselves into believing that we are not free.

The existentialist response to this escape from freedom has been, briefly, threefold:

- First: It is an irrefutable and irrevocable fact that we have free will—at least in one zone of our total experience.

- Second: To escape and thus avoid facing the fact of our freedom solves nothing, but increases the already existing problems.

- Third: Although freedom may be painful and may lead to guilt and anxiety, it is not as painful as the escape from freedom.

Once we have mustered the courage to understand, to accept, and to face fully the absolute existence of our free will, we will discover that it can give us unequalled power to handle our fundamental problems. To accept and to understand one's free will is to have reached maturity, to have developed the capacity to live life fully. The word "existence" is used to signal this belief in the factual reality of the freedom that arises out of our free will.

THE NATURE OF OUR EXPERIENCE

The belief in the existence of our free will is grounded in a focus on the nature of our experience. We must first understand the philosophical commitment to the centrality and validity of our experience in general. This is a method of knowing with the cumbersome name of "phenomenology." This means we must treat as fact only what we call authentic or original data, those experiences which are presented to us in immediate consciousness.

Theoretically, the most satisfactory way to develop a theory of being a person is through the careful description of the introspective data about our human nature, that is, about our general experiences of existing as human beings in the world. The only access we have to our innermost nature is through the process of self-reflection and introspection.

If we marshal the forces of closely examining our experience without assumptions or presuppositions (another aspect of what is called phenomenology) and focus on our inner life, we make an important discovery: As we observe with care the nature of our actions, motives, intentions, and general behavior, we discover there is a locus (or some unique episode) at the very heart of our being beyond which we cannot go. And that we call our free will. We all know it, we all feel it, we are it, but we can't talk about it.

Let us take a simple experience as an illustration: I eat a piece of pie. As I look inward, I recognize that I in fact *chose to eat* and I *choose to continue to eat* that pie. I recognize I could *choose* to stop eating it at any moment—although in fact I may find that I do not stop. In retrospect, I may interpret my action to mean I could not help myself, that even though I was on a diet, I was unable to stop eating. A more accurate analysis of the actual experience, however, discloses that I *chose* to continue eating: I *chose* freely to break my diet. That is how the eating of the pie appears to the observer and experiencer of the act. And that simple point, integrated into our lives, has monumental implications. It lends substance to the pithy little phrase that I am indeed "the captain of my soul."

Further examination of the unique experience of choice shows, at least to the immediate consciousness, that it has no antecedents. Nothing related to the event in question came before the first choice: we decide spontaneously; we decide *ex nihilo*—out of nothing. The spontaneous origination of action is our own; it is self-determined. In sum, if we examine our actions and decisions introspectively, we discover they possess a unique and irreducible core which can be described by the phrase "free will." The existence of this unique quality described appropriately with the expression "free will" is an unmistakable fact of our experience. Any explanation of why this fact exists, why we ate the pie, takes place after the act, after the original choice. We choose the explanations of free will. Free will is prior to reason and prior to causes.

It is true, of course, that the fact of free will is vague, elusive, and perhaps unclear. However, its existence, its actual presence in experience, is nevertheless certain. It is as vague and as certain as anxiety, joy, a toothache, and love. The action exists and manifes itself as a ubiquitous and important fact. The fact of free will is pervasive—we are never without it. In fact, the statement, "I experience my existence but not my free will" is utterly without meaning. Free will identifies itself with the heart of our being.

FREE WILL IS PERVASIVE

The experience of free will is not a minor structure of consciousness, but is present whenever we are conscious, and it is relevant to whatever occupies our attention. Let us assume I sit down and do nothing. I may be inactive, but I am nevertheless conscious. In examining the structure of that present indolent consciousness, I discover I spontaneously and freely initiated my inaction. I feel I could just as easily have initiated some other, vigorous action. Furthermore, I am free to continue my inactivity or to initiate some change. The consciousness of that ever-present capacity is the awareness of my free will or freedom. Many of us repress the consciousness of that freedom and, conversely, the recognition and utilization of that freedom can give us the power—in fact, that is the only source of power—to make our lives mature, meaningful, successful, and happy, or, in a word, authentic. We are responsible.

THE CHARACTER OF FREE WILL

Free will is qualitatively absolute and infinite but quantitatively relative and limited. Our experience of free will can be better understood by looking at three elements that characterize it: spontaneity, self-determination, and choice.

Spontaneity

Actions and inactions may be *thought of* as externally determined, and not spontaneous, but they are *experienced* as spontaneous. A free act manifests itself literally as coming from nothing.

If we are skeptical and argue that nothing can occur without a cause or without an antecedent relevant state of affairs, then the philosopher answers that this belief in a more universal determinism is a prejudice of our scientific thinking. The true spirit of science allows the facts to speak for themselves. The facts of the experience of free will are that certain acts of ours appear as truly, unequivocally, and unmistakably spontaneous—even arbitrary. Even though our past, our culture may try to drive us to act in a certain way, it does not determine that we do it. We always have the choice not to follow the dictates of our environment, granted we often pay a price for choosing our own path.

In a fundamental sense, any free act has significant parallels with the religious conception of the creation of the world. God is conceived as having created the world out of absolutely nothing. In the same way, an act called "free" is experienced as springing from nowhere and from nothing. We possess a quasi-divine power—the power to initiate events from nowhere and out of nothing. In a real sense, we have the power of creation. We cannot create a universe, but we do create a world of action, of character, of happiness, and of a meaningful human existence.

The Spontaneous Choice
in Every Decision

Let us assume you are in despair because you cannot get along with your boss. The situation is leading to depression, ruining your workdays and similarly affecting the relationship with your colleagues. It even affects your relationship with your children and puts a heavy burden on your marriage. You have a number of choices. You can indulge yourself in the existing emotional tension, feel deeply sorry for yourself, and exacerbate the entire situation until you have a nervous breakdown or your boss, colleagues, or family start to give up on you. The more common response would be to quit your job and face the crisis of unemployment and economic hardship.

The alternative is to examine the situation objectively and engage your environment in such a way as to make every effort to confront your boss even at the risk of losing the job. You can never truthfully say, "I've tried it all and it has failed." As long as you have breath left to live, you need not give up trying to improve the circumstances. To give up the struggle is not inevitable; it is a spontaneous decision. One choice that is open to you is to totally lose your individuality, give up all the things that you wanted from work, merely to avoid the conflict and for the sake of employment. You can allow your boss to make all decisions and completely define the nature of your relationship. Or, with significant risk, you can attempt to renegotiate the relationship or demand to be moved to another position.

The irrefutable fact is that in such a situation any of us does, in effect, adopt one of those choices. The alternative of not making any choice at all is unfortunately not open to us; it is not an alternative for anyone. In fully committing ourselves to one of these paths of action or behavior (and let us assume for the sake of argument that these are the only ones open to us), we are making a spontaneous decision—a decision which, strictly speaking, has no necessary link between it and the past. We cannot say that our past life conditioned us to choose the particular response that we in fact adopted, since our choice between the alternatives of accepting or rejecting our past also is experienced as totally spontaneous. The decision to explain our choice by explaining our past is still freely willed. We may decide as we did in the past; but we may also decide in a manner altogether contrary to our previous behavior. If in the past we were rational, we may now decide to be irrational. Conversely, if earlier we were emotional and volatile, we may decide henceforth on a rational path of action and behavior. If we have a pattern of quitting in the face of conflict, we may now stay and attempt to face it.

In making any of the above decisions, we create the flavor of our lives, the tone of our existence, the structure of our world of work. We create our essence out of that total structure, literally out of nothing. We create our world in the same sense as God created the universe—spontaneously.

The spontaneous character of human consciousness is the source and explanation for the agony of decision making. Either we leap or we do not leap. All decisions carry with them the element of danger, loneliness, and chance: in a word, one of the essential characteristics of the experience of free will is that it is a spontaneous expression. In that spontaneity lie both the burden and the power of free will. This is made clearer in looking at major decisions, but the principle holds true in all of our choices.

Self-Determination

The second element of our freedom is self-determination. A free act is an act performed by the individual—by the very essence and core of his or her individuality. It is an independent, self-reliant, and autonomous act. The person who chooses is as unique as the act itself. The element of self-determination makes clear the uniqueness and irreplaceable value of every human being. The spontaneity of a free act is made concrete and real by ourselves and not by others.

In resolving your conflict with your boss, you know that the decision that will either save or wreck your career is not only a spontaneous creation, but is your own personal commitment. You *are* that decision. The weight of the decision, as well as the glory or the disaster of its consummation, lies squarely and totally on your own shoulders. The sense of power, responsibility, and divinity that accompanies your insight into spontaneity is enhanced by your recognition that the decision makes and defines you as a human being. You create yourself—your own person, your own character, your own world, your own values—with and through the exercise of your free will.

Choice

The third fundamental dimension in the experience of free will is that it invariably is accompanied by the consciousness that I-could-have-acted-otherwise. Every experience of free will is the inexorable realization that a choice has taken place. To exercise the full expression of your freedom is to commit yourself to a choice. To act freely is to choose. To choose means to be aware—or to have the disposition of becoming aware—that alternatives were open and that you picked one of these not only spontaneously out of nothing, but also with self-determination.

In the example of having a problem with our boss, no matter how we comport ourselves, we will have engaged in a deliberate choice, not acted automatically. We will always, upon careful introspective, self-disclosing examination, discover a certain structure within our agonized existence, a structure of the form "I-could-have-acted-otherwise." Each act, in fact, each state of being, contains recognizably within it such an "I-could-have-acted-otherwise" structure. The *affective,* or *feeling,* recognition of that structure is called "guilt." In our problems, actions, and decisions we always have alternatives—that is what the element of choice points to in the experience of free will.

Choice Is Not an Option

If I fall asleep at the wheel of my car and get into a serious accident, I have to accept the tragedy as the consequence of my free will, that is, my choice. As I got sleepy driving, I was confronted continuously by the alternatives of either stopping or moving on. And as the clock ticked away, I continuously and freely chose between the alternatives. However, the fact that I had to choose between these alternatives was not in turn subject to choice. Choice exists, it is not an option. In choosing to keep driving, I freely chose to take my chances. In other words, the careful analysis of the act of driving—an act which may lead to death—shows that it contained all three elements of free will: spontaneity, self-determination, and choice. My possible death was thus a consequence of my free choice. To be equipped with the clear knowledge of the structure of one's free will gives one the maturity to avoid tragic mistakes. Our free will and our understanding of it are perhaps our greatest resources.

Three Consequences

In sum, our free will discloses that it is composed of three elements or dimensions. Our free actions are spontaneous—they arise out of nothing. Our free actions are self-determined—they are our own personal, individual creation. And, finally, our free actions are choices among alternatives—that at bottom we always could have acted otherwise. There are three consequences in the quality of our lives stemming from the knowledge of these pervasive characteristics of our freely willed actions.

First, we achieve a sense of power and importance. We recognize that we are individuals with dignity, that we are people who count. The lowliest and the highest of us all possess the power and the importance that are given to us merely through the insight that we are born free—born with free will—and that nothing can change this fact.

Second, the fact that free will is an essential constituent of what it means to be human suffuses us with a sense of divine mystery and kinship. We are endowed with a basic similarity to our conception of God, who is, after all, envisioned as a Creator and as one who "created man in His image." This characteristic of free will gives us a holy charisma—it makes the heart of our soul or mind, of our inwardness, the most precious thing in the universe.

Third, the understanding of free will gives us a sense of supreme accountability: the willingness to accept responsibility and blame for all of our acts is a central ingredient in an authentic existence.

RESPONSIBILITY IN OURSELVES
AND IN OTHERS

To feel responsibility for one's actions is not merely a desirable frame of mind, but is above all the recognition of a fact of human existence, a fact that follows directly from our understanding of our free will or freedom. That respiration brings fresh oxygen to the blood and removes old carbon dioxide is not merely a desirable characteristic of our human constitutions. It is also and foremost a fact of our physiological nature. In the same sense, the existence of responsibility is a fact of our spiritual nature, of our general experience of existing as a human being in the world. We are accountable to the world as it exists, whether we like it or not.

That responsibility is a fact rather than an opinion is important in the face of the current prevalence of ethical relativism. Words such as "obligation" and "value" are not to be analyzed as feelings—as was done so eloquently by mid-twentieth century philosopher Charles Stevenson—but as important states of consciousness, states that define our existence.

What existential philosophy argues for, then, is a person who never gives up; we are to be people who are always looking to themselves as the genuine source and essential fountain for the improvement of their life situation. In keeping with this line of reasoning, blaming other people or external circumstances for our problems, misfortunes, failures, and meaninglessness is not an insight into the "true" nature of things, but merely a cheap and eventually ineffectual form of escape. To blame others merely means making a decision to avoid the responsibility which ultimately and inescapably is one's very own.

It goes, of course, without saying that people who go through life with the attitude that all events are fully and totally their own, personal, and inexorable responsibility are likely to exert much more effort toward succeeding as persons than those who always ascribe difficulties to fate and say they can do nothing about events. The true existentialist, however, goes far beyond this already commendable resolution to accept responsibilities.

The existentialist view holds that we have no choice in the matter of accepting responsibility for the quality of our lives. That responsibility is ours by birth, by virtue of the fact that we are human, in the same sense that our heart is ours by birth. We are in fact responsible for success as well as for failure in life, irrespective of whether we are prepared to accept and assume such responsibility.

THE LEGITIMATE USE OF PRAISE AND BLAME

To accept responsibility also is to recognize that praise and blame are a part of our lives. To sort this out, we must, therefore, distinguish subjective responsibility or blame (the responsibility or blame of oneself) from objective responsibility or blame (responsibility or blame of another). We need to affirm the value of subjective blame, and question the value of objective blame.

The two expressions have different meanings: The fact that they are used in ordinary language as if they had one and the same meaning (as is true of the word "death" in its two meanings—"death of myself" and "death of another") is of fundamental importance. We repress that distinction and the linguistic ambiguity offers us a convenient out. We hide the distinction because it is painful. To admit to the repressed existence of the distinction between subjective and objective responsibility (and blame) is as painful—but just as salutary—as any urgent medical operation.

Subjective Versus Objective Responsibility

Precisely what is this difference? In the case of subjective responsibility and blame, the experience of one's own free will is present, whereas in the experience of objective responsibility or blame, that experience of free will is absolutely absent. For example, let us assume—contrary to what actually occurred—that in 1962 when President Kennedy sent troops to the University of Mississippi, the results had been a short-lived civil war. Let us assume further that many people had died, that the University of Mississippi was finished as a center for higher learning, and that the United States was greatly embarrassed in her foreign relations because of these events. With this hypothetical situation as background, let us investigate the distinction between objective and subjective blame from the perspective of the President of the United States, in whom rested ultimate responsibility for seeing that the law was obeyed.

Objective responsibility in this case is responsibility or blame as it would be assigned by a court of law. In our hypothetical situation, it is relatively simple to ascribe objective responsibility and assign objective blame to the Governor of Mississippi, who contributed to a violation of a legal and legitimate court order and encouraged public disobedience of the law. In terms of objective blame, the President cannot be held responsible for the situation, since he was merely fulfilling his obligations to that office.

From the point of view of his inner life, the President's situation is more complex. From his own subjective perspective, the President knows the decision to send troops was his. He had to choose between fulfilling his obligation or avoiding it. Furthermore, it was not merely a decision to send troops. After the initial decision to support the court order, the President had to decide the details of that decision. In our hypothetical illustration, if federal troops had been better trained, better equipped, had arrived more promptly and in larger numbers, if greater efforts at conciliation had been made—such as a personal appearance of the President at the university—perhaps (but only perhaps) the postulated blood-shed and destruction could have been averted. From the point of view of his own conscience, the President must assume full responsibility for the initial decision to support the law and all the ensuing decisions on how to carry out and continue his initial choice.

Since, whatever the outcome, he is merely fulfilling his legal obligation, he cannot be blamed objectively if the outcome is sour. On the other hand, from the point of view of his conscience, of his inner life, of his sense of free will, he must assume full and unqualified responsibility and blame for absolutely every decision that he makes. Regardless of the legalistic and objective circumstances, he knows subjectively that he could have acted differently. Each step was his own, self-determined, spontaneous, freely willed choice. Because of the fact that he subjectively knows that he could have acted otherwise, he must assume full subjective responsibility for the events. It is a fact that he could have chosen differently, history and the Constitution to the contrary. Nothing can alter this contrarian possibility as a fact of human nature. And as long as that fact exists, the decisions—regardless of external circumstances—are free and his.

There is no law that demands JFK hold such a subjective attitude; it is simply a recognition of an inescapable characteristic and trait of human responsibility. An immature person will decide to reject subjective responsibility. But it is folly to reject the facts. For one who decides to reject subjective responsibility our language has a ready-made excuse and alibi: in our language, the distinction between subjective and objective responsibility is obscured. If we choose, we may equate and thereby confuse the two kinds of responsibility. But all this equating means simply that we decide to repress clarity and understanding about subjective responsibility.

FACING UP TO RESPONSIBILITY

One of the keys to a meaningful existence is to decide to face and to accept subjective responsibility. That decision means that we are willing to assume responsibility for all our actions as well as omissions, regardless of how scandalous the behavior of others may be, and regardless of the number of excuses offered to us for avoiding subjective responsibility.

In this sense, a mother is totally responsible for the type of persons her children become. From the point of view of objective responsibility and blame, this stringent ethic is, of course, false. The quality of children's lives depends on much more than their mother's personal actions. It depends on the quality of the father, of the schools, of relatives, on the economic situation of the family and nation, and on what they, themselves, brought into this world.

But from the point of view of subjective responsibility, a mother can do much to counteract any difficulties and problems in areas that are usually thought to be beyond her control. Every minute of the day she has to decide between adopting either the attitude of "I can't help it" or that of "I'm absolutely determined to do something about it." By recognizing that even under the most adverse circumstances she does impact the lives of her children and that there is no clear limit to her potential impact, she is far more likely to control her life than she might otherwise. The expression "subjective responsibility or blame" is merely a phrase that suggests that fact—a person must choose continually between either accepting events as they come or manipulating and improving them. In other terms, you must decide whether to accept or reject your personal accountability for the world in which you live.

In sum, the fundamental distinction between the two facts in our experience as human beings that are called subjective and objective responsibility is this: in subjective responsibility and blame, the sense of free will is present; in objective responsibility and blame, it is absent. The experience of responsibility with free will is structurally distinct from that experience without free will. When a court assigns blame, the judge must examine the objective facts and not be concerned with his or her sense of free will. In our own lives, however, we must always remind ourselves that whatever another person may do, and regardless of how blameworthy the actions of another may be, we must nonetheless freely assume full responsibility for all our own actions, omissions, attitudes, and their consequences.

IT IS NOT THEIR FAULT

This framework of free will should help make it clear that decisions and responsibilities are those of individuals, not of amorphous entities such as institutions. This consequence follows from an analysis of the fact of free will itself.

The attempt to let decisions emerge spontaneously, as it were, from institutions is a widespread contemporary practice which often serves to blur—and thus hopes to escape—the very nature of free will itself. Such an effort often leads to distortion of the most basic human characteristics, to procrastination of necessary decisions, and the dilution of responsibility and of the solutions proffered; it leads to cowardice where courage is essential, or to fool-hardiness when restraint is in order.

In essence, of course, there is nothing wrong in the marvelous democratic process of reaching decisions by vote or by organizational consensus. Not only is it often the case that many heads are better than one, but—central to considerations of human dignity—all individuals in our society must have the right to participate in decisions that will affect them as individuals or as members of that society. However, when decisions are placed at the feet of organizations, the temptations of hiding in the collective in order to avoid the burdens of personal responsibility are great indeed. Since many individuals fall prey to the temptation of being anonymous and do not assume the responsibility that is theirs, we often find the situation in which the results of organizational action, due to the narrow interests of the organization, are really inimical to the interest of the members of the larger society and are contrary to the intentions entertained individually by the very people responsible for such a communal decision.

Chapter 2

CHOICE, REALITY, AND WILL

Every act we perform is, in its foundation, a free one. If we never forget this fact about our human existence, we shall never be loath to assume willingly, cheerfully, and effectively the responsibility that is ours to begin with.

WE NEVER ACT LIKE MACHINES—that is, automatically. We cannot be machines, even if we wish to be. This means that all conscious acts are in effect choices among alternatives. That there exists a choice means that we-could-have-acted-otherwise, so that when we exclaim, "I really had no choice in the matter," we cannot be understood to mean literally what we say, that we were helpless. Translated by philosophical insight, the sentence means that we

Adapted from Peter Koestenbaum, "The Power of Freedom," in *The Vitality of Death: Essays in Existential Psychology and Philosophy,* Westport, CT: Greenwood Publishing Co., 1971 (originally reprinted with permission from *International Forum for Existential Psychiatry* 1, no. 2 (Summer 1966): 208–218 and 1, no. 3 (Fall 1966: 323–337)).

decided or chose to do as we in fact did, either because we were intimidated and acted out of fear or because of some other, perhaps more rational grounds. This stance declares that all states of consciousness—including those we ordinarily call "choices" as well as those we like to term "inevitable actions"—disclose a core experience of free will or, in the word of psychiatrist-psychologist Karl Jaspers, an "Urentschluss"—an "archetypal" choice.

CHOICE AND THE NATURE OF HELPLESSNESS

If every one of our acts is a choice and that choice is free, then whenever we act consciously and deliberately, we also experience at the core of our action the sense of free will. In spite of the widespread feeling of helplessness and the avoidance of accountability in the culture, all states of consciousness consist of alternatives among which we must choose. Mature and authentic individuals are fully conscious of the fact that they must choose, since free choice in actions cannot be avoided; i.e., that is not one of the alternatives open to them. Although we are free to choose, we are not free to choose to choose. This weight of always choosing can become unbearably heavy. So, ordinarily, only when anguish accompanies the consciousness of our ever-present free will do we actually name that a choice. But that is a mere linguistic idiosyncrasy.

We always make a deliberate and persistent effort to keep in mind that every act we perform is, indeed, in its foundation a free one. If we never forget this fact about our human existence, we shall never be loath to assume willingly, cheerfully, and effectively the responsibility that is ours to begin with. Success in life and ful-

fillment as a human being are intimately tied to the clear and constant consciousness of this principle.

This means all statements of helplessness, all claims of it was
not my fault, are factually incorrect. Despite any claims that I may
make about the presence of coercion, the force of circumstances,
or the lack of choice, each of my acts could have been performed
otherwise—or, as a final alternative, it could have been omitted altogether. Of course, the alternatives themselves are not infinite,
but there are always more than one. The statements "I could not
help myself" and "I had no choice" have, if taken strictly, no experiential correlate. They are rather emotive expressions of a double free choice: choice A is to perform act a, and choice B is to
suppress as far as possible the consciousness that act a is the result
of choice A.

Every Act Is Free

By saying "I had no choice" (and meaning it), we have chosen to
betray our human nature. We have, in that sentence, freely chosen
to resign from the human race and join the animal kingdom or the
technocracy of machines or electronics. But even while making
this dehumanizing decision, we have not really succeeded at all in
shedding our humanity, for, after all, the decision to be like an animal or like a machine is a free—that is, typically human—act; it
is an act that neither animal nor machine nor chip can perform!
Even the attitude or decision that there is "really" no choice discloses itself to be a major and a free decision about the kind of person we are going to be. Once it is clear, however, that we are
humans—in Sartre's famous words, that we are "condemned to be
free"—we will give up our futile and self-destructive efforts to deny

our very nature. On the contrary, we will accept our nature and face, with redoubtable resoluteness, the problem of making our life meaningful.

Often, what makes it difficult to realize that all acts are free choices is that frequently all the alternatives open are unpleasant and painful. To be free certainly does not mean that the alternatives of paradisaical pleasure and bountiful bliss are invariably open to us. To identify free will with pleasure is naïve. To be free simply means that there are always alternatives among which we can choose, even if none of the alternatives are ones we are pleased with.

THE LOCUS OF FREEDOM

Let us be certain that we understand what in our human experience is free and what is not.

First, as stated above, whenever we act, we choose among alternatives, and this is one of the stubborn characteristics of our human existence. Second, the precise alternatives open to us are not themselves subject to our free will. The particular nature of the alternatives is simply one of the invariant and overpowering characteristics of the world around and within us. Given these limitations, we must understand nevertheless that we constantly choose, regardless of how we may deny it. The consequences of this knowledge—in the Socratic spirit of "know thyself" and "virtue is knowledge"—is emotional maturity.

Freedom Where We Least Expect It

Most of us are unclear about the pervasiveness of choice and about the extent of freedom. For example, what freedom does a political prisoner have as he walks to the firing squad? As is usual in such an extreme situation, the precise distinctions between free choice and alternatives are simplified. The fact that he walks to his death is, in a pitiful and somber sense, a free act nonetheless. We can say the prisoner is not free to choose only because the alternatives open to him do not include escape to freedom. But whichever his choice in the narrow range of possibilities, he thereby still determines the kind of person that he is, the quality of the character he possesses. The prisoner's alternatives are these: he can meekly and obediently walk to face the firing squad; he can obey under dignified protest; he can fight and attempt to escape, considering it perhaps more honorable to die in the effort to escape—and perhaps take one or two guards with him—than to die meekly; or he can attempt suicide.

The alternatives themselves are fixed. Also, that he must choose among them, that he must adopt one of these paths of action or inaction, is also fixed and determined. He will, of course, choose one of them. However, which of these he chooses is a matter of his absolute free will, i.e., it is spontaneously self-determined. One might well argue that these alternatives are insignificant: they all end in death. Of course they do. However, this is an example of a terminal situation, and cannot be examined in isolation. Had the prisoner thought clearly and consistently about his freedom, his life might not have reached this impasse. After all, a firing squad is a symbol of one possible end point in a life-long series of choices. Had he recognized and fully claimed his freedom earlier, the prisoner would either have chosen the possibility of a firing squad when his life and his liberty were still realistic alternatives, and then his present predicament is clearly suffused with his free choices, or he would never have allowed himself to reach this situation in the first place. The illustration clearly points out that even when it seems least likely, we cannot act consciously without at the same time making free choices.

It may come as a surprise to the prisoner that his meek walk to the firing squad is the result of the same free choice that would have been his fiercest and most violent rebellion. The relatively simple insight that all our acts are free choices is a major step in enabling us to conduct our lives with the ingredients of emotional maturity, namely, reason, intelligence, foresight, and courage.

A FIRST-PERSON CHOICE

Staying with the context of an extreme freedom-limiting justice system, another example should further clarify both the ubiquitous presence and the irrevocable importance of free will.

A fifteen-year-old boy—from a dismal family background, and low in native intelligence—has committed a crime and is brought before a judge. In thinking through the problem of the sentencing, the judge asks herself how much freedom this boy had. Would not any human being faced with a like undesirable background and low intelligence react in the same way and also commit a crime? If the judge could but determine whether the boy's action was free or not, she would also know what kind of sentence it would be right to pass. If the boy was "free" when he committed the crime then he must be held responsible for his action and treated accordingly; he must then be punished. On the other hand, if he was not free to act otherwise—if his past and present circumstances fully determined his actions—then the boy should perhaps not be punished.

It is fortunate, maintains the judge, that there are "free-will experts" in our society whom she can consult. She asks a number of behavioral scientists whether the boy was or was not free to do otherwise when the crime was committed. That is, she orders a sanity hearing. The judge believes that sentencing depends on an objectively ascertainable scientific fact, namely, whether that boy was really free when he committed the crime.

The judge's approach to the situation is based on an altogether erroneous analysis of the experience of human existence. It ignores the ubiquitous character of free will. That ignorance is not accidental, but, in turn, a deliberate choice. It is the choice to attempt to circumvent the anxiety of choice. Unfortunately, such an attempt is futile.

Free will is always a first-person phenomenon. The question of free will is germane only to the decision of the judge, not to the boy's crime. Contrary to the traditional analysis of the situation, the judge's dilemma is not about an objective fact but about a subjective decision. A fact is discovered—which involves no pain—whereas a decision is agonized. She wants to avoid making a difficult decision by hoping for a factual answer to what is really the philosophic problem of free will and determinism. She seeks to establish definitively whether the boy was free or not.

But from the point of view of practical morality, the real question for the judge is: "How shall I decide?" or "On what grounds shall I decide?" She has a number of alternatives. She may choose that her decision will rest on the factual solution to the problem of whether that boy was really free or not. Her decision is then based, not on the actual and objective freedom of the fifteen-year-old boy, but on her free and spontaneous decision to make that issue the determining factor and on her eventually free decision to consider the philosophical problem of free will definitively settled in her appraisal of the boy's life situation.

On the other hand, the judge may choose to adopt the attitude that, irrespective of the age and circumstances of the offender, it is her solemn duty to make clear to society that the arm of the law is inflexible and powerful. In that case she has to decide that the full weight of the law shall descend on that boy. Or, the judge may adopt an attitude of sympathy and try to understand the boy. Her sentence will then reflect, not the strong arm of the law, but her effort to rehabilitate the boy. Finally, the judge may choose not to worry much over the matter and let precedent, some rule-of-thumb, or some formula decide.

WILL LIES WITHIN

The real locus of the problem of free will is in the inwardness of the judge herself. She has to contend with the inescapable existence of her own personal free will. She is faced, let us assume, exclusively with the above four alternatives. The alternatives are fixed, and so is her need to choose. Between these two impenetrable barriers her freedom is both her purgatory and her paradise—it is total. In that region of the judge's human existence, her freedom is absolute; once again, it is commensurate with God's freedom in creation. The judge hopes to circumvent her anguished epiphany through the inefficacious strategy of calling on the experts.

Genuine Options

It follows that all conscious acts are choices, and that these choices involve basic decisions. The judge cannot avoid the full personal weight of the value decision. She must decide whether to follow the laws, precedent, and tradition, and precisely to what extent. She must decide how humane she is to be or whether she should be indifferent to individual suffering; she must decide how to react to the moral code in which she was reared. All these are indifferent choices, but are what William James has called "genuine options." To have total responsibility for a situation is not a legal requirement but a fact of human existence. That is the meaning of responsibility-in-me and subjective responsibility or blame. It is important to understand and experience that existential reality about our humanity. Without that insight we are subhuman.

Since ultimate responsibility rests on our own, very personal shoulders, in the last analysis, we can ask no one else to make a decision for us. Ordinarily, when we say "no one else can decide for you" or "you must make up your own mind," we make reference to an ethical ideal rather than a factual state of affairs. We mean that it is childish and immature to allow others to decide for us. We mean that each of us must be independent and thereby decide for ourselves. But the existential meaning of self-reliance is much more radical and profound than a mere ethical cliché. It might be truly wonderful if, upon occasion, we could pass on the burden of making decisions.

The fact is, however, that such an alleviation of responsibility is not possible. It is not one of the alternatives open to us. If we understand rightly the nature of the human condition—which is that we are free—we recognize that it is not possible to deny responsibility. We cannot appeal to any being other than ourselves for final decisions. We may appeal to someone else, but that is not a final appeal. We, personally and freely, make the decision which determines to whom we are to appeal. Shall we talk to a minister? to God? to our spouse? to our boss? to a parent? to our child? to a psychoanalyst? to a friend? to a neighbor? No one can be consulted for this primary decision. And the nature of the response is a function of this initial decision of whom to consult. Furthermore, once we have received the requested advice, the decision of whether to adopt it or to reject it is again solely our own.

FREE WILL AND OBJECTIVE REALITY

Just as we call what in our experience is given us as free, our freedom, or free will, so we must have a name for that which is given to us as fixed and "objective reality."

The ancient Stoic philosophers were already familiar with such a distinction. They referred to our freedom or free will as the class of "things that are in our power." They meant by this expression that we are legitimately entitled to call our own only those things which no celestial or terrestrial power can take away from us. Since, by this definition, most things are ours merely on loan—including our heartbeats, our happiness, our fortunes, etc.—the things that are truly ours are very few indeed. They are, in brief, our character (our integrity, dignity, our sense of duty and purpose) and our ability to resign ourselves to fate—to accept cheerfully the frustrations and limitations that life has in store for us. Although these two "possessions" are sparse ones indeed, our success in life as human beings depends on the recognition of the limits to our freedom. The remaining goods for the Stoics were "things that are not in our power." These include not only the obvious, such as the weather and the stock market, but even those things over which our control is partial but nonetheless limited, such as health, friendship, and success in business. No dedication to any cause is fully mature if we are not also prepared for failure.

Two Forms of Reality

Authentic existence and emotional health depend, first, on the ability to distinguish between free will and objective reality and, second, on the readiness to accept both the responsibility of free will and the inevitability of what we cannot change. We must also distinguish between two kinds of objective reality (Figure 2.1). The alternatives among which we must choose are fixed; this is one kind of reality. The fact that we must choose, and that in any conscious situation a choice is unavoidable, is also an instance of what we have no control over. This second type—the inevitability of choice itself—is what makes freedom as burdensome, onerous, and terrifying as it really is. The specific number of alternatives open to us, as well as the necessity to choose among them, both are unchangeable. Free will is the result of the combination of these two,

Figure 2.1.   The Geography of Freedom

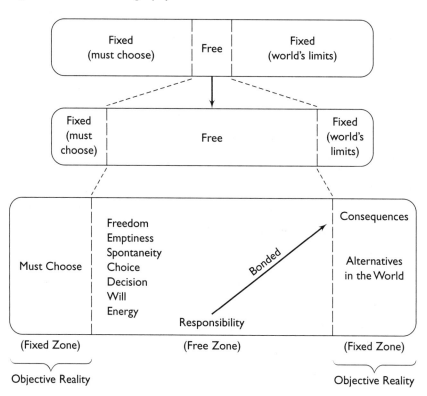

since within the confines of these limits our freedom is total and our power over our lives, absolute (Figure 2.2).

The mature individual recognizes that these two kinds of realities exist and that they exist in every situation. Furthermore, we are able to recognize all the alternatives open to us, not just a few that have been selected neurotically, out of self-pity, or on the basis of wishful thinking. The immature person recognizes neither all the available alternatives among which we are free to choose, nor—

and this is perhaps even more important—the fact that a choice among them is nonetheless inevitable. Whatever happens, we have chosen, whether or not we admit to ourselves the existence of that choice. The knowledge that we are condemned to be free elevates us to a position of power over our lives and destiny. The clear recognition that to be indecisive is in itself a deliberate and free choice—a decision the consequences of which are likewise our full responsibility—will liberate us from that indecisiveness.

Figure 2.2.   Degrees of Freedom

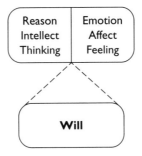

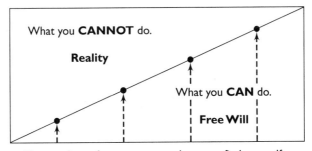

You are always free, no matter where you find yourself.
Can you leverage and maximize that freedom?

What are your degrees of freedom?

Inevitable Choice

Let us illustrate these points with a sketchy analysis of the experience of exhaustion, common today in feeling overworked and pulled apart at the edges. First, there is the inevitable and overwhelming feeling of exhaustion, or the difficulty in getting anything done. While the exhaustion is a matter of fact, there is an aspect of the experience of exhaustion that confronts us with the choice of either recognizing the realities of life or hiding these realities. Why is one tired? That question can be answered, often by the individual herself, and if not, by professionals in the healing arts. We may discover the real source of exhaustion from an objective appraisal of our physical, emotional, and economic life; or it may be necessary for us to make those or similar discoveries through a medical examination or psychological counseling.

In other words, whether or not I am informed of the objective nature, source, and possible remedy of my exhaustion is the direct result of my conscious and deliberate choice. Just as we can walk freely without verbalizing that activity, and without being deliberate about it, so also we can make choices that are, in effect, free and deliberate and for which we are fully responsible without articulating these clearly at the time. At each moment, we can discern that there are choices at the basis of all of our actions. On the other hand, we may choose, with equal freedom, to repress that fact, to endeavor to convince ourselves that either these facts do not exist, or that they are not as they appear, or both. In other words, I may choose to deceive myself into believing that the need to work so long and hard is an inexorable fact, that it is just one of those things, and so I choose to do nothing about my situation.

The Revelation of Our Freedom

We are constantly faced with whether to fight our situation constructively or whether to accept it fatalistically. If our overwork and exhaustion are due to inefficient management of our life, and if we have decided to accept the reality of that situation, we must make the choice—every minute of every day—between fighting that situation intelligently, by restructuring our life, accepting it, relishing it, feeling sorry for ourselves, or doing nothing about it.

All that freedom needs is the knowledge that I have such choices, as Sartre shows in his description of the reality of human freedom.

The Resistance

We were never more free than under the German Occupation. We had lost all our rights, above all the right to speak; we were insulted daily and had to remain silent, we were deported, because we were workers, because we were Jews, because we were political prisoners. All around us on the walls, in the newspapers, on the screen, we met that foul and insipid image that our oppressors wanted us to accept as ourselves. . . . All those who were aware—and what Frenchman was not, at one time or another—of some information about the Resistance, asked himself anxiously, "If they torture me, can I hold out?" Thus the question of freedom was posed, and we were brought to the edge of the deepest knowledge a man can have of himself. For the secret of a man is not his Oedipus complex or his inferiority complex, it is the limit of his freedom, his ability to resist torture and death. . . . at the depth of this solitude, others were present, all the comrades of the Resistance they were defending;

a single word was enough to trigger ten, a hundred arrests. This total responsibility in total solitude, is it not the revelation of our freedom?[1]

Situations III, 11–13

THE GIFT OF FREEDOM

Understanding our free will eventually leads to security, amelioration of anxiety, and reduction of the sense of meaninglessness. There are fundamentally two ways of reducing anxiety and with it achieving security. One way is to be persuaded that, in some sense, we are not alone in the universe, and that there is absolute justice or right. For example, if no one agrees with me, even if I feel abandoned, I can gain sustenance from the thought and the feeling that, after all, I am right, that there is some absolute in whose hands I rest. This solution is unreliable; not only does it depend on arguments which have been questioned, but it ignores and escapes the basic fact of subjectivity or inwardness.

The second solution is to be fully and firmly rooted in our own subjectivity, and thus build security within those difficult and lonely confines. This latter solution can be effected by realizing the reality of our freedom and understanding the structure of that freedom. The problem of "escape into objectivity" is a major and separate issue. In brief, the belief in objective solutions to basic problems is a decision to escape the subjective burden of responsibility that these entail. In the last analysis, the decisions are ours, and once that fact is recognized we can discover the great sense of security that this insight into the nature of our subjectivity provides.

The sense that life is meaningless is partially due to the feeling that we have no genuine control over our lives. Focus on our free will, however, calls attention to our full creative powers. Free will is thus a symbol of hope. To realize that we are free can give us the strength, energy, vigor, and determination to make life meaningful.

Chapter 3

DETERMINISM AND THE CASE AGAINST FREEDOM

The decision for determinism is a free choice to deny freedom.
Our last free act—after which no further free acts are possible—
is to deny that we are free.

T IS STILL FASHIONABLE, even after a century of existential thought, to be convinced that freedom is not a fact or, even worse, that it may be simply a dream. The fundamental existential position is that freedom is real; it is not an illusion. Free will is a pervasive and legitimate experience. But free will also transcends our experience, so that any denial of consciousness—or of what is sometimes called the "transcendental" realm—is also a denial of the possibility of freedom. Philosophy has an ethical responsibility to

Adapted from Peter Koestenbaum, "In Defense of Freedom," in *The New Image of the Person: The Theory and Practice of Clinical Philosophy,* Westport, CT: Greenwood Press, 1978, and "The Power of Freedom," in *The Vitality of Death: Essays in Existential Psychology and Philosophy,* Westport, CT: Greenwood Publishing Co., 1971 (originally reprinted with permission from *International Forum for Existential Psychiatry* 1, no. 2 (Summer 1966: 208–218) and 1, no. 3 (Fall 1966: 323–337)).

society to establish with finality the reality of free will. The exigencies of human dignity and personal meaning can no longer tolerate the denial of our central and unequivocal core of freedom.

We know that existential philosophy tries to describe, without bias or assumptions, the human condition. It does not argue, nor does it seek to prove; it merely describes—with sensitivity. Therefore, any attempt to strictly *demonstrate* or *prove* that free will exists—as would also be the case with proving the existence of God—is an error. Those who doubt the centrality of our freedom will maneuver us to consent to the false notion that free will is the conclusion of a lengthy argument chain, resting on unexceptionable axioms, or that it is the result of some intricate experiment, resting on a bed of statistics. These approaches have the dangerous tendency to place freedom among the world's objects, whereas in truth, freedom is a structure of inwardness, an element of subjectivity. Free will is an *experience*. It is an irreducible experience, and therefore it has the authority of all primary and uninterpreted data.

STAGES IN THE SELF-DISCLOSURE OF FREE WILL

Before we can accept our freedom, we do battle with it. Self-consciousness of our free will goes through four distinct, clearly discernible, and progressive stages, each closely related to development of our recognition of the meaning of existence.

Stage 1.
Repression

The first step in the recognition of free will is its repression or, in Erich Fromm's words, "the escape from freedom." We rationalize away our free will. Consider the case of Helen, a partner in a business that is struggling, for the first time in its history.

Helen focuses on her partner, Tom, whose part of the business has been weakening over time. She agonizes over how to deal with him, tends to discount him continually, and finally confronts him with his poor performance and inability to meet his commitments. She knows Tom has not been pulling his weight for some time but, due to their friendship and the long history of their relationship, has ignored the problem and fooled herself into thinking things would improve.

Tom is thoroughly contrite and seeks help from Helen, but she continues to feel betrayed, refuses to forgive him, and expresses an extraordinary amount of anger toward him. She feels the situation is hopeless and looks to end the relationship. Helen's disappointment toward her partner has been quietly smoldering for ten years, but she has never permitted herself to express it. She had doubts about Tom for over a year and was witness to their deteriorating relationship, but said nothing, preferring not to think of it. By precipitating the crisis, and justifying it with the results of the business, she found an objective excuse, that is, a rationale, for expressing her anger. She believes that his performance is the cause of her anger, while in actual fact it was her ten-year-long doubts that had contributed to her partner's disappointing results.

She feels her anger is caused and justified by Tom's failure. The anger is thus, in her eyes, not a free act, nor is the decision of what is just and what is not her own. In other words, she has maneuvered herself into a position in which her angry behavior appears to be not free in two important senses. First, the release of anger is

not free because Tom's performance caused it, not her own decision, and second, she is relieved of the decision of whether it is
moral or immoral to express anger (a problem that occasioned her
delay in manifesting anger) because the social order justifies or ap-
proves of her anger under these circumstances.

This complex situation represents a not uncommon repression
of freedom. It is repression of two kinds of freedom—that she played
a part in causing the situation by not dealing with Tom sooner, and
that she packaged her anger in her concern over the state of the
business. Her behavior is thus not experienced as free. Rationalization, in this case, temporarily allayed her anxiety.

Stage 2.
Anxiety

The second stage in the disclosure of one's free will leads to anxiety.
Free will is an enormous burden—as existentialists have repeatedly
pointed out in such phrases as "man is condemned to be free" and
"dreadful freedom." The burden is both causative and axiological.
To know we are free means, causatively, that each of us creates the
life we lead and the person we become—i.e., our actions—and ax-
iologically (in terms of values) that we choose a particular system of
universal values out of an abyss of nothingness.

That picture of a person, that realization of one's own nature,
if understood with its full affective impact, is difficult to bear. When
Helen, in our example, realized how her own free choices were behind her earlier repression and how she freely made events happen
to project her own free will onto her partner, she experienced great
guilt and anxiety. She wished she had never developed that insight,
regardless of how it served her.

Stage 3.
Mastery and Release

The third stage in the disclosure of free will is a sense of power, control, strength, integrity, and consequent self-confidence and peace of mind. Helen, in our example, eventually came to understand that her anxiety about her free will was caused in part by her fear that she might choose the wrong acts and the wrong values.

Once she recognized that these are merely choices—that right and wrong are her choices in turn—and that free choosing, free creation, is the prime divine attribute, she felt an extraordinary sense of release. She realized her life is her own and that success and failure in it is entirely in her hands, regardless of how the business does. She felt master of the situation and acquired the competence, ease, and grace in structuring her life that we find when the most accomplished playwright manipulates a script's characters and situations.

And Helen was free to discover sources of her disappointment toward her partner that were more basic than anything she had heretofore had the courage to face. As a consequence, her sense of betrayal subsided and she reorganized her life in a way that gave her a genuine sense of meaningfulness. She was then free to deal with Tom, her partner, in a direct way that was clear, unclouded by her displaced anger and deep disappointment.

Stage 4.
"Peak Experience"

The fourth and final stage in the disclosure of free will is the *summun bonum* (highest good) of philosophical thought; it is the experience of the miracle of being in one's own person; it is the realization and appreciation of the fact that we exist; it is the experience of the concretion, mystery, wonder, and marvel of our existence. That experience goes beyond the goals of traditional coaching or even psychotherapy. By the exercise of free choice the individual ceases to be a disembodied consciousness and becomes the rich and full person of passion, or, in the words of Spanish philosopher and educator Miguel de Unamuno, the "man of flesh and bones." This can be a profoundly religious and aesthetic experience.

As she looked back on the marvels achieved by the discovery and exercise of her free will, Helen had some profoundly moving philosophical experiences about the worth of life, the marvel of being. She felt true joie de vivre. She felt joyous over the mere fact that she was alive—the practical situation of her life was altogether adventitious. She saw that she was free and she proved it to herself by exercising that free will. She richly experienced what Abraham Maslow has called "peak experiences." Such results are indeed worth achieving.

Poet and playwright Archibald MacLeish expressed it when he said, "The world was always yours; you would not take it."

THE STRUCTURE OF DENIAL

And what of those stuck in denial? What is the frame of mind, the world view, the perception of reality of a person who says that free will does not exist? Or a person who insists on a deterministic and mechanistic world view, who perceives the world as predictable?

The Determinist View

First of all, the determinist does not *prove* that every event has a cause; it is *assumed*. A determinist freely chooses to make this assumption, since there is no way to arrive at it except to choose it.

But as soon as we discover and understand that an assumption is indeed chosen—that it can come into being in no other fashion than through some kind of archetypal decision—then we have recognized the primacy of choice and the certainty of free will. Thus in existential philosophy we do not seek to prove anything but only to describe the primary and raw data of uninterpreted experience.

If we now describe a determinist philosophically, we see that it is impossible to portray one's inner conscious structure without inserting the root fact that one arbitrarily, freely, and without rational or experiential grounds *chooses to view the world in terms of the assumption that every event has a cause which fully determines it.* There can be no other explanation.

The determinist says, "I shall consider meaningful only those events, sentences, and occurrences for which I can find an antecedent and determining set of situations or causes." And then, simply, "I assume that every event has a cause, and I assume further that the cause fully determines the nature and the existence of that event. If I can*not* find a cause for a specific event, I conclude that it has not yet been discovered but that at some future time will be."

It is clear that the determinist does not *argue* for a position but *assumes* it before any argument takes place. The existentialist rejoins by appealing to the facts of experience rather than to blind prejudice. No matter how conclusive may be the experimental evidence, the determinist will always demand that we continue the search until something is found that satisfies our criteria of *cause.* If we still fail, they will insist that we cannot find the cause, not that it does not exist. And this situation will never change.

The scientific outlook, which includes the medical model of the person, thinks of people as objects (the ghost-in-a-machine theory of the person). Researchers who function within this model are therefore subject to the same a priori demands for causal explanations as they would expect to apply to any physical object. But when we begin to integrate into medicine other theories of being, then we can overcome this archetypal decision for determinism. We then become capable and willing to realize that, since persons are not objects but also transcendental subjects, i.e., conscious egos, a legitimate place for free will can be found in behavioral science research. To be specific, we begin to accept the idea that we play a part in choosing our own illness. Medicine, psychology, and psychiatry change drastically when free will becomes fully integrated into these fields as a meaningful and logical truth, one which is completely consistent with the most rigorous application of the scientific method.

Choosing Cause and Effect

The consensual world makes a *decision* to perceive the world as having causes and it *chooses* to be blind to contrary evidence and experience. No real empirical evidence is brought to bear on the validity of the deterministic position.

That we have not found the cause for cancer can never mean to the scientist that cancer does not have a cause. On the contrary, scientists redouble their efforts and spend more energy and money than before to search for it. Thus, if there should ever be an event for which we do not know the cause, we never say that it does not have one, but rather that the cause is hidden. And common sense is absolutely rigid on this point. We are a culture of determinists, and the determinist assumes—in fact, *insists*—that everything is determined. The phenomenological disclosure is that we do not *discover* this fact. Indeed, the requirement that every event have a determining cause then becomes the very test for meaning itself. Unless our experience can be interpreted as cause-and-effect sequences, we choose not to understand it. Our selective perception does not notice an event if it does not appear in a cause-and-effect context. Determinism is therefore a decision about how to perceive and interpret experience; it is not a scientific discovery or description about the nature of our human experience. That is how the deterministic frame of mind operates.

Deciding Against Freedom

Thus, determinism is *freely* chosen and the belief in free will is *freely* denied. Determinists *freely* choose and accept the assumptions that they make. They are personally *responsible* for making these assumptions. They are not *forced* to accept them. Nothing in their nature coerces them into making them. However, our culture and the scientific outlook, common sense and the consensual world, do encourage us to make these assumptions. But there is another deeper reason why this is so. Religion has called it the Fall of Man. Others call it materialism or plain ignorance of the philosophical realities of human existence. We might here call it the objectivist fallacy—the rejection of subjectivity, of consciousness, of the reality of the silent and solitary center. Objectivism is the malaise of our age, and the convulsions of the resultant symptoms are almost beyond coping.

In sum, a careful phenomenological analysis, one that is sensitive to the intentionality of all experience and fully recognizes the reality of the transcendental dimension—the realm of pure consciousness—present in all experience, discovers a zone of freedom every time determinism is asserted, every time the world is perceived or conceived as causal. Determinism is a conscious act, a constituted (constructed) meaning, and as such it emanates from a center; and one of the defining characteristics of that highly specific center is its freedom.

In particular, the decision *for* determinism is the decision *against* freedom. It is a free choice to deny freedom. That decision is made deep in the unconscious, deep in the personality, deep in the body, and deep in the roots of society. The decision *for* determinism is thus an archetypal one, that is, one of the very first decisions (logically *and* chronologically) made and continuously being made whose effect is to organize the most basic structures of our world. Furthermore, determinism is repressed self-deception; it is philosophical suicide. Our last free act—after which no further free acts are possible—is to deny that we are free. This process is the mechanism of dehumanization and the dynamics of depersonalization. Because of the pervasiveness of this denial of freedom, we live in an age of alienation, an age that cannot manage its freedom-induced anxiety.

A determinist *freely chooses to reject any consciousness of freedom* because of the pain, agony, and suffering—in short, anxiety—which accompanies that discovery. Freedom is a volcanic discovery; there is superficial merit in aligning oneself with the forces that deny and resist it. But ultimate authenticity can never be achieved without being in possession of the fullness of one's freedom.

A MENTAL EXPERIMENT

To better understand your own connection to determinism, you might perform the following exercise. Put yourself in the frame of mind that says, "I cannot accept free will; there is no free will.

Even though I cannot immediately recognize the causes for my actions, thoughts, and feelings, as I explore myself further and increase my learning I do begin to discover these causes. Eventually I will uncover the antecedent situations that forced me to accept certain ideas, and to speak as I do and be the kind of person that I am. As Jane or John Doe, I have been *determined* by the causes in my background to talk and to write about *free will.*"

Now that you have fantasized yourself into this deterministic position, try to describe it. A careful phenomenological description of your own frame of mind should make it clear that you are *choosing* to be a determinist. All experience is intentional, and so is the experience of determinism. Even the deterministic world design is perceived by an ego and is constituted by an ego. And all acts of constitution contain an element of freedom, since they can be chosen, rechosen, preserved, and undone.

Furthermore, in choosing determinism, you are also choosing the consequences of determinism. These are, among others, that the universe is explainable, not mysterious; that the universe is rigid, not loose; that the universe is predictable, not unpredictable; and that the universe is clear, not ambiguous. In choosing determinism you deny the shadow region (Jung's term) within you, which is represented by the objective *ambiguity* of the world and by its subjective correlate, the absolute *freedom* for self-definition. The choice for a deterministic world view is furthermore the decision to avoid responsibility. Your world has now been constituted as rigid, and as purely black and white. The gray areas, which are ambiguous and retain their flexibility to willingly accept our projections, have been blotted out.

A deterministic world view therefore gives the illusion that it protects you from anxiety. Specifically, the free choice of determinism shields you from the anxiety that is inherent in the dual indeterminism of human existence itself. In sum, the decision for determinism says, "I will not *look* at my freedom. I will not *accept* a world view that tells me that I am free. I will use my freedom to *deny* my freedom. I will use my freedom for *self-deception*." That is the voice of the neurotic anxiety of freedom.

CONSEQUENCES OF KNOWING THAT WE ARE FREE

Realizing the fact and nature of our freedom makes us mature; it gives us the reins of our life—we can exercise control, direction, and command over our own existence. We each become, in short, an individual, with all the satisfaction, concreteness, solidity, and security that this implies. Successful and authentic living and action require a constant consciousness of the fullness of our freedom and the corresponding responsibility and control.

Accepting Responsibility and Accountability

Another value of deeply understanding free will is that we may, as a consequence, be more willing to accept our responsibility. Once it is clear that we cannot avoid responsibility—regardless of how we choose—we are better prepared to freely accept this responsibility. Our energies will be channeled into fulfilling our responsibilities intelligently rather than into futile attempts to avoid them. It is a sign of grave inauthenticity and immaturity and a sure sign of failure in life to be unwilling to consciously accept the responsibility that is ours by our very nature.

The willingness to accept full responsibility—that is, to be accountable for all the implications of our actions—grows directly out of accepting the fact of our free will. Once the inevitability of accountability is recognized, we will be inclined to place the full blame on ourselves rather than on others or on objective situations beyond our control. We may thus avoid the dangerous choice of fatalism. Once we are clear about the fact that, whether we like or approve, we are fully accountable for the general character of our lives, for our actions and omissions, only then will we resolutely take the stance that we are willing to assume these responsibilities. When we see the inevitability of a demand, we can willingly engage in its execution.

Embracing Risk and Decisions

Another consequence of the insight that we are free, in the sense that we have free will, is our willingness to take risks. Life is a succession of risks anyway; yet the quality of our lives differs from bad to good to the extent that we take risks grudgingly or freely and willingly.

Any decision is a risk and entails a commitment to a set of values and a type of personality. Decision involves risk and commitment. The risk varies with the momentousness of the decision. But to realize that risk is an inevitable, albeit unpleasant, ingredient in choice makes risk not a surprise to be avoided but an impenetrable barrier to be stoically accepted. Say someone resigns an important post to make a point of principle; the person resigns in protest. Such a decision means he or she accepts responsibility, full responsibility, and accepts risks. A courageous act cannot be performed without the clear-cut realization of the nature and of the existence of the structure of free will.

People in mid-life may be faced with the following decision: shall they continue with their present job until retirement or go into business for themselves? They may think the choice is between security and risk. This is not true. There are risks either way. Fundamentally, if they keep the job, they risk mediocrity in later life, personal dissatisfaction, years of an unlived life. On the other hand, if they open their own business they risk at least temporary financial failure. They must realize that they cannot avoid risk. Risk is part of the structure of our free will, and we must learn to live with risk as well as with death. We must learn to accept that fact, and accept it cheerfully. We must live with risk as we live with the necessity for food, drink, and sleep. When that necessity is recognized and accepted, the decision to go into business for yourself becomes relatively easy. You can make it on rational grounds. In this way you will be serving your own authentic interests best of all.

Experience Is Where We find It

Whereas the validity of logic and scientific experimentation is not to be denied, the acceptance and defense of freedom avails itself of more primitive methods. We must appeal directly to the basis of all knowledge—immediate experience. And we must be equally open to the transcendental as well as the empirical dimension— the zone of the subject *and* the region of the object. We must be willing, in searching for the facts of immediate experience, to refer to the world and to reflect into our inwardness. When we gaze into our inwardness we see with clarity—and with both hope and anxiety as well—our transcendental freedom; we perceive it also as irreducible, primitive, and primordial.

Chapter 4

THE EXISTENTIAL
UNDERSTANDING

What it means to be a person is your creation. The meaning of human existence, our provenance and destiny, the essence and definition of us all— these are not found or discovered; they are invented.

T HE PERSPECTIVE ON FREEDOM examined so far is at the heart of an existentialist view of what it means to be human. This chapter takes us deeper into the belief that each person is free or, more accurately, is a living freedom—and thereby accountable. At this point we want to look at the whole of what constitutes the existential viewpoint, including some summary of what has gone before. Following this chapter, we will go into more depth about the elements introduced here. Here is the fundamental architecture that supports our exploration of freedom and accountability.

Adapted from Peter Koestenbaum, "The Existential Crisis in Philosophy and Psychology," in *The Vitality of Death: Essays in Existential Psychology and Philosophy,* Westport, CT: Greenwood Publishing Co., 1971 (originally reprinted with permission from *Explorations,* no. 7: 26–41).

What we have stated is that freedom and accountability are inherent qualities of our existence. They are present all the time and do not have to be nurtured or induced, as much of our culture and many of our institutions believe is required. On the contrary, it takes conscious (or unconscious) effort to create conditions where people do *not* act accountably and do *not* experience the power of their freedom. The struggle to deeply experience our freedom and to live with the weight of full accountability for the world we have created is in itself not a problem to be solved, but rather what can give meaning to our lives.

THE EXISTENTIAL VIEWPOINT

The underpinnings of our beliefs about freedom have been named "existentialism." It is the close study of the person that leads to this theory of human existence. Existentialism is a unique method of inquiry that attempts a complete statement of the human condition, that is, a total view of what it really means—in its very last essence—to be human, or to exist as a human being in the world.

There is much popular misunderstanding about existentialism that treats it as a justification for unrestrained behavior and a countercultural literary style—even as a fad. It is not a morbid world view nor does it preach despair; it is not atheism, communism, or nihilism. In fact, it is only partially true that existentialism stands for what have unfortunately become the clichés of individualism versus conformity, the search for identity, boredom with luxury, and other popularized social criticism.

It must also be made amply clear that existentialism is not an atheistic philosophy. Existentialism is beyond the distinction between theism and atheism. While the decision about God is one of the most important decisions one has to face and make, the decision is ours exclusively—and so are the consequences. There are no absolute standards on the basis of which each person can determine the reality of God. The existence and nature of God have been ascertained on the basis of principles that individuals freely choose to accept or reject. In other words, the final responsibility for the solution of the religious question is a matter of free will: we must opt for or against God from the depths of our own inwardness.

In essence, existentialism today is a disciplined, systematic theory of being in general and of the person, within it, in particular. In fact, the frontiers of knowledge in philosophy, psychiatry, and theology have converged on one and the same image of the person. Existential philosophy, associated with names such as Kierkegaard, Nietzsche, Sartre, Heidegger, and Jaspers, agrees with the insights of depth psychology, such as those of Freud and C. G. Jung, and further leads to the kind of demythologized theology that has found acceptance with Bultmann, Tillich, and Buber.

Let us cut through all the highly technical, esoteric, and sophisticated verbiage about existentialism and examine in plain terms a few recurring themes in the emerging existentialist theory of being alive. We begin with the idea that we each create the world that we inhabit.

WORLD-CONSTITUTION

Fundamental to existentialist theory is the view that the world as it appears to us is our own creation (or co-creation), and we must assume responsibility for it. Suppose that the bricks out of which we can build a universe are a chaotic kaleidoscope of colors, shapes, sounds, smells, moods, hopes, fears, joys, pains, ideas, and movements; there is no up and down, no inside and outside, no "I" and no "other." Out of this anarchy, we organize a world for ourselves. We subdue the disordered shapelessness into a world by choosing one out of an infinity of possible structures. This act is called "constitution" or "construction." World and self co-create.

Imagine that you gaze reflectively for a long time on a stream of water rushing out of a faucet. Under these conditions, what do you *really* see as opposed to what you *think* you see? You are confronted not only with a conglomerate of sounds, colors, shapes, and motions, but also with associations, feelings, fantasies, and moods. The sound may become a color, a color may translate itself into a sound. You may associate with it the sound of sweet nothings whispered in love on a beach, the vigorous grip of your father's stentorian voice, the peaceful endlessness of time, or the sad swift loss of the fleeting present. This is what is there, in the world, before you have organized, interpreted, and reconstructed it. If, in organizing those experiences, you stress the voices, if you interpret moods to be external and colors internal, then we will accuse you of hearing voices and being abnormal. If, on the other hand, you organize the material into *running water* that mesmerizes you so that water is *outside* and associated emotions, voices, and moods are *inside,* then you have restructured the raw material in a normal way. Normal and abnormal are not absolutes; from a purely logical point of view they are equal. Normal and abnormal are freely chosen value ascriptions around which you have decided to organize your experience.

The most important conclusion to be drawn from these considerations is not that the stream of water—as stream rather than voices—is your creation, but that what it means to be a person is your creation. The nature of a person, the meaning of human existence, the provenance and destiny of men and women, the essence and definition of us all—all these are not found or discovered; they are invented. The supreme and most difficult creative act in world-constitution is the creation of ourselves. We invent ourselves as either God-fearing or as conceited and proud. We sometimes constitute our world so that our role is a noble giant, a Prometheus or a Zeus, or we project ourselves as insignificant and anonymous pipsqueaks in an infinite expanse of space and time. We choose ourselves as either heroic or cowardly, as sensuous or ascetic, as self-centered or altruistic. And we choose ourselves as either at home or alien in the world.

Creating our world is a dialogue; therefore we talk of co-creation.

At the focal point of our self-constitution there always is a value. That value becomes the absolute around which our world is organized. But that absolute is chosen by you out of an empty abyss, chosen arbitrarily but with total responsibility. The existentialist believes in the existence of absolute values, values to which you are totally committed and for which you will die. You are therefore free of the cowardice of the relativist—the person with no opinions, no convictions, no commitments, and no substance. But the existentialist also believes that we have freely chosen those values to be absolute. They are not *discovered* as absolutes; we have *invented* them as absolutes. In this way the existentialist is free of the chauvinism and intolerance of the fundamentalist—the person for whom there is but one correct opinion . . . and he or she happens to hold it. In addition, our creation of absolute values, far from making us weightless like the relativist without backbone, endows us with a powerful and concrete human existence.

QUESTIONING OUR ASSUMPTIONS

We must be cured of our propensity to accept the uncritical everyday world view as the correct image of ourselves. Here are some fundamental presuppositions—about ourselves and the world—that are not borne out by a close philosophic analysis of the facts of immediate experience. These assumptions are really our inventions, and each of us, in assessing human kind, must be open to questioning them, because through their disclosure we discover what we really are, as opposed to what we have been told about who we are.

Assumption 1.
"I am awake."

Dreams can duplicate all conditions of the waking state, even to the extent that we can dream that we are awake. That the distinction is clear and final and that the waking state is real, whereas the dream state is illusory, are not given data from our experience but are aspects of our choice in how to constitute our world. In many ways we do not know when we are awake and when we are asleep, and in fact the more we explore our own history, the more we discover how un-awake we have been.

Assumption 2.
"I am a body first, with a mind or soul contained within it."

You assume you are "a ghost in a machine," in the words of British philosopher Gilbert Ryle, an isolated mind-body complex. In actual fact, you experience yourself to be more like a vast sea of consciousness (called "transcendental consciousness," "*Sein,*" or "being") within which the world takes shape and moves. In that sea you have constituted anchor points, hard cores or nodules of presentations that we call "things" or "objects."

When you attend a lecture, the speaker appears as part lectern, part person, and part wall. But you, in a synthesizing act of conscious constitution, separate these areas of the given continuum into three independent *objects:* lectern, person, and wall. Furthermore, you associate the sounds with the person, not the lectern. But most important of all, *you do not experience yourself to be only your body, or even your personality.* On the contrary, your body is but one item within that vast sea of consciousness that you experience yourself as being. You experience first the room, then other bodies—your consciousness reaches out to them, *is* them. Only later do you reach out and identify with your own body. The newborn child does not automatically separate his or her body from that of the mother. In fact, when very young, infants are likely to experience the mother's breast as part of themselves, but not their own foot. Eventually, of course, your body becomes an item of the first importance within that sea of consciousness (which you are). The fact that we experience the self as not permanently connected to either our body or our psychological states has not been an uncommon insight connected with certain ascetic religious practices. Sometimes the self is experienced as less and sometimes as more than the body. You are emotionally attached to the body. You see it as a vehicle with which to perceive the world and with which you reach out to the world and show yourself to the world. If the attachment is excessively close, any threat to your body becomes a threat to being itself. The psychologist calls it narcissism, and it logically leads to unreasonable fears of death (thanatophobia), disease, the sight of blood, hypodermics, pain, etc.

A case illustrates this point.

Alicia was an eighteen-year-old girl with an exceptionally militaristic and domineering father. She had gained thirty pounds in her first semester of college, suffered severely from asthma and emphysema but refused to give up smoking, did not attend classes regularly, and failed many of her courses; she stayed out at night far beyond her curfew time and, in general, refused to take any parental advice. She had seen two psychiatrists, but refused to continue treatment and rejected hospitalization. She was unable to look into the future, to get a grasp of what lay ahead: it was a total blank for her.

After considerable dialogue, she found that the following existential interpretation of her condition allayed some of her anxieties, subdued her depression, helped restore her ability to look ahead, and placed her in a receptive mood for further counseling. An interpretation that she felt was useful to her was as follows:

Her father's authoritarianism had prevented her from experiencing her own existence through normal channels of self-affirmation, self-esteem, feeling attractive, education, popularity, etc. The situation became so desperate to her that she resorted to an individual's final form of self-assertion: She said, "No!" Because her father had symbolically appropriated her body, since he in fact insisted that she be but an extension of himself, she experienced her body not as part of herself but as part of him. As a consequence, her negative self-affirmation was directed against her father and his appendages—which included her body. Her need to feel her existence could be expressed only by saying "No!" to that part of her father most readily accessible to her, namely, her own body. She therefore worked at destroying it. This may appear to be a convoluted analysis, but emotionally it made sense. In her depth, she had "freely chosen" to construct her world in this fashion. But once she sensed that freedom, she also had access to rebuilding that toxic structure.

Alicia had constituted her world in an inauthentic fashion, a fact that can be realized only after we understand the distinction between *my awareness* and *my body.* She responded to that existential description with an *Aha!* experience; that is, she felt that it helped her to put her life in its proper perspective and increased her control over it so she could begin the process of reconstruction.

Assumption 3.
"The ego is split from the external world by an unbridgeable gap."

The philosophic question of mind-matter interaction is related to the presumed irrevocable chasm between the inner world of subjectivity and the outer world of objectivity. In actual fact, however, such a gap is our invention—that is, uninterpreted. Pure experience discloses an individual-world continuum. We could also argue, for example, that we are a vast sea of consciousness, which is, in fact, itself such an ego-universe continuum, which we then in turn sever artificially into two incompatible regions.

Assumption 4.
"Each person is a homunculus (a tiny person) within an infinite universe."

Confronted with the totality of being, I am a nothing—a nothing in infinite space, a nothing in infinite time. My power is like nothing, and my knowledge is, in the words of Socrates, only about the fact that I know nothing.

This view of a person is contrary to the facts of "scientific" experience. It applies to a body, but not to awareness. And we are our awareness, first and last. The view that a person is a nothing is an image in our own minds, an image we ourselves have constituted. Rather than being a nothing, our subjectivity or "inwardness" (as Kierkegaard called it) is the very foundation of everything. Our inwardness has the power of world-constitution or world-construction, and only words such as "divine" and "holy" can describe this potential adequately. The supreme power of creativity found in each person's inwardness is encapsulated in Aristotle's and Aquinas's conception of God as the Creator: the First Mover, First Cause, and Ultimate Substance. And it is written in Genesis that "God created man in His image," that is, as a creator. A far cry from being nothing.

Assumption 5.
"The person is not free. Our physical and spiritual life is the result of determining forces beyond our control."

We discussed this in the previous chapter and repeat it here for emphasis. This common, albeit strange assumption, that our life is the effect of causes beyond our control, is especially strange in view of the fact that we *do* experience our free will. For the existentialist, to espouse universal determinism or fatalism and to say that what we are, what we believe, and what we do are events beyond our control—that these are determined by heredity, environment, or divine edict—is merely to have made the deliberate and free choice to avoid recognizing responsibility over the life that we do in fact possess. Determinism is rationalization; it is deliberate self-deception because the burden of freedom is too heavy.

This is exemplified in the problem of Abraham when God asked him to sacrifice his son Isaac. Abraham knew what to do, because God told him. His real problem was not that he had to sacrifice his son, but that he had to decide entirely on his own whether that command was the voice of God or a mere hallucination. And even God could not help him there. In a crisis, we each experience the anxiety that our total freedom brings to the situation. At these moments we are in the role of God having to create a world of values. There is no appeal beyond our own final decision, but we must nonetheless take full personal responsibility. We only resolve the crisis when we take full, deliberate, clear, and conscientious charge of the situation. We *make* events happen, not allow ourselves to drift into them. We, not fate, became the master of our life. In other words, we mature.

THE SOURCE OF ANXIETY

Questioning these assumptions—that we are awake, that we are a body with a mind in it, that we are separated from the external world by an unbridgeable gap, and that we are so small and our life is the result of determining forces beyond our control—creates high anxiety.

W. H. Auden called the twentieth-century the "Age of Anxiety." Anxiety overarches our landscape not only because of the obvious—such as hot wars, cold wars, nuclear threats, mass propaganda, overpopulation, revolutions, emerging nations, social change, highway deaths, air pollution, and the like—but preeminently because of our geometrically increasing introspective self-knowledge. Oedipus, by solving the riddle of the Sphinx, delved deep into the human condition, yet he was punished with patricide, incest, despair, blindness, and infanticide for his knowledge. So were, perhaps, Adam and Eve. To know ourselves means to know anxiety, since anxiety is the drill that strikes gold at the heart of each of us.

Anxiety Is a Cognitive Emotion

Prior to any interpretation, anxiety—like all moods—occurs to us as an integral part of the world. As in the example of the way we constitute our view of the water streaming from a faucet, it is our own subjective reconstruction, structuring, or constitution of the world that decides to place the anxiety that suffuses the world before us *in me* and locates the colors, shapes, and sounds of the world *outside of me*.

In addition, we must recognize that anxiety is not an ancillary phenomenon. On the contrary, it is exceptionally pervasive—just as darkness is ubiquitous at night. The shift is that the experience of anxiety is not an undesirable pain but is, in fact, a fundamental clue to the authentic structure of the human condition.

Anxiety Carries Powerful Messages

What does anxiety disclose? We discover the answer, if we do not fight or repress anxiety but allow it to develop its message to us.

Meaninglessness

If we are honest with ourselves, we uncover the truth that we place certain irrevocable demands on life (total satisfaction or happiness, for example) and that, conversely, life places irrefragable demands on us (that we meet the demands of our conscience and our roles). A man who in his own eyes fails in his role as father feels that he himself has robbed life of meaning. Or a woman whose lifelong profession offers her no satisfaction is overpowered with the knowledge that life has failed to give her meaning. These truths are experienced as anxiety.

Anxiety is therefore a clue that we in fact experience life as empty, boring, pointless, and meaningless, although we may at the same time be terrified to admit it.

Nothingness

Anxiety shows that we are in the presence of our supreme dread, anguish, *angst*. Its name is "nothing," and its essence is the extinction of all value and of all being. Death is a common symbol for that nothingness. However, if we follow rather than fight anxiety to wherever it will lead us, we make additional and extraordinary discoveries. We realize that our supreme anxiety and our supreme values coincide. We are anxious about losing the things that matter most.

We discover, for example, that the highest and perhaps only meaning that life has to offer is found in the concrete and clear experience of one's existence. We experience the succulent richness of our existence in pleasure, courage, nobility, achievement, sacrifice, and responsibility. When all is lost, we can still experience the reality of our existence by simply saying, "No!"

Anxiety is the threatened loss of that existence. But if we now continue the introspective analysis of anxiety, we discover that the coincidence of our highest aspirations and deepest fears is even greater than we thought. For, what happens when we reach the nadir of despair? Does being cease? Not at all! Quite on the contrary, a solution is offered: Courage. The theologian Paul Tillich called it "the courage to be."

The Swiss psychoanalyst Medard Boss cites a case in point (rephrased here)—the translation of anxiety into security.

An unmarried woman psychiatrist had the not uncommon nightmares of being engulfed by snakes. Since she was also an artist, she would draw her dreams. Nightly the snakes approached, and as they were just upon her she would wake up in a terrified sweat. It was suggested to her that she give in rather than fight her anxiety, that she let the snakes approach her and that she look them straight in the face and try not to wake up. She did allow the snakes to come closer and found that their faces were horrible, ugly masks, ready to consume her. She continued this until one night she actually allowed the spine-chilling snakes with the blood-curdling masks to come closer than ever before and literally to engulf her. To her unbelieving, dreaming eyes, the heads turned gradually into a single head from which there emerged the figure of a lissome, delicate, beautiful, and sexually interesting young girl—the kind of person she had always wanted to be but never was. Her ultimate anxiety disclosed her genuine—and suddenly acceptable—feelings to her.[1]

Despair

It seems that we can choose our lowest despair as our highest goal precisely because that is the one way we can savor and see the fullness of our existence. If we permit anxiety to go even further than we have discussed up to this point, we discover that ultimate anxiety discloses the indestructible presence of consciousness. When, in the abyss of despair, the soul's dark night of nothingness finally arrives, we are still very much conscious; awareness is still around us everywhere. The idea suddenly comes to us—like a divine insight—that even total despair annihilates neither our consciousness nor our ego. In fact, "nothingness" is a term bereft of all meaning except as a fear confronting an ego.

It is impossible for the human mind to even imagine what could be meant by the elimination of its existence. This insight—that there can be no such thing as nothing, that each individual is a consciousness that cannot even imagine the nonbeing of that very same consciousness—is the rock bottom foundation for all ultimate security. It is a direct, experienced return to the very *ground of being* that we are. Thus, anxiety is the threshold that leads to the understanding that the consciousness and the ego (which is not the same as *my body* or *my person*) cannot be thought of as not existing. Depth psychology has sometimes symbolized the search for this insight as a desire to "return to the womb"—which presumably symbolizes ultimate regression, ultimate security, ultimate refuge. In theology, this intuition reappears as an argument for the existence of God, where God is conceived as an *existens a se*—a being that is not contingent but exists by virtue of its own inner necessity; a being whose essence is its existence.

It thus appears that through total anxiety we can achieve total security. And total security means permanent recognition of the reality, fullness, and concretion of existence. That conclusion may be stated epigrammatically by rewriting Descartes' famous *cogito, ergo sum* (I think, therefore I am) into "I despair totally, therefore I exist necessarily."

Some of my female colleagues have remarked that giving birth has been simultaneously their greatest and their most despairing moments, their most fulfilling and most anxious experience, their greatest pleasure and their gravest pain. This is a good illustration of what we may call the anxiety-security syndrome, the basic form of which is that we value anxiety, for it helps us to discover our necessary existence.

Death

We finally come to anxiety about death, which we will take up more fully later. Sartre writes that "man's project is God." For the theist this means that our goal as human beings is to imitate, glorify, and obey the living God. To the atheist this same statement means that each of us seeks to become an infinite being, a being traditionally represented in the myth of God. On either interpretation, the great paradox is our inexorable finitude. Anxiety is really anxiety about death, since death is our most dramatic limit, our sharpest reminder of our finitude. The presence of death leads to anxiety, but it also leads to courage, strength, and integrity, and makes clear what our genuine values really are.

A LARGER VIEWPOINT

Given our brief summary of the existentialist position through the themes of constitution, anxiety, death, our final responsibility for our values, and our need to feel the texture and substance of our existence, let us now examine how these may affect specific issues in the larger culture.

Democracy

Existentialism can provide a modern philosophic foundation and justification for the democratic way of life. The cornerstone of democracy is the dignity and even sanctity of the individual. In accepting democracy, we may have vague notions about the religious conceptions of a soul and of its relation to God; perhaps we know something about the theory of natural law, on which Jefferson based his views of democracy. Perhaps we are even familiar with Locke's *Treatise of Civil Government,* Mill's *Essay on Liberty,* and Rousseau's *Social Contract.* In all these cases the justification for the dignity of humankind is either oblique or based on complex metaphysics that are difficult to understand and have been, and can be, severely criticized.

A much simpler justification for democracy and the dignity of the person stems from the existentialist analysis of inwardness. We may call it the principle of "reverence for subjectivity." A careful description of the world leads us to the conclusion that our innermost subjectivity is the foundation for the structure of the world and the existence of those absolute values which guide the process of world-constitution or world-construction. The human race is indeed an Atlas who carries the world; our vision literally illuminates the world to make it what it is. How can anyone who understands that show disrespect for any human being? To understand the meaning of subjectivity is to automatically revere it. "Virtue is knowledge," said Socrates. To know about virtue is to make one virtuous. To know about the necessary existence of consciousness is to be grounded.

Free Will and Responsibility

According to this position, each of us must take total responsibility for his or her life's situation because, in most cases, one could have acted or chosen otherwise. Such an attitude may lead to an overburden of guilt but it also results in a sense of power, control, and direction over the quality of one's life. Each person must be reminded that a human being is "a being who has no excuses." But it must be made clear that total freedom is a sacred fact of life and not a moralistic reproach. Furthermore, those who instill this knowledge of responsibility in others are human too, and must as a consequence assume total responsibility for their impact.

The situation is no different for managers or parents. Each must assume total responsibility for the situation. When an employee or child has a problem, then, according to this analysis, that person is fully responsible both for his or her role in this person's existence and for the solution. But similar full responsibility rests on the manager or parent. Each one is *fully* responsible since it is a fact of human existence that he or she can influence the situation to an extraordinary degree. Not only is each individual responsible for the solution of another person's problem, but is likewise responsible to make clear to others their own full responsibility in turn. I can always do far more than I do or think I can do. And for that vacuum I am also responsible.

Thus, from this seemingly extreme point of view, the manager is totally responsible for the welfare of employees, but that responsibility extends also to support the belief that employees are fully responsible for their lives. The statement "I am responsible for you" implies the statement "I am responsible for teaching you that you are responsible for yourself." This ostensibly paradoxical approach of relegating responsibility without any personal exoneration is called the "sense of subjective responsibility." Responsibility has the same magical properties of knowledge and of wisdom. You do not reduce your share of it by giving all of it away to the world. In fact, you increase it. The point here is to clarify free will and accountability as core structures of human existence more than to prescribe management techniques.

Paideia: The Creation of an Adult from the Child

Leaders and managers—for optimum effectiveness and because of their position at the fulcrum of society—must not only be competent professionals but, even more important, authentic human beings. Engineers can program computers effectively with skill alone. They need no humanity for it. People leading others, on the other hand, cannot fulfill their role with skill alone. They need the potential for encounter with others as an authentic human being. Therefore, the leader-manager must be thoroughly grounded in the science of being a whole person.

The way we lead or manage, and the way we construct our institutions, depends on our theory of what it means to be human. Today's goals are often based on unclear theology, outdated political philosophy, uncritical common sense, and the youngest of our sciences, psychology. Existential philosophy, applied to psychology, has been an attempt to develop a way of thinking about what it means to be a human being in a way the fits the unique nature of acting as a leader.

Values

Leaders must make clear, to themselves as well as to those they lead, that everyone has the responsibility to choose a commitment to values. To live is to have such a commitment. We have made a choice of values, whether we like it or not, even if that choice has been the repression of the issues involved. Each of us is a god with respect to our values. We choose whether to accept our religion, our parental admonitions, leadership from a boss, and our culture. We choose whether to rebel and strike out on our own or whether to accept what the environment offers us. We choose whether to concern ourselves with values or to ignore the problem. And in choosing the values we choose also the consequences of our choices.

Whether we like it or not, we are fully responsible for our relation to values, but at the same time our decision is final and is true by virtue of the fact that we have made it. It is the leader's responsibility to instruct the people on the gravity of this situation, its inevitability, and the extraordinary power and dignity associated with it. That is the existential method of leadership.

Language

Language is a basic form of self-transcendence—going past where we are now. It must be understood in the same expressive and temporal sense as music, painting, and the dance. But beyond that, language is also a form of world-constitution, world-construction. Our peculiar mode of structuring our world—including all the assumptions of the uncritical world view that we discussed earlier—is built into our language. For example, the declarative and subject-predicate structure of sentences embodies the chasm between world and ego. Language says, "Ideas exist in the mind." Language creates a partition between ideas and mind, making the latter into a container. But that distortion results only from the preposition "in" and the fact that we separate mind and ideas instead of making them one and the same, such as "the ideamind."

Both of these aspects of language should affect our understanding of what we call "the skills of communication." In the first place, it is a mistake to think of language as principally concerned with communication. It is above all an act of self-creation through expression and an act of world-creation through self-transcendence. The teaching of language becomes then partially the teaching of unhesitating self-expression and world-creation. Discipline and rules must be introduced slowly and judiciously. Communication proper appears when language is directed toward the encounter with another human subjectivity.

We need to take seriously language as a means for self-transcendence—reaching out to the world, striving for more than we are. When we write or speak, it needs to have the quality of free-associative expression, where the important thing is the continuous flow of the self through language into the world and not disciplined orthography and syntax, not even logic. Discipline can be introduced as *support* to expression (in the case of communication) rather than as a brake to expression (which is too often the case). Language, as self-transcendence, is self-expression reaching out toward another inwardness, another receptive consciousness. The self-expression element can be cultivated by encouraging the free flow of language and the encounter with others it makes possible.

Finally, speaking, writing, and even listening must bring joy, since they are the only sure index that self-transcendence is open, authentic, and successful.

Part I

IMPLICATIONS

WHEN WE DECIDE that supporting freedom is in the interest of our institutions, we shift our thinking about management. Who needs to be managed? Who does the managing? Does control have to be engineered or might it find its own level? These are not new questions, but our thinking changes in the context of this discussion about freedom. The challenge is to welcome and institutionalize the existence of freedom with as much enthusiasm as we have welcomed and institutionalized the need for boundaries and the need for constraint. The belief that freedom must be managed and actually feared, as opposed to released, has led us to our current bureaucratic set of practices. Here are some implications of choosing a faith in freedom that up to now we have conferred upon control.

1.
EMPLOYEES DO NOT NEED
TO BE MOTIVATED

The moment we accept that each person is constituting the world in which they live, we stop thinking that the job of managers is to take responsibility for the morale and motivation of people who work for them. Human motivation is an individual decision, not an environmental consequence. We currently act as if people are not inherently motivated, rather that they go to work each day and wait for someone else to light their fire. This belief is common among managers and employees alike. The belief that management is responsible for employee actions is the perfect defense, for each side is quick to blame the other for their disappointments.

It is one thing to hear employees blame management for their lack of motivation or even performance; it is another thing for managers to swallow the bait and believe it. We have accepted the idea that managers are responsible for their employees' attitudes and behavior, so much so that in some organizations, managers are evaluated and paid based on employee ratings of their manager.

All people are also responsible for their own morale. If employees want to be depressed, then why would we steal from them that right? This is not to deny that there are some managers whom no one wants to work for, who abuse their power and should not be managers. But, their employees still have a choice about how to deal with them. They have a choice to stay or leave, to join together to demand a change, to ignore management and get on with the work, or to unionize and structurally institutionalize their power.

When top management or a staff group conducts an attitude survey of employees that asks how they feel about management, they collude with the part of employees that does not want to be responsible for their own experience. It legitimizes the idea that employee well-being is in the hands of management. Plus, when top management gets the survey information, it is rare they can find really useful ways to act on it.

It is right and human for managers to care about the motivation and morale of their people, it is just that they are not the cause of it. Managers should ask for feedback from employees about how they could improve as managers, but they ask this out of their own interest and desire to learn, not for the sake of their employees. If we decide to view employees as free and accountable, then we stop fixing them.

Also, if we want to hold on to the belief that managers and employees create each other, why do we believe that motivation only flows downhill? Who motivates the managers? Does it make sense to believe that it is the employees' job to be responsible for the morale and motivation of those above them? If a manager is depressed, do we expect employees to ask what they are doing to depress that manager? Do we ever ask what new skills they need to increase top management's spirits? Not often.

2.
REWARDS DO NOT EXPLAIN AND DRIVE BEHAVIOR

The most sacred and widely accepted belief in organizations is that rewards, in the form of praise and compensation, drive behavior—that people will only do what is institutionally rewarded. What does not get rewarded does not get done. Touch this belief and your fingers get burned.

Without getting too deeply into the specifics of compensation (there is a whole chapter in *Stewardship* on this), what is relevant here is the belief that instrumental barter is fundamental to our organizational relationships. We think that the institution must purchase what it wants from people, just as it purchases every other resource. If we want a certain behavior, we have to order it and put money on it.

Alternatively, if we accept that employees are choosing their actions freely and of their own accord—and are thereby choosing the world they want to live in—we would keep barter and pay in perspective. We would put it on a back burner, make it fair and transparent, but not fundamental. It would cease being a universal solvent. We would then stop turning to economic solutions to problems whose source lies elsewhere.

This would put an end to devices such as golden handcuffs, hiring bonuses, and staying bonuses. We would make employees stock owners because it seems right to us since they are actively creating the wealth of the organization, not because it will change their behavior. We might question the elitist distinctions we make by having different pay systems for executives, managers, and workers. One effect would be to disconnect executive pay dramatically from stock price, since there is little hard evidence that this helps create a healthy future for an institution.

The specifics, though, do not really matter. What matters is the recognition that human beings cannot be purchased; they are not possessions or assets of the organization who are reducible to simple market transactions. And if, despite this argument, it still seems to you that employees are primarily driven by pay and promotion, then take this as the product of a world you have chosen to construct, a picture you have chosen to paint.

3.
THE ORGANIZATION DOES NOT HAVE TO DEVELOP "ITS" EMPLOYEES

When we decide that each employee is a freedom and an accountability by nature, then employee development becomes simply an opportunity for self-definition. It is no longer the responsibility of the organization to develop "its" people. Even the possessive term "its" implies that the employee belongs to the organization, that the organization owns "its" people. If we stop possessing people, then our organizations can support learning and have a stake in learning, but are not responsible for it. People would be required to choose their own way of learning, defining their own learning goals, and figuring out how and when to pursue them.

Management would give feedback to employees, be happy and disappointed in them, but it is the employee who decides what change is needed. The implicit bargain around performance—that if the employee exceeds management expectations, then management will in some way take care of the employee—would disappear. The institution will always make demands, reward and punish individuals, but the rewards do not become a bargaining chip. In reality, rewards and punishment come to each person with the same predictability as the weather: it can make a big difference to us, but the idea that we can control it or ultimately predict it is foolish.

When people are forced to face the reality of their own freedom, and that management no longer possesses them, they see that their future is in their own hands. While the rewards that management has to offer may be of value, they are no longer compelling.

They cease to be an excuse for our actions. If I know that my freedom is my birthright—that my future is mine to create—then I will no longer be foolish enough to look longingly at the organization and ask them what I should become or what they have in mind for me. Ambition gets redefined as a pursuit of individual and organizational purpose, not a pursuit of advancement, progress, or appreciation. And the idea that we would ask the organization to "promote" us would make as little sense as asking your partner in business or in life to "promote" you.

This mindset also changes the nature of the training programs we offer. They will demand more participant initiative. Participants will join in defining their goals, constructing the form of the learning, and being responsible for its success. Training will stop being something *done to* or *for* the employee, but something *done by* and *with* the employee. Individuals are responsible for co-constructing their lives and so also their learning experiences. The idea that people do not know what they do not know is no longer used as a rationalization for high control teaching to supposedly empty vessel students.

Evaluation also is an important bellwether or symbol of our stance on freedom. When we ask people to evaluate a meeting or learning event, we should ask them to evaluate how they themselves did, not what was done to them. If we continue to decide what people should learn and how they should learn it, we will forever have to convince them the learning is good for them. We will continue to sell them on learning, mandate or nominate their attendance, and they, in turn, will act as if learning is an entitlement instead of a privilege. When participants enter the room of a learning event knowing full well that they chose to be there, the social contract of their learning has shifted dramatically. It is no longer up to the instructors to prove their own value and relevance; it is clear from moment one that the learner is responsible for the value received.

This is more than a shift in semantics; it is a shift in the social contract. It breaks the parenting bondage. It also dramatizes the cost of our freedom. And we move in this direction not because the employee is asking for it, but because we are committed to the well-being of the institution and to a world based on real life. The existing deal between institution and employee, despite the free agency rhetoric of the last few years, is still based on the unreal belief that the institution owns the employees and therefore is morally and operationally forced to motivate them, reward them, and develop them.

One more element of human resources is for us to reassess our thinking about whom we hire. We now screen people according to their past. We use criteria that have little basis in fact. We want people who have attended certain schools, achieved certain levels of education, chosen certain rites of passage. Little of this is based on fact; it is more an issue of class. School class and social class. One of the blessings of the Internet revolution is that it has made visible the possibility that people can contribute according to their inherent talent, and not the accident of their family or educational history.

All this requires each of us to face our own faith in the possibilities of our freedom and the hope that that encourages, that we will create chosen accountability to replace the purchased and mandated accountability that drives our conventional wisdom. What reassures me in seeking a different way of thinking is that the current wisdom is not working very well. Our institutions may often seem successful, but they are so despite being a breeding ground for entitlement and passivity, not service and activism.

4.

LEADERSHIP IS ABUNDANT, NOT RARE

Leadership is the willingness to initiate the world, to involve others in producing what did not exist before. This is the exercise of freedom, which means that leadership includes the task of confronting other people with their freedom. If we would shift the discussions of freedom from worrying about boundaries to worrying about how to maximize local choice and flexibility, we would expect leadership instead of searching for it. Our beginning assumption would be that people are capable of using their freedom in service of the institution, and we would not put so much energy into setting hurdles that require people to demonstrate their worthiness to act freely.

Leaders would also accept the idea that employee expectations of leaders are unfulfillable and need to be confronted. Leaders do not exist to meet the expectations of followers. We confront people with their freedom when we respect their own capacities, and this gives us the freedom to say no to them. Clearly, explicitly. Too often our lips say yes, and no is left to the expression in our eyes.

Leaders exist to use the breadth of their position to see where the institution should be placed in its marketplace. We need a vision about where the enterprise should be headed; we do not need a vision from leaders about how we should behave and what values we should embrace. Employees have a deep sense of values and can be as trusted to live them out as fully as we trust our leaders. At what point did integrity become a quality defined by organizational level?

If leaders want to walk their talk, work as a team, listen well, and send single, consistent messages to the world, let them do it for their own sake, not for the sake of low power people. We are condescending to each other when we think that leaders carry a special and unique role model burden of expressing the humanity of the institution. If we eliminate leader as cause and employee as effect, this will work to eliminate the class structure in our institutions and reduce the social distance between levels. The privilege systems that differentiate by level and class do not serve the institution well; they only serve to reinforce our fear of democracy and our belief in a special ruling class. Leadership in an environment of freedom and accountability stands for each person being a manager, a leader, all responsible for the well-being of the larger world.

Those in power do have the responsibility of using that power with some grace. They need to take the idea of liberty seriously and work to eliminate oppressive controls. This is mostly an exercise in restraint. We need to stop managing people's time, managing their expenditures, worrying about on-the-job Internet journeys and personal phone calls. Go light on supervision, maybe even get rid of the word. Who has super vision anyway? Most of us end up wearing glasses regardless of our institutional level.

Although this might all appear soft-headed, it is actually the opposite. It creates a culture in which people are held somewhat brutally accountable for meeting their promises and commitments. When we expect people to act as freely choosing individuals, we take away their excuses, de-legitimize their ability to blame others, and we put light in places where they or we once hid. This would begin to give us a real world.

Part II

THE POTENTIAL OF ANXIETY

A^{S} INDIVIDUALS, we spend enormous energy defending against anxiety, and this is reflected in our organizational life. We try to construct a workplace where anxiety is reduced to a minor distraction. The common managerial injunction, "Don't bring me problems, bring me solutions," is a good example of our defense against the ambiguity and uncertainty of life.

Much of what we usually describe as bureaucracy—caution, slavishness to rules, needing many approvals before doing anything—is really a defense against our inherent anxiety. We usually don't attribute our caution to our own experience of anxiety; we are more likely to attribute its cause to our bosses or our subordinates, or anyone who happens to be in our field of vision at the moment.

This pervasive point of view, that my anxiety is caused by the external world, is placed in question by the philosophy expressed in the next three chapters. Peter outlines the revealing and transforming potential of anxiety. He opens the possibility that this experience of tension that I have been running from, and that organizations are organized to deny, needs to be embraced, welcomed, and accepted.

The implications of this point of view are enormous. If we could learn to live with anxiety and see it as a positive key to our own well-being, and not something erasable or caused by others, we could then drop our defensive routines. We could begin to trust ourselves more and to trust each other. We would be less fearful of people in power, for we would realize that the grief we thought they brought us was in reality unavoidably self-inflicted.

THE FRUITS OF YOUR PATIENCE

A friendly caution. You may grow weary of all this talk of anxiety, and of having to absorb concepts such as "consciousness" and "transcendence" that come with definitions that slip away one minute after they have been articulated.

It is also possible you may at times become impatient with continually dwelling on subjects that seem to hold a negative cast and language that often confuses more than clarifies. The common response to philosophy—at least for most of us—is to drift and lose some interest. This response, in itself, is interesting for it is likely a measure of how embedded we are in rationality and science as a way of explaining our experience. There is no language that the larger culture has less patience with than the language of philosophy.

The first response to philosophic thinking and language is to want to get practical. "How does this apply to how I operate in the real world?" "Give some practical examples where these ideas have built successful organizations." "Why can't you use words that I am familiar with?"

This impatience, while fair game and valid, is also an example of the theory being presented in the book, for the impatience is an example of the experience itself—it is our anxiety. And we want to solve it. We want to transform anxiety—an experience, a feeling, a reaction—into some action that will make it go away.

Our institutions use speed and time as the argument for action. We feel that reflection, introspection, inward thought take too long. If something cannot be done quickly, it is not worth doing—there is something wrong with it. This is true at every level, whether it is the hunt for quarterly earnings improvement, the need for a shorter cycle time of a new product or process, the desired training time for new skills, or the search for a living God. We value speed over depth and action over insight.

While of course there is a marketplace requirement for timeliness and we know there are just so many hours in the day, our desire for speed and concreteness is more than a rational response to environmental requirements. It has invaded every aspect of our lives. I can't watch television without a remote control, I need quick service on vacation, I even want to know the gender of my unborn child.

OUR RESPONSE TO ANXIETY

All of these qualities of modern culture can be viewed as a way of life in the information age and the new economy, but they can also be seen as symptoms of how we manage our own anxiety, which is to escape it or eliminate it. For much of my life, in fact until I ran into Peter and his philosophy, I viewed anxiety as a weakness, a problem to be solved. In the terms of the following section, I was anxious about being anxious. One place this became visible was when I had to make a presentation for my work.

As with many of us, the prospect of public speaking created great stress. I would worry about the talk, I would over or under prepare for the talk, I would carry too many transparencies, PowerPoint® slides, and even then, in some dark moments, I would imagine my escape. I would wonder what would happen if I did not even show up for the talk. How far could I get before I would have to pay a price for my irresponsibility?

At one level you might say that what I needed was more confidence, more practice perhaps, some training in public speaking, or some private affirmations I could speak to myself to shore myself up. While all of this might help some, these actions represent a solution to a wrongly defined problem. The presentation was not the problem.

The problem was my response to the experience of being afraid, or anxious—what existential philosophy would call my neurotic anxiety. What I did not realize for too long was that the tension I felt about speaking to groups was a sign of life. It was anxiety that was dragging me more actively into finding my own voice, facing my wish to present a perfect face to the world, helping me find my own legs to stand on.

At some point, although the physical experience of the anxiety was disconcerting, I began to see it as water into which I needed to dive—that the anxiety was an invitation to move toward those things I had tried to avoid. This revelation shifted my response to the fear, and I actually got pretty good at speaking to groups. I still do not really enjoy the speaking, but it gives meaning to the ideas that I care about and gives me a platform from which I can engage the world.

THE PROMISE OF ANXIETY

This instinct to treat anxiety as the enemy drives a great deal of our behavior at work, in the so-called real world. The workplace raises for each of us a bundle of anxious emotions. We worry about our bosses and how they feel about us. We carry the burden of promises we made that we may not deliver on; we are embroiled in territorial disputes, and budget pressure, and on it goes. We spend enormous time and energy trying to solve these pressures by applying more structure and definition. We fill out feedback forms on our bosses. We develop complex project management protocols for our promises. We meet endlessly, trying to define and negotiate territory. We spend endless resources on information technology in the belief that if we watch money more closely, it will go farther.

The insight of philosophy gives us a chance to see all of these responses to our anxiety as futile attempts to eliminate or solve what are inherent qualities of being a human being. This insight has the potential to save us time and resources if we could reframe the question and stop trying to fix what in reality is not a problem, but a signpost that something important is on the table. Anxiety is designed and built into the experience of being part of an organization, especially one that survives by delivering results. The moment we shift our thinking about our experience, in the ways Peter writes about, then new possibilities open up for our institutions.

THE LANGUAGE
OF FREEDOM

There is a fine line between philosophy, religion, and spirituality. They all occupy the domain of feeling, experience, and consciousness, which balance our more common focus on data, reason, and science. The language of philosophy, religion, and spirituality—while it is about real life and is based on the fact of who we are—is more like poetry than engineering speech in that it seeks those areas of life that are paradoxical and defy clear measurement.

The language of philosophy is poetic and complex by design, for language is a primary way that we express our freedom and, in a sense, acknowledge it into existence. The common language of the culture in place, sometimes called the default culture, is anything but poetic. It is primarily the language of engineering and economics and some psychology. In our organizations, we use the language of results, outcomes, negotiation, and barter. We talk of systems, strategy, and appraisal. Schedule, metrics, and milestones. Data and information management. Competency models, modifying and prescribing desired behavior. The bottom line and the ones above it become the point.

The language of freedom is quite different. Even the word "freedom" seems traditionally out of place in institutions. But if we want to come to terms with our freedom, then we are taken into the language of the poet or priest. The language akin to deepening our experience uses words like "forgiveness," "destiny," "confession," "compassion," "wisdom," "feeling," "guilt," "transformation," and "revelation."

These words not only describe the world of the soul, but they in fact create it. If we want our organizations to become more humanly habitable, more supportive of developing the capacity of the person, and also more focused on service than on economics, then it begins with a shift in language. The language is one of the challenges of a book on philosophy, for purposely using language that defies definition becomes a political point. The language we use declares where the power lies.

Will we decide to take the language of philosophy, and perhaps religion, and force fit it into the mindset of engineering and economics? Or do we bring the unadulterated language of the soul and heart into the world of work, and thereby occupy some of the space formerly held exclusively by rationality and scientific proof? The final answer will be that we need both ways of constructing the world, which is why we included the idea of accountability in the title of this book. It is a declaration that we need both economist and philosopher defining the nature of our institutions. It is a mistake, however, to smooth over the political significance of the words we use by getting too chummy too quickly.

It is because words like "revelation," "guilt," "forgiveness," and "compassion" seem somewhat out of place in many (not all) institutions that the use of these words is powerful. What is at stake is the answer to the question of who defines reality—the economist or the philosopher? In western culture, the economist has had full rein in defining what counts and deciding how we measure how we are doing. This is inevitable in a materialistic, consumer driven society.

SHIFTING THE CONTEXT

The fact that we are increasingly interested in the subjects of freedom, meaning, and destiny, though, means that something's blowing in the wind, and has been for some time. For several years now books on soul, poetry, and spirituality have sold well into the organization marketplace. These books and ideas, however, have stayed on the periphery; they have been used more as coping strategies to make outcome- and control-driven organizations more tolerable. What has not happened, though, is any real shift in the basic context of our organizations, which would be to believe that philosophic insights are essential to the survival of an institution and provide a basis for governance.

The reason for shifting the context from economics to philosophy is to create a culture of accountability. We are in a period where accountability is under assault. Entitlement is strong and people feel less responsible for the whole. We act as if the question, "What's in it for me?" is a reasonable and useful one. We are free agents and loyalty to any one organization is disappearing. In communities, we live in the isolation of our TV room and back yard. We treat government and public education as if they belong to someone else.

The focus here on an existential view of human freedom and human destiny demands a level of personal accountability that our institutions and culture have not contemplated. If we continue to have to hold people accountable, then we will continue to get compliance and miss the value of accountability that is chosen. Our language is the starting point to discover accountability that is chosen as a consequence of claiming our freedom.

Chapter 5

THE FACES
OF ANXIETY

To run in anguish from anxiety is futile, since anxiety will not go away
any more than our breath will go away. To be "cured" of anxiety makes
as much sense as to be "cured" of heartbeats or of metabolism.

A NEXT STEP in understanding freedom is to explore our desire to escape from it, for there is a cost to our freedom, and
that is the anxiety that accompanies it. We need to change our
mind about anxiety and learn to embrace it. We reclaim our freedom when we come to terms with the anxiety that is associated
with it. This chapter goes into some detail about the redemptive
qualities that an existential understanding of anxiety offers us.

"Anxiety" is a common word in the English language; it is
a family of experiences drawn from the life-world; everyone who

Adapted from Peter Koestenbaum, "Description of Anxiety" and "Diagnosis and Value of Anxiety,"
in *The New Image of the Person: The Theory and Practice of Clinical Philosophy*, Westport, CT: Greenwood Press, 1978.

reads these pages can use the word "anxiety" correctly. In addition, each of us has our own theories about anxiety. As a result we will have used that word as a principle of organization for our own life and that of others. Our intent here is to explore the philosophical background of anxiety, to use it as a principle of organization that has moved from the pinpoint of the individual to the universe of being itself. We must endeavor to describe anxiety without the ordinary assumptions that any science, especially psychology, expects us to make.

EXISTENTIAL AND NEUROTIC ANXIETY

Philosophers make an important and well-known distinction between existential and neurotic anxiety. Neurotic anxiety is not a separate type but rather a dysfunctional derivative of the basic anxiety, which is existential. Existential anxiety is healthy and is the natural condition of the person when in a state of self-disclosure. Neurotic anxiety is diseased and is the denial of existential anxiety. Existential anxiety leads to creativity, whereas neurotic anxiety leads to symptoms of ill health. In other words, neurotic anxiety is a function of existential anxiety. The function is negative. The function is denial. The basis is existential anxiety. This distinction is important because it reverses the conventional view that all anxiety is pathological. We no longer need to be surprised that our attempts to "cure" anxiety do not work!

Existential Anxiety

Existential anxiety, also called authentic anxiety, is the unique aspect of human experience that reveals our truth of what it means to be human. As such, it is a healthy, normal, and desirable phenomenon, something to be cultivated and cherished, to be chosen voluntarily, and a condition that leads to strength, peace, and creativity. Existential anxiety reveals the structure of being. It reveals the reality of consciousness, our nature as a field, the abyss and the search for ground residing in our depth, the vastness and the anguish of our freedom, and all of those characteristics of our essence needed to achieve true health.

Yet it turns out that we human beings—because of our tendency to conceptualize our experience in terms of external objects alone rather than in terms of a first person, I-am-the-subject-that-is-the-object field (the ghost-in-a-machine theory as opposed to the field-of-consciousness theory of existence)—fear our own nature. We deny the truth about ourselves, and we deny our source of insight. We try to kill the anxiety that is in reality the messenger of the gods.

When anxiety is denied our nature is denied. And that denial leads to conditions of inauthenticity called, variously, mental illness, neurosis, maladjustment, maladaptation, melancholia, and so forth. But above all, the denial of existential anxiety leads to a lack of meaning in life, to an existence without a task, to a condition of despair—because we *must* live yet *cannot* live. William Blake was not far off the mark when he said that "if the doors of perception were opened, we would see every thing as it is, infinite." He should have added that anxiety (as authentic and existential) is those "open doors of perception."

Neurotic Anxiety

The denial of existential anxiety is called neurotic, inauthentic, or pathological anxiety. Neurotic anxiety includes the fear of anxiety. It is second-order anxiety, that is, anxiety about anxiety. When we are anxious, we experience the truth. But when we are anxious about being anxious, we are sick and needlessly limit our potential for enjoying life—and we do not experience the truth.

The mechanisms by which we deny existential anxiety are endless: repression, projection, displacement, as well as rationalization, reaction-formation, dissociation, compulsion, obsession, compensation, sublimation, and on and on. What is denied by all of these strategies, directly or symbolically, is existential anxiety and the truth about being. This denial is experienced as an unhappy life, or worse.

Causes and Costs of Denial

The specific causes for the denial of existential anxiety are various and we will list but a few. Philosophic ignorance or general misinformation is the common cause for the denial of existential anxiety; specifically, materialism and the dominance of scientific rationality are prime cultural culprits. Fear and the avoidance of pain, as if these were intrinsic evils rather than conditions to be evaluated in perspective, are also causes for denial.

These causes point out that if we deny our existential anxiety we are still immature and seriously underdeveloped in view of the vast potential for self-understanding of which a human being is capable. As a result, the price we pay for the denial of existential anxiety is severe. The dominant consequence is to restrict our life.

Limiting Life.   Rather than fulfilling our potential, denying our existential anxiety seriously limits the realization of our range of possibilities. This is an act that *deliberately* limits life for the sake of protecting it from anxiety. "Sacrifice living but at least be protected from sensing anxiety" is the operative rule. Note the emphasis on the word "deliberately." People can be held responsible for limiting themselves. Their reasons may be good and logical, given their environment, but the reasons for not limiting themselves are even better. Holding people responsible enables them to discover their free will, which is a fact of existence, and puts them in touch with the only device known that can help them—the power of their freedom.

Symptoms and Dysfunctions. Another consequence of denial is the formation of symptoms, the most obvious being some form of illness. But there are other conditions properly called "symptoms" that result from this denial. Sexual dysfunctions are a good illustration, as are the difficulties many people have in allowing for intimacy in relationships.

There are also behavior dysfunctions, which include difficulties with non-intimate human relationships, and spiritual dysfunctions, which refer to the impoverishment of the life of consciousness, to the loss of meaning occasioned by a lack of spiritual values.

Self-Deception. In denying our anxiety we pay the price of self-betrayal. At the core of many a person is the dismal fear or recognition that we have betrayed ourselves by not fulfilling our possibilities. That is the underlying sense of worthlessness and self-contempt that is the root of many an inauthentic existence. And no amount of rationalization can convince us that there are excuses or exonerating circumstances for our self-betrayal. Conscience is merciless and indomitable.

A life of neurotic anxiety is thus an existence of self-deception. Freedom is used not to grow and be strong, not for joy and love, but only to disguise itself. When we use our freedom to hide our freedom from ourselves, we are expending all our precious life-force, libido, and the temporal stream of consciousness that runs through us on the single goal of self-deception. The quintessential price that emerges from denying existential anxiety and thereby producing neurotic anxiety is a living death and a life of intolerable self-immolation.

BEFRIENDING ANXIETY

Existential anxiety is a unique, *sui generis* experience. Like the concept of being, anxiety does not lend itself to classification. To describe it is therefore difficult and mostly metaphoric.

Anxiety Is Unique

As a result of its uniqueness, anxiety occupies a pivotal position in grasping our freedom. It is fundamental to achieving an understanding of personality and of human existence. It is the one phenomenon that does not give us conceptual analysis alone, as would be true of a logical truth, nor does it give us experience alone, as would be the case with a feeling or an emotion.

Anxiety is unique in that it is a concept-feeling phenomenon. And our first discovery in the careful analysis of anxiety—that is, in our assumption-free description of it from the distance of reflection—is that anxiety is elusive. It cannot be readily classified or described; it cannot literally be named. It is indeed unique. And we will shortly see why.

Anxiety Is Normal

Contrary to conventional psychological theories, anxiety—as existential anxiety—is not an illness, not a disease, and not a dysfunction, neither mental nor physical. Therefore, it is not something about which we should be embarrassed, or something which makes us feel inferior or inadequate. We should not worry about it or want to get rid of it. On the contrary, anxiety must be recognized as healthy, normal, and natural. It gives us strength because it is creative; it can give us joy because it is alive. It need not lead to dysfunction but can be the raw material for an authentic existence. We must examine anxiety in terms of a growth and knowledge model, rather than in terms of a disease model, which is the traditional view.

Anxiety Is a State of Insight and Health

Furthermore, anxiety cannot properly be called a feeling or an emotion, although these may be its accompanying characteristics. Again, the contrast between conventional psychological and existential descriptions of anxiety is radical. One can still a feeling with behavioral desensitization techniques—ventilation in psychotherapy, or medication in psychiatry. But existential anxiety cannot be silenced, and we should not attempt to do so. To treat anxiety with a head-on collision is like expecting to understand physics by burning the textbook.

The results of this philosophically proposed shift in our perception of anxiety—from being an illness to not being an illness but a deeper state of insight and health—are that we can cope confidently and in a relaxed manner with anxiety, rather than feel obligated—as we would on the basis of the disease model—to escape or deny it. To run in anguish from anxiety is futile, since anxiety will not go away any more than our breath will go away. To be "cured" of anxiety makes as much sense as to be "cured" of heartbeats or of metabolism.

Once we have accepted anxiety as right and proper, we can begin to build creatively on the experience. That new peace and relaxation removes blocks and releases the natural flow of energy that accompanies the perennial stream of the field of consciousness that we are. We therefore no longer feel obliged to assault anxiety destructively with Thorazine, Prozac, or divorce, with straitjackets or alcohol, or even with Librium and psychotherapy. To confront anxiety with the conviction it is the enemy drains us of our natural creative energies because we must uphold an artificial structure, a self-concept contrary to the philosophically discovered elements of human existence.

Anxiety Is Philosophical Perception

The preferred metaphor for anxiety that comes close to symbolizing what is essentially its indescribable nature is that it is a *revelation*. Anxiety is cognitive, an illumination, a seeing. In fact, anxiety is the act of philosophical perception itself. To be anxious, in the pure sense of existential anxiety, is to stand on the mountaintop that reveals being to us. Anxiety is our window to the truth about being. The book that supposedly helps you to think philosophically and to act on its philosophic insight should hold one simple instruction: "Permit yourself to be anxious!"

THE PAINFUL QUALITIES
OF ANXIETY

Anxiety is also the experience of chaos and death, that is, of the world's disorganization, the withdrawal of consciousness from its worldly attachments and identifications. This is always painful, but it is equally obvious that such an experience is a prerequisite for meaningful change and growth. This makes possible a reconstruction and invokes the full use of our transcendental freedom.

Anxiety Is Deconstruction

Thus, anxiety reveals directly the truth about being. Because it is the experience of detachment, anxiety gives us the world free of belief systems, world views, world designs, and other constructs. Anxiety can reveal being to us before the constitution or construction of the ego, soul, or self. It has the potential to show us that perhaps even the ego is merely an accent on eternity, a derivate construct rather than an irreducible atomic core. The converse also follows, namely, that these constructs—all our attempts to treat anxiety as a disease or eliminate it—have a psychological function: they are defenses against anxiety; they bind anxiety. They help us manage anxiety, escape anxiety, and pretend that we can avoid it. Anxiety is the illumination that invades us when these defenses are no longer in operation.

As an illustration that anxiety means both deconstruction and revelation, and that we have a tendency to defend ourselves against this anxiety by invoking—through magic or other ceremonies— tried and habitual belief systems, consider Norma.

Norma is deeply interested in meditation. Also she has frequent nightmares about tornadoes, typhoons, hurricanes, earthquakes, and other encompassing disasters. She routinely wakes up and feels the need to drink a glass of warm milk. One oversimplified interpretation might be: her nightmares mean destruction and emotional letting go, and with it the mystical revelations that she secretly longs for. This sort of dream, like many others, is actually a covert form of wish-fulfillment. While anxious about falling apart, she at the same time desires it. Drinking warm milk, on the other hand, is a regressive phenomenon—back to early childhood. After each traumatic experience she automatically repeats her earliest childhood experience of the world. It was then that her first sense of having some control over her life began, and she hopes it will be repeated each time after a dream through the magic of her milk-drinking ceremony.

A deepened response and understanding for Norma would be to accept the health and normalcy of her anxiety (tornadoes) and to take charge and responsibility herself for courageously reconstructing her world according to her own decisions and choices—that is, those values and lifestyles which present themselves to her in meditation as *right*. Above all, however, she begins to fulfill in her dreams what she seeks while awake: transcendental illumination, truth in meditation, religious integration. To carry out that program in real life is to assume personal responsibility for tolerating anxiety and its revelations.

Anxiety As a Possibility

Anxiety is thus an experience belonging to the expanded possibilities of human existence. It discloses the consciousness that, depending on our terminology, we are, or that courses through us. Anxiety is the experience expressed by the metaphor of a young child totally connected to his or her mother who is suddenly cut off from her (through her death, illness, or deliberate abandonment). The child, understanding nothing but experiencing everything, is left with a pure look, an objectless consciousness, an intentional stream that says "Mommy! Mommy!" but faces only a wordless blank.

If we think of the death of the biosphere as the paradigm for anxiety—as our concern for the environment makes obvious—then the image of an earth-deprived existence is a further metaphor for transcendental or pure consciousness or freedom. As said before, the philosophical image of transcendental consciousness is not produced by personal experiences such as separating from our parents early in life. The contrary is true; the loneliness of pure consciousness is a truth about being. We have developed the images of separation and abandonment in order to dramatize metaphorically these philosophical realities and to incarnate the abstract philosophic truth in the life of flesh, bones, and in our origins as children. Anxiety thus opens up the full realm of the transcendental dimension, the realm of eternal consciousness, and absolute freedom. That is the realm where the source for all meaningful and deep answers of life are to be found.

Kierkegaard defined anxiety in this way: "So when the danger is so great that death has become one's hope, despair is the disconsolateness of not being able to die."[1] It seems that the psychological metaphors of rejection, abandonment, and separation used to describe anxiety are most effective in eliciting both experientially and conceptually their underlying philosophic meaning.

ANXIETY REVEALS TRUTH

We cannot of course deny the obvious, in that from a common sense point of view many people literally *suffer* from anxiety. Nor do we mean that this despair is covert joy. However, two causes account for this condition of distress. First, the anxiety may be neurotic anxiety. Our defense against anxiety may no longer be effective in repressing the insights that our unconscious demands us to disclose to ourselves. The rhinoceros, which was a baby when we got it and lived docilely in its wooden cage, has now grown to a full-sized, ill-tempered monster that can no longer be contained by the fragile pen. It is now breaking loose.

The second cause for the upsurge of unmanageable anxiety is that we have no, or limited, toleration for the truth. We thus fight to be blind. That is our crisis. We also discover—a point to which the psychiatrists Thomas Szasz and R.D. Laing have been sensitive—that our friends and society around us are terrified by our visions of the real truth. Like the fate of visionaries of an earlier age, the social consensus is that we are heretics possessed by the Devil and must be purified of our contamination by the *auto-da-fé* of burning.

The "normal" condition is to have much of the philosophic truth about us permanently repressed. The more this truth can be tolerated, the more authentic is the individual. Many individuals can tolerate little and would rather die than see it. Part of the problem is social bias against seeing the world as it is. Ignorance of philosophy leads people to recoil in terror when philosophic truth becomes revealed.

TOLERATION FOR ANXIETY

Authenticity is a function of how much and how well we integrate the negative aspects of life into our existence. Toleration for anxiety measures our capacity to cope. Authentic individuals are not unanxious, but have enormous capacity for being comfortable with anxiety. They have well-toned psychic muscles.

The experience of tolerating anxiety is difficult to describe. Imagine you are a skydiver who, upon reaching a certain speed, ceases to accelerate downward. Still not opening your parachute, you feel as if you were sleeping on a cloud. You leap into the abyss and discover that the abyss supports you. Anxiety is tolerated when you abandon yourself to it and gain strength and stature, reality and authority. It is like dreams of falling. At first we try to arrest the fall; and that feels like a cramp. Then we relax and abandon ourselves to the fall. At that moment we achieve ego-strength through the toleration for anxiety.

How to acquire toleration for anxiety? Can it be cultivated? In the final analysis, toleration is the result of an archetypal choice. Toleration for anxiety—and thus a self-actualizing lifestyle and an authentic existence—is a condition that can be brought about fully through our own efforts.

Earl is a man with four children. He lost two sons—to him an absolutely irrecoverable tragedy. His wife *chose* (in existential terms) not to cope and had a total breakdown, becoming as dependent on his most meticulous care as a tropical plant would be in Alaska. Not only did he have to cope with his own feelings about this disaster, but he had to protect and provide a home for his remaining children. Suicide was not an option for him primarily because his remaining children had an ethical claim on his continued and sane existence. His situation was terrible; there can be no question about that. But whether he would open himself up to the enormity of anxiety and allow it to engulf him, to permit it to swallow him like a whale, or whether he would deny it, close his eyes, run away, blame others, or suffer a psychotic episode—these were his free choices.

The decision is difficult only because the alternatives are equally painful and because Earl would give anything—as would many of us—not to be confronted with these two disagreeable options. Other than that, however, he is completely free and his freedom is easy to carry out. For him, tolerating anxiety is no more and no less than a simple decision.

This decision is another manifestation of the archetypal—that is, foundational, deep-in-the-soul—decision to be a whole person. The statement "I cannot make the decision to tolerate anxiety" is an incomplete analysis. This is a statement of intention, not a factual condition of the person. The subjective or inward path leading to it requires the following complete statement: "I, as a pure freedom, choose not to make the archetypal decision to tolerate anxiety." We have difficulty with the second statement only because we somehow feel it is inherently wrong or false. However, at the archetypal level, right and wrong have not yet been established (that is, constituted or constructed); therefore, to choose toleration is really no better than not to choose it.

THE VALUE OF ANXIETY

We have up to now covered many negative aspects of anxiety. But it is only neurotic anxiety that is really negative. Existential anxiety, even though mistakenly feared, is a very positive experience. It is important to end this definition of existential anxiety by being more specific about anxiety's positive values. What, exactly, does a person feel in a fully blossoming state of existential anxiety?

To Feel Alive

First and foremost, anxiety is the concrete experience of living. To be anxious is to feel alive. Consider these questions: How does it actually feel to be alive? What is and how can we describe this sense of existing, this fact of being? The answer is anxiety. Anxiety is the conflict of polarities. It is the oscillating stress that makes us aware of the fact that we exist, the tension between contradictions and thus the vibrancy of life itself. *To be* and *to be anxious* are therefore synonyms. The excitement of being a body, of being sensuous, of being finite are the richly concrete experiences described by the phenomenon of existential anxiety. Anxiety is an openness to being; it is a receptivity to reality; it is being properly fitted to absorb existence.

Anxiety forms part of a continuum that we can call excitement, excitation, or the throb of life. One extreme of that continuum we call anxiety and the other, joy. The similarities are more important than the differences:

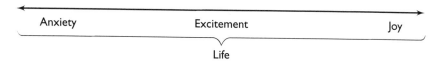

From P. Koestenbaum, *The New Image of the Person*, p. 235 (Westport, CT: Greenwood Press, 1978).

However, we sometimes cut off anxiety from the continuum and think it to be bad and alien:

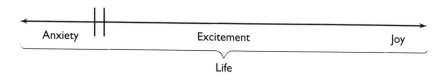

From P. Koestenbaum, *The New Image of the Person*, p. 235 (Westport, CT: Greenwood Press, 1978).

When we do that, we *deny* the truth about anxiety. Anxiety as part of this continuum is existential anxiety. In an inauthentic life that anxiety is denied. And cutting it off is what we call neurotic anxiety. Merely understanding this point can put your anxiety in perspective. Experiencing and then applying or integrating it is even more meaningful.

Each of us spins our past like a cobweb. We see what our empty consciousness has created by looking at our past. But we no longer *are* that past—we only *were* it. We are now and always a-present-creating-its-past. Thus, the experiences of ambition and accomplishment are the values inherent in the reality that is anxiety, since they are the process of creating the past. Consequently, anxiety informs us of the meaning of life because anxiety is that meaning. To be anxious is the meaning. Anxiety discloses our substantiality to us. It tells us how to go about creating our past. And to create ourselves in the future into a concrete past is what we mean by the content of the meaning of life.

To Find Meaning and Growth

Second, anxiety is the motivation to meaning. A life without anxiety is static, like a rock. Anxiety introduces disequilibrium; it creates an imbalance that develops a goal of resoluteness. The *search* for meaning is brought about through the phenomenon of anxiety.

A third value of anxiety is that it arouses us to the significance of love and compassion; it alerts us to the incontrovertible need for care and concern. Anxiety proves to us the value of tenderness. The emptiness of anxiety, its sense of isolation, separation, and abandonment, urgently points to the axiomatic need for closeness, oneness, and intimacy. What is there to share if it is not one's anxiety?

Fourth, anxiety is also the experience of time, and with it, of futurity and hope. Anxiety discloses our structure as intentional beings; it therefore purifies for us the experience of time that we are. And being time, we are also that toward which time moves, which is the future. And in disclosing to us our futurization, anxiety is the experience of hope.

Finally, anxiety is the experience of creativity. All creative acts—artistic, loving, scholarly, scientific, political, social, and so forth—are born of anxiety and made possible through anxiety. All great creative people have translated the experience of anxiety into the act and product of creation. Time and creativity together fashion growth. Anxiety is thus essential to growth. In fact, the experience of anxiety *is* the experience of growth.

Chapter 6

SOME REVELATIONS
OF ANXIETY

The presence of anxiety does not mean that we are sick
but that something within us is trying to be born.
To grow is to experience anxiety. There can be no growth without it.

W E HAVE SAID that anxiety is essential to understanding
what it means to be a human being. We now explore
some of what anxiety reveals and what happens when these revelations are suppressed.

The revelations of existential anxiety can be ordered into several types, each revealing a unique characteristic of being human:
birth, evil, grounding, freedom, death, individuality, and *guilt.* We
will spend some time in this chapter talking about birth, and briefly
touch on freedom, death, and risk, which are explored at length

Adapted from Peter Koestenbaum, "Birth" and "Provocation of Anxiety" in *The New Image of the
Person: The Theory and Practice of Clinical Philosophy,* Westport, CT: Greenwood Press, 1978.

in other parts of the book. The ideas about guilt, individuality, and being grounded are also covered in other sections. They are all mentioned here to show the complete continuum of insights that anxiety offers us. We also delve into some of the particular manifestations of anxiety in the workplace and outline some ways of acknowledging, or even provoking, anxiety as a way to freedom and growth.

BIRTH AND REBIRTH

The first type of existential anxiety is the anxiety of birth or the anxiety of being born. It reveals the fact that to exist authentically is to permit oneself—even encourage oneself—to be born and reborn. The presence of anxiety does not mean that we are sick but that something within us is trying to be born. The experience of anxiety can be the realization that an old self is dying and a new self is trying to appear. To grow is to experience anxiety. There can be no growth without it.

This means that the presence of anxiety may well be the experience of growth itself. To interfere, hinder, or impede this growth is the equivalent of shoving the baby back into the womb, when what is needed is to tolerate the pain so as to facilitate the wonderful event. The wise person is glad to feel anxiety and recognizes it as a friend. We encourage our anxiety and with it facilitate the birth of our own meaning, our own project, fulfillment, and integrity. The fool fears anxiety and squelches it with repression or drugs—and suffers the loss of meaning as a result. It may not be an exaggeration to say that in avoiding anxiety salvation was of-

fered to us and we were too blind to see it and take advantage of the opportunity.

If we do not feel anxious, it may be appropriate to encourage it for the sake of rebirth. For our learning or transformation to be effective and truly reconstructive, we must seek out the maximum amount of tolerable anxiety. The changes that occur in intensive transformational experiences do so by undermining our deepest suppressed assumptions—a condition of grave anxiety. Such anxiety must be encouraged for rebirth to take place. We can mobilize the anxiety of birth, and thus facilitate growth, when we are given first of all—by life events or another person—a "shocking" assessment of ourselves. However, when the "shock" comes from a friend or helper, the person must be the equivalent of an artist. The shock must be loving, and it must be perceived as such. And it must occur in a genuinely supportive environment. It must also be based on an accurate assessment of our project or our being-in-the-world. The shock must be strong enough to undermine the old and nonworking world design of ourselves, but not so violent as to arouse more anxiety than we are able to cope with. It is this shocking and anxiety-producing experience, this quick grasp of the new possibilities of one's existence, that makes the arousal of the anxiety of birth worthwhile.

RECLAIMING OUR FREEDOM

At these moments, we discover how grossly we have neglected our freedom, how we have neglected taking charge of our life. Our whole existence reflects the absence of our freedom. Through the anxiety of birth, we can see in one flash how life can be reorganized in its very foundations. We often discover that throughout our life we have allowed external circumstances, publicly broadcast values, and accidental relationships to determine what is to be of meaning in our existence. We suddenly realize the philosophic fact that we do have an inner foundation, an internal resource, and that this ground is of far greater importance than whatever our social environment could possibly offer.

We also realize that the world in general and history—if not our immediate social world—will support and respond to our inner voices and values. In addition we discover how we have never learned to affirm ourselves effectively, to assert ourselves irrevocably. Our old self-concept is life-denying. The anxiety of birth is the experience of a new possibility: life affirmation. It is also the actual experience of this transition. We are helped to discover the philosophic fact that we can choose, literally, to be reborn to be someone else: unmistakable and consistent self-affirmation is as close to us as our pre-birth decision of self-denial.

There may be a childhood origin or explanation for our old self-concept. As children, it probably was logical, rational, and reasonable to respond to our early situation as we in fact did: we relinquished our freedom, we developed an other-directed identity, and we became self-effacing. In short, we tried our best to adapt to the childhood world by approximating as closely as possible the state of nonexistence.

A five-year-old boy overhears his mother: "Junior has grown in the last year. Thank God! We feared he'd never be of decent size!" At this moment we experience how the mother blames her son for being short. She expects him to solve her own feelings of inferiority. The five-year-old is expected to take on his mother's burdens. He must take responsibility for being too short to satisfy his mother—at five years of age! The child will internalize that perception of him, accept it as his own, and go through life thinking of himself as too short, and deservedly crippled.

A father, complaining about the cost of an item while shopping for his little daughter, tells the salesperson—in "jest," of course—"She isn't worth even two dollars!"

It is logical for these children to learn to experience themselves as ungrounded or as not existing. As adults, in mobilizing the anxiety of birth, we are given the possibility to transform ourselves from nonexistence to existence.

Virtually each of us, when grown, will need to learn that our self-image is philosophically without foundation and perform an act of massive reconstitution and reconstruction. To do that is to experience the anxiety of birth. To the extent that this process occurs, we experience existential anxiety; but to the degree that we fear we cannot handle this existential anxiety and therefore choose to deny, fight, or repress it, we are experiencing neurotic anxiety. Existential anxiety leads to health; neurotic anxiety produces symptoms.

In an authentic existence we are, as in the myth of reincarnation, reborn again and again. Birth therefore also means rebirth. It also means the forward movement of life, the experience of time, growth, and with it the embrace of hope. Birth comes after death just as a beginning comes after an ending. The process of birth involves the risk of novelty and the risk of death. Rebirth is like the second discovery of fire in Teilhard de Chardin's beautiful words, "Someday, after mastering the winds, the waves, the tides and gravity, we shall harness for God the energies of love, and then, for the second time in the history of the world, man will discover fire."

But birth can only be accomplished through anxiety. That is true of both biological *and* philosophical birth. Rollo May points that out in his book *Existence,* when he calls attention to the interesting etymology of the word "anxiety." The German "Angst" and the English "anguish" derive from the Latin "angustus,"which means narrow and difficult. And that word comes in turn from the Latin "angere,"which means to press together.

The word "anxiety" thus seems to give us a direct confirmation of the fact that in the primordial dawn of humankind's consciousness, biological birth and philosophical anxiety were recognized as connected. For our purposes we must remember that birth—as the experience of growth, transition, change, transformation, and creativity, including what Carl Rogers means by his apt phrase "becoming what one is"—is an anxiety-producing experience. Without birth there is no authentic existence; without anxiety, or at least the toleration for anxiety, there can be no authentic existence.

DEATH IS THE BEGINNING

In the phenomenon of birth, the pain or anxiety is in the ending that precedes every beginning, the ending of the familiar that also makes room for a beginning. Snow White and Rose Red are good examples of one's need to die (an anxiety situation) before one can live. Snow White dies by the poisoned apple (anxiety) before she is kissed by her prince and brought back to life and fulfillment (birth); Rose Red sleeps for a hundred years (death, anxiety) before she is rescued by her prince (birth) for a life of meaning. All fundamental changes in life follow this pattern. The increasing presence of anxiety is not a sign of regression or failure but a sign of openness and hope. It is a sign that an old world is dying to allow a new one to be born. A simple but subtle example can serve as illustration.

Lilly was successful in her job and was deemed a high potential by every company she worked for. Her life was devoted to her work. She worked long hours each day. After some time, she began to develop anxiety and some unexpected changes appeared in her life. She observed that these changes were happening in her behavior, but she did not feel that she was making them happen through deliberate choice. The changes were these: increased anxiety, switching companies for a better job, and feeling more and more stressed, despite the unbroken path of success.

In the newest job, however, her boss told her to spend less time at work and to stop worrying so much about her own progress. She should become more of a teacher to others and be more concerned with the next generation. Her initial response to her boss's advice was disturbing. She for a time began to dislike her boss, and her respect for him as a leader declined.

Over time, however, the suggested changes gradually and unexpectedly emerged in her life, and the psychological meaning of this was profound. Her compulsive work before had been a panic reaction to her lack of self-confidence as a leader and executive. Her incessant toil anesthetized her against feelings of failure. Her new boss asked her to reduce her work time, which made practical sense due to the strain on her physically and on her capacity to give quality attention to what was in front of her. Fewer hours meant faith rather than panic as her mode of being-in-the-world. She filled the empty time (which had initially produced anxiety and panic) not with self-deceiving busywork—taking more university courses and compulsive exercise—but with teaching and thereby learning.

Teaching and learning are interchangeable activities. The theologian Alan Watts once said, "I don't know much about death. I think I'll write a book about it!" An old Hassidic saying is "The teacher learns five times as much as the student." Sometimes the coach benefits emotionally more from coaching than does the player or subject. For Lilly teaching meant reflecting on work in addition to just working. It was at that time that she started listening more and inviting feedback from others. She had not noticed the connection between asking for feedback and teaching. Both are experiences of reflection and distancing.

For Lily, teaching also meant contact with others and self-exposure. Those were expressions of faith in the larger purpose of her existence. To *be* does not only mean to be in control and to construct or constitute. To be can also mean to let be and *deconstitute* or *deconstruct*. That was for her the fundamental experience of birth. *Her big change was the discovery of faith in nature,* including her own nature. She had made a quantum jump of growth. She had broken the barrier that had stopped her from becoming a significant executive. All of that growth occurred against the backdrop of anxiety. The task of her self-development was *not to interfere* with this growth process. Only toleration for the anxiety of birth and the knowledge that existential anxiety is healthy can make possible her transformation from a driven, self-absorbed manager to a genuine leader.

BEING ANXIOUS ABOUT BEING ANXIOUS

Anxiety has a tendency to rise when in the presence of anxiety. This is true in our experiences at home and in our communities, and often most dramatically at work. Another way to say this is that anxiety is highly contagious. It is contagious in the sense that all insight is "catching" and all knowledge is "communicable." Existential anxiety is contagious because insight is communicable—even without putting it into words through declarative, abstract language. Neurotic anxiety—because it cripples existential anxiety and distorts the possibilities of existential anxiety—is also contagious. Its residue is transmitted in human interactions.

In other words, a person with neurotic anxiety communicates nonverbally, and from the unconscious to the unconscious of others, the bitter struggle of repression and struggle against the existential anxiety raging within. Just as the heart of an atomic explosion starts fires all around it and in distant places, so does the neurotic anxiety of one human being remind others close by of their own unresolved struggles. If a highly anxious person enters a room or participates in a discussion, the anxiety levels of the others are raised to a high pitch. That is often the reaction we get from meeting a schizophrenic. We are upset by the meeting but do not understand why. As a result, we are likely to put it out of our mind. But what we have just experienced is the contagiousness of anxiety—our own anxiety heightened by another's.

PING PONG ANXIETY

One of the most difficult problems in being a manager or leader— or in having some power over others, which includes consultants and other helpers and healers—is dealing with the anxiety of those around us. And the hardest part in this is the fact that anxiety in the subordinates, clients, bosses, or others arouses our own anxiety.

There are two important issues here: first, an employee's anxiety arouses anxiety in the manager or helper. Second, the manager or helper's own anxiety provokes anxiety in the employee, or boss, or any other person. Both conditions interfere with growth and learning.

The practical problem of anxiety in the workplace does not revolve exclusively around the question of how to act toward the anxious person. It also concerns itself with how to regard the anxious manager or helper who is dealing with another anxious person. Moreover, and all too often, the manager or helper provokes anxiety in the employee or client. We then frequently have a situation in which the anxiety originates in the manager or helper and then through its contagiousness reappears in the employee or client, where it is then treated (or mistreated) as part of the latter's symptoms.

Considering simply the manager for the moment, what goes on when a manager's anxiety is transferred to the employee? This is a strictly neurotic and inauthentic situation. It does not occur when the manager experiences authentic—that is, existential— anxiety but when it has been distorted into neurotic anxiety, and

when the manager uses an employee to work out his or her own anxiety. A simple example: managers who are excessively worried about where they stand with their own boss tend to control much more tightly the work of their subordinates.

What kind of people are these anxiety-provoking managers? Their initial anxiety may be based on their own personal situation or lack of philosophical self-disclosure, their lack of self-consciousness.

Unresolved Anxiety

People who exude provoking waves of anxiety because they have not resolved their neurotic anxiety into its existential underpinnings, who have not worked through their own inauthenticity, will have difficulty being in a managing position. Being a competent surgeon, for example, is not in itself enough to make the physician an authentic healer. Even though the surgeon performs the healing function while the patient is supine and unconscious, it is the personal contact both before and after surgery that provides the frame of mind which—as many experts on holistic and psychosomatic medicine now maintain—will help ensure a speedy recovery, not to mention the purely moral issues involved. Same with a manager. Managers may have the surgeon's knowledge of the business of the organization, but their own way of managing anxiety may keep them from really building an effective human organization.

The Burden of High Expectations

A second common reason for the existence of inauthentic anxiety in managers is based on a dual fear: they feel incompetent; they feel they cannot handle the specific problem confronting them, a situation typical mostly early in people's careers, in other words the first thirty years. And they may also feel that they cannot meet the excessive expectations of their employees. The dying patient expects to be saved; the surgical patient wants a painless operation; the alcoholic thinks the therapist holds the cure; the client with a bad marriage assumes that the counselor will transform years of bitterness into a future of uninterrupted bliss; and likewise, employees expect their bosses to ensure them high ratings and successful careers.

These expectations are often categorical demands. Managers who take on these expectations or internalize unwarranted demands either have no inner-directed sense for their own self-image—and thus depend entirely for what they think they are on how others perceive them—or they have the need to think of themselves as a kind of god. They are therefore flattered when employees recognize them as such, but also dismayed when they discover what a trap that narcissistic and egomaniacal need turns out to be.

Abuse of Power

A third form of manager anxiety, an anxiety that is contagious through provocation, results in the subtle expression of sadistic impulses. All managers and helpers can be tempted to abuse their power. Imprisoned by their own lack of self-awareness, they may take out their own desires for absolute power and immunity on the people they are meant to serve. They heap on verbal abuse, they can be remote and unreachable, they can set standards no one can reach, and on it goes.

Certain inherent and unavoidable aspects of management—as well as medicine and therapy—are of a provoking character and thus produce anxiety in the employee, patient, or client. Having power over others, be it in a management, coaching, or helping role, unavoidably involves invasions of the privacy and violations of the integrity of the employee or client. Employees lose control over their own territory—their body, feelings, and world view—that is legitimately theirs and theirs alone. This problem can be greatly ameliorated by helping employees create their own boundaries and, as this book is about, their own experience of their freedom.

WHEN MANAGERS PROVOKE ANXIETY

In general, provoking anxiety is part of teaching commitment and character. In this context, and others, provoking anxiety can be legitimate or illegitimate. It is legitimate, and thus an authentic act, when the assaults on another's security are both necessary and unavoidable *and* you use every known device to avoid provoking unnecessary anxiety. Not using all safeguards is a provocation. People who create havoc in those around them and do not see this may need to be pushed into greater awareness. If we do this too aggressively, in front of others for example, we are abusing the relationship. The provocation is illegitimate if it is unnecessary. We are talking now about the much subtler abuse of another's security and privacy and disregard of their sensitivities when more thought and increased competence could avoid stressful situations.

One area where the legitimate use of provocation gets complicated is when employees complain about their boss. We call it "being challenged." Their complaint may or may not be valid. In fact, the complaint of induced or provoked anxiety may often be no more than an inverted wish or a covert desire by the employee or client to remain a victim. On the other hand we could assume that an employee or client feels violated and has in fact been violated (on some objective criterion we need not go into). Provoking a conversation about the conflict, perhaps by accusing the employee or client of expressing a secret wish, may have some value. The result of this interpretation may well be that the employee is shocked into taking full responsibility for what happens. If the employee does not like it, then he or she will do something about it.

To Provoke Anxiety Authentically

Freud said that anxiety is necessary for growth. Too much ends the consultation. Too little neutralizes progress. The Golden Mean of provoking anxiety (stretching, challenging) produces change and growth. Following are a few suggestions on the useful provocation of anxiety.

First, managers and helpers must be healthy themselves. Specifically, those who hope to facilitate the development of authenticity in others must also be authentic. This does not imply that we must not be neurotic. In fact, a manager with problems is often more sympathetic and helpful than one with none. It does mean that, as an authentic person with power over another, we must possess the permanent possibility for establishing and maintaining distance from our own problems and those of the employee or client. If we have problems, we must be able to recognize them, put them at a distance and out of action. In short, the authentic manager or helper may be neurotic (which to a point we all are), but must place the neurosis in suspension.

In addition, an authentic manager or helper permanently makes the binding decision—a commitment that has its origin within the region of consciousness exposed by an understanding of freedom—to be devoted solely to the interest of the employee as a human being. We pledge never to use or exploit them, for our own or the institution's neurotic purposes.

Our commitment to freedom and accountability exposes several characteristics of consciousness that must be invoked by any authentic manager or helper, regardless of their psychological health: their freedom, rationality, objectivity, and capacity for maintaining distance. They must be capable of making the decision, which is to be permanent, that all dealings with their employees or clients have their origin in the realm of reason and not in the empirical realm of feelings, in the existential realm of freedom and control and not in the empirical realm of deterministic subservience to impulses.

Another rule for the management of anxiety in a management or helping role is to be honest about feelings and shortcomings. The honesty in question is not only with ourselves, but with our employees and clients (which is an act of courage and thus a free commitment to the other's reality and integrity). Managers create a relationship with great learning potential, if they can share with the employee their own anxieties about their relationship, their own inadequacies in their role and way of relating to subordinates. An honest articulation of this issue of manager anxiety can be the hallmark of an existential encounter.

True, employees will find it more difficult to project their unconscious on that kind of an honest manager. But they will early in the relationship be exposed to the dual notions of personal responsibility and human finitude. That exposure will make up for whatever difficulty there may be in employees being disappointed that a manager will not take on their projections. This means that leading by authoritative suggestion—which many employees and clients demand tacitly—is ruled out by the type of existential honesty we are discussing here.

ANXIETY REVEALS A BEGINNING

We have said that to be born—to be renewed—makes sense only if there is some kind of death or ending connected with it. Consider the following symbol of the death-leads-to-birth, ending-means-beginning, or anxiety-reveals-birth process:

From P. Koestenbaum, *The New Image of the Person,* p. 243 (Westport, CT: Greenwood Press, 1978).

It can be a helpful illustration of the anxiety of being born into a new job or work relationship, a different lifestyle, a new world design, or a new personality.

The total situation is good, normal, and healthy, but is also anxiety-producing because of the negative, downward, and regressive turn the lines take. In fact, the loop—which is the essence of birth—is experienced as anxiety. Anything that tends to allay anxiety also flattens the loop. And that, as would be true of any wheel, stops its progress. The initial curve moves down, representing a negative, depressive, and unsatisfactory work situation, lifestyle, or self-concept. The final curve points forward and upward— the traditional symbols for self-transcending expansiveness in space and futurization in time. The loop, which is the anxiety zone, is the needed change of direction.

We can state this situation formally as follows. If the existential anxiety of birth is denied through any of the many defense mechanisms, then we reach a state of pathology or neurotic anxiety that is characterized primarily as being uncreative. Life is then experienced as dry and pointless, and joy is relegated to the escape from meaning in busywork, job, hobbies, fights, resentments, and the neglect of body, mind, and relationships. However, if we accept the existential anxiety of birth as revealing an important structure of human existence, if we welcome it as a messenger of salvation and hope, then our life will have taken a fundamental turn from jejune death to joyous birth.

RISK AS A WAY OF LIFE

The existential anxiety of birth is the anatomy of the experience of risking. To learn to risk, to use risk judiciously, and to press risking just beyond the comfort point are birth-giving acts. The answer to risk-denial (the neurotic anxiety of birth) is to be prepared to take risks. If systematic risking becomes a way of life, then life becomes a perpetual birth. Both the prominence and the tragedies of the Kennedy family resulted from systematic risking as a lifestyle. This family has become a cultural archetype for each of us.

Each of us has to decide for ourselves whether or not we have risked enough or excessively.

Each revelation of anxiety has political implications as well as psychological ones. The anxiety of birth describes well the agony of our age. We are a dying age, but *ipso facto* also a birth-giving age. The convulsions of the present age are, it is true, the last gasps of a dying age, a dying image of the person, a dying value system, and of a dying world view. But they are also the labor pains of birth. This anguished hope assigns to us a three-fold task: we must understand the age that tries to be born; we must not interfere with that birth by pushing the infant back into the womb; and we must facilitate the birth, help it to be what it is striving to be. In summary, we must understand and facilitate the transition of our age from one of technology to one of inner-space exploration. We must, together, invent the new symbols and meanings for the age that wishes to be born. We must allow ourselves to be the prophets through which our culture invents these symbols—such as the looping birth sign above. This is not a time to lose faith in our future, nor is it a time to lose our nerve. The knowledge that we are in a historical anxiety-of-birth cycle can give us and our institutions hope and meaning for the future.

Chapter 7

_____

COPING WITH THE ANXIETY OF REBIRTH AND FREEDOM

_____

Anxiety is our window to the truth about being. The book that supposedly helps you to think philosophically and to act on its philosophic insight should hold one simple instruction: "Permit yourself to be anxious!"

S TRATEGIES FOR COPING with the existential anxiety of birth revolve around courage and learning how to risk. Contending with the anxiety of birth means coping with the existential anxiety of affirmatively welcoming birth *and* coping with the neurotic anxiety of denying birth. Coping with anxiety philosophically involves both an avoidance-reaction and an approach-reaction. The general rule with neurotic anxiety is to recognize it as ignorance and suppression. We counter it with philosophical understanding and

_____

Adapted from Peter Koestenbaum, "Coping with the Anxiety of Rebirth" and "Coping with the Anxiety of Freedom," in *The New Image of the Person: The Theory and Practice of Clinical Philosophy,* Westport, CT: Greenwood Press, 1978.

deliberate provocation. *Understanding* or appreciating means we know anxiety is healthy, and *provoking* or challenging means we neutralize the suppression with a deliberate attack.

The general rule with existential anxiety is to hear its message and then live it. Living it means developing strategies for coping with rebirth and freedom. This involves winding our way through many of the following paths:

- Entering into healing relationships (i.e., encounters with others),

- Mapping the decisions that have formed our freedom,

- Using language to construct our experience of freedom,

- Translating anger into a constructive force,

- Taking risks,

- Choosing to live our lives as examples of choosing meaning, and

- Refusing to surrender.

RELATIONSHIPS

An absolutely basic principle of our freedom is that *all healing occurs in relationships*. Although absolutes are always dangerous, it is safe to say that pure self-help is rare and what heals is the relationship between two or more persons. There are reasons for this. Authenticity often requires that we replace the suppressed premises by which we live. Self-help, more often than not, is based on the very premises that cause our inauthenticity. We need an encounter with another person—either as model or as challenger—to bore into those root premises.

Contact

Successful changes seem to depend more heavily on the quality of our encounters, even with professional therapists or coaches, than they do on theories of behavioral science or the particular belief system of those we come into real contact with. While the details of each person's encounter and growth are highly specific, there are general characteristics that can be defined.

For example, an hour of profound quality contact between two people is successful in proportion to the depth of encounter, contact, sense of oneness, and continuity that has been established. It is the time spent in this transcendental healing atmosphere (reflective consciousness to reflective consciousness)—rather than in the specifics of a theory of the person that may have been transmitted or in the impersonal application of technique derived from the behavioral sciences and used mechanically—that is the actual healing process or coping strategy for anxiety.

Anxiety reveals the cosmically significant consciousness which I am and which connects me with others. To be *healed* means to acquire the confidence that this anxiety can be tolerated. These phenomena occur in an expanded consciousness. That is why all healing occurs in relationships. That is the therapeutic meaning of encounter or being-with. In other words, when we say that all healing of anxiety occurs in relationships, we must recognize that interpretation, advice, coaching, teaching, and understanding do not heal as well as does the actual relationship of two people, the actual experience of being-with.

It is in this state that reside both the *freedom* for reconstitution or reconstruction needed for in-depth change and the sense of *eternity* and indestructibility that provide the ground for self-confidence and the courage needed to act.

Commitment

Another aspect of a relationship—in addition to the element of contact—that heals anxiety is commitment. One person—be it a loved one, a friend, a therapist, a coach, or a colleague at work—makes a commitment to be with a person as long as needed. Commitment is based on a human need and not a commercial transaction or a business requirement, although these are perfectly legitimate and often important ingredients of the growth-producing transaction. The fact that one party may be getting paid to be helpful ensures equality, avoids exploitation, and shows respect to the economic realities of our existence.

Regardless of the context, for commitment to be an ingredient in a healing relationship, it needs three characteristics: it must be *inner directed*, *"forever,"* and *an action*.

Inner Directed

Commitment must, first, be *inner directed*. Its source must be within the person. We decide to make a commitment to another person. We do not do it out of pity or obligation, or for profit. We do it in response to objective need, on the basis of a rational ethical posture, as a result of an independent decision about our own lifestyle and personal or professional development, and in voluntary responsibility to the presence of another human being in need.

Only the ethics of eighteenth century philosopher Immanuel Kant explain this kind of motivation. Conventional psychology assumes motivation to be based on instinct, need, habit, pleasure, satisfaction, approval, conditioning, reward, or some form of self-interest. All these causes are of empirical, that is, worldly, origin—they are events in the realm of objects. We need to add the transcendental dimension, the realm of pure consciousness and awareness, to helping another person. In this realm, the region of pure observing and witnessing, motivation by sheer choice is a meaningful concept. An act is chosen on rational grounds alone, and that choice is adopted without pushes or pulls but spontaneously and autonomously, that is, freely. The categories of reason and freedom, which are the motives for a truly moral act, have their origin and meaning in the transcendental realm, the zone of pure consciousness. That is the Kantian ethic and that is the definition of an authentic commitment. One person owes nothing to another. The client owes no emotional debt to the coach. This commitment is fulfilled when healing has occurred, and then one perhaps fades away and becomes but a flicker of a memory. We choose to offer help, as a friend, or even manager, even though we know this will eventually neutralize the other person's need for us to practically zero.

Forever

Second, a healing commitment must be *"forever,"* in the sense that it will cover a finite period in the other person's life, and during that time—with all the usual ups and downs—the helper will not abandon the relationship. And that guarantee includes, at least theoretically, provisions against illness, change of residence, death, and suicide. In other words, if the one abandons the other *for any reason whatever,* that act is to be interpreted as a failure committed by the coach. For the life of the need, one's commitment is permanent.

An Action

Finally, commitment is an *action* and not a reaction. Commitment does not depend on the cooperation of the other person or their friendliness, nor even on their responsiveness to help. The person knows the helper is there, committed to them in the sense that the door is always open and he or she is always welcome, understood, and accepted. There is an intense ethical core to coaching.

Implementation

To act in support of the growth of another, two simple rules must be followed. If you are a leader, a manager, a helper, a coach, or a friend, you must offer to be-with, make encounter possible, invite connection. You do this with understanding, compassion, patience, and perseverance, especially if you are dealing with a disturbed or rigid person. You can also challenge the other person by stating categorically that the absence of deep relationship is a source of their anxiety. In highly impersonal and distant relationships, such an absolute challenge is helpful.

If on the other hand you are in the employee, client, or patient position, then take the initiative and ask that someone of your choice *be with you.* You are entitled to this; you have a claim on life that it give you the right to relationship when needed. If you understand that in demanding an intimate connection you are neither attacking, squelching, nor suffocating anyone, but simply affirming a human fact, then you will also discover that the world can be surprisingly responsive and supportive. The world will in fact thank you for your demands. If one person is not responsive, another will recognize your right.

> A front-line supervisor described the effects of her meetings with her manager-coach as "soothing." She said she was a better supervisor after the sessions. The reason she gave was simply that the being-with which defined the coaching relationship with her boss gave her a sense of peace—that is, security and self-confidence—and this feeling carried over to the office and was transmitted to her team.

The supervisor was referring to the benefits derived from the simple fact that once a week she existed in a transcendental relationship, self-to-self reflecting on her life and on her relationship with her coach. A transcendental relationship is when two people reconnect at a higher level of consciousness as they "reflect" on the previous, so-called "engaged" aspect of their relationship. During the week, employee and boss *engage* and *argue*. In coaching they *reflect* on their *arguing*. In so doing, they connect at a higher level.

> Several employees were making significant changes in their lives. One was going through a divorce, another was moving away from parents, and a third was changing careers. They committed to meet once a week to share their progress and frustrations at a nearby coffee house.

All three primarily needed support. But it is not enough to say only that much. They needed a home, a headquarters, a base of operations, a ground, a source. And that was found in the experience of the intimacy of pure consciousness that an authentic relationship can and should provide. Only within a relationship with another as foundation was it then possible to make use of the philosophic insights embodied in these existential views. They were able to come in and talk. They felt understood; they felt connected; they felt safe.

In both of these examples we see transcendental characteristics: expanded consciousness and no empirical (that is, physical or emotional) demands. The expanded consciousness spelled security; it was a taste of ground. The absence of practical demands spelled an ethical relationship in both cases, which means that people they respect made a commitment to them. It was this relationship that gave them the strength and the base from which to reconstruct their lives.

> A manager goes into a period of depression. He loses energy and commitment for the work and most other things from which he once took great pleasure. Some months before he mentioned that the demands of his bosses and employees had become unendurable. He perceived being with them as burdensome. Intimate, being-with, transcendental experiences were not part of his professional, intellectual, or personal equipment. To him all relationships were about fixing something, something that followed from his exclusive reliance on the engineering mindset.

This manager's alternatives were aloofness—which limited his capacity to manage—or to have authentic relationships with the people around him, which he perceived as unendurable and crushing burdens. He needed, we might say, his own being-with, that is, being-with himself. In other words, he needed to say no to his employees and bosses. His exclusively problem-solving orientation wormed itself deep into his psyche and rendered him incapable of the transcendental relationships that could have saved him.

SIGNIFICANT OTHERS ARE WATCHING

Another effective coping device is to recognize that our response to anxiety serves as a living example for other persons on what to do with anxiety, how to manage it, and how to cope with it. And those watching to whom we should pay attention are the so-called "significant others." Your children are watching if you are a parent. Your patient is watching if you are a therapist. Your wife is watching if you are a husband and vice versa. Your constituency is watching if you are a political leader, and so are your colleagues. Managers are watched by employees, and generals by their armies. The teacher is watched by the student, and leaders in literature and the arts are watched by the world.

To Be a Living Example

All the individuals in your "audience" may be tempted away from their integrity and need you to set an example. In the United States, for instance, it is the president who has the maximum opportunity to serve as example, an opportunity often neglected. To realize that your authenticity—that is, your coping with anxiety—is being watched by and serves as an example for significant others is a potent stimulus toward taking charge of your anxiety management.

When Jim divorced his wife, the court gave her custody of their three children, aged eight to three. His marriage counselor felt Jim had little choice in the matter. After the divorce, Jim found it harder and harder to be with his children. Jim went to court and got no relief. In fact, and as one would expect, his former wife's hostility increased with each court action, exacerbating an already bad situation. (Of course, often this situation is reversed, and it is the former husband who makes life miserable for his divorced wife.) Jim had exhausted all legal actions and turned to his boss for advice and support for coping with his anxiety.

The essence of the device suggested to Jim by his manager is that his actions—as well as his emotional health—be focused not on what they will do for him but on serving as an example to his children, even given only sparse contact with them.

Translate Anxiety into Meaning

Jim coped with anxiety by translating it into meaning, by realizing that it is the core ingredient of meaning. He restructured his life from the narcissistic pursuits of pleasure and self-fulfillment to the other-focused (not self-focused) goals of charity, love, commitment, obligation, and even duty.

Jim demonstrated to his children that maintaining a relationship with them was a lifetime project, which if it does not succeed today will perhaps succeed tomorrow, or next month, or next year, or possibly in the next decade. They may hate him today but they might also perceive him and his relationship to them a few years hence in a better light. He exhibited loyalty to them in his life (given the irreversible fact of the divorce). Even if they never respond to him, someday they may realize that their father made a lifelong commitment to them under difficult circumstances.

In short, Jim coped with his anxiety of having left his children by defining himself as a loyal person, as a father whose essence is the eternal, unqualified, and inner-directed (which means that the decision stands, with or without response from the children) commitment to his children. In so doing he knew he was choosing this self-definition not for his benefit but to serve as a model for his children. He acted not out of a need for self-satisfaction but because his children needed him. He expressed through his life the kind of commitment that was described above as an inescapable ingredient in the therapeutic encounter. They would always know the quality of person that their father was. They would also always experience the power of the choice for relationship, because the irreversible inner-directed commitment to them had been made.

The opposite of this commitment was illustrated by a newspaper article in which a young comedienne responded to a question about the whereabouts of her father with "I don't know what he's doing; but I'm sure that whatever it is, it's illegal," to which her father responded with a $4 million lawsuit. For a father to sue his daughter is the grotesque antithesis of commitment. An authentic father would not make what amounts to an anticommitment to his daughter.

Reveal Feelings and Share Experience

A second step in the technique suggested by Jim's manager was to share—whenever possible and at a level of depth and openness that seemed appropriate—his negative feelings of guilt, failure, frustration, and anger with his children. But he also shared his positive attempts to cope, his feelings of love for them, and his decision to be determined to succeed with them; he did that by demonstrating to them that he was the model of a good father. He taught them, in words and by example, that he loved them, that he cherished them, that he trusted them, that they were important to him, and that he respected them.

Refuse to Surrender

A third aspect of Jim's coping device was that he would choose strength, courage, success, and life-affirmation, rather than surrender to despair through alcohol, hostility, drugs, neurosis, neglect, psychosis, retribution, or bitterness. He demonstrated to his children that strength is a choice—open to all. He chose to affirm life not as much for himself as for the sake of his children. They needed his self-affirmation.

Jim's meaning in life became to teach his children how to develop into authentic individuals by serving as their example. It is difficult under normal circumstances to serve one's children as a model of authenticity. In Jim's case, with guilt and inaccessibility added, the difficulty was increased a hundred-fold. His task was that much clearer; his authenticity that much more precious; his example that much more inspired. It was up to him whether he would betray them or not. To betray himself was bad enough. He could, however, live with that. But to betray his children was more than he could face. Consequently, he had no choice but to choose to cope with his anxiety.

If Jim can show his children that he can cope honestly and maturely—and thus successfully—with one of his life's most difficult problems, then he is giving them his noblest gift and leaving them the richest inheritance there is. And that is an authentic solution to the problem of coping with anxiety. The anxiety is not overcome; but it is internalized, integrated creatively into life. It is tolerated and is translated into strength and health.

ANGER

Anger is one of the most important and effective coping devices against anxiety, for anger is protest, and protest is proof that the indomitable human spirit has not been squelched. Indifference is the absence of a core, the experience of being an empty shell. Indifference is an ego that is hollow; it is only an envelope. Anger, however, is the experience of the archetypal decision to be an ego, a self, a core, an identity. Anger is the last vestige of self-affirmation. You may have been squelched since childhood. You may never have been fully confirmed as a child. Your parental message in life may always have been "You're not quite good enough. In fact, you can never try hard enough to satisfy me." If you grow into an indifferent adult, you will have been defeated. But if you grow instead into an angry adult, you will maintain the posture of protest. Your anger is your self-affirmation.

But anger is negative. Your next step is to translate that anger into something constructive and creative. That translation is not sublimation but is the continued growth of the anger. Anger is not a pure emotion. It is the brutal, direct, and unadorned life-affirmation in the face of ultimate threat. In translating it into something constructive, you do not transmute it into a socially acceptable emotion or lifestyle. Instead, you develop further the self-affirmation that is the anger and expand it into the world. Perhaps you are now ready to proceed from anger to a life of excellence, accomplishment, and competence. You will then gain deserved respect, recognition, and even power. You will not need to apologize or hide, because your expanded self-affirmation is a contribution to your organization, community, and society.

> Jill is a middle-aged woman with three grown children who complains she has an unhappy work situation. Her relationship with her boss is one angry episode after another. Yet years of working on the relationship, she says, have brought about no changes other than to intensify the anger. Whereas in fantasy she wants to leave the job, she is surprised that in actual fact she does nothing to change things. On a deep level she prefers the status quo. In her work there is anger everywhere: from her to her boss, from him to her, among colleagues.

Anger need not be directional; it is rather the pervasive horizon against which a person's life is experienced. Jill, it seems, is not really unhappy at all. She *believes* she *should* be unhappy because that is what the social model demands. She could have a "happy" job by totally squelching her anger. Then society would approve. The truth lies elsewhere. Jill needs self-affirmation and not social approval. Her anger—which is safely embedded in her work—is her self-affirmation. Jill is happier being angry than having a "good" work situation. In fact, she does have a good job because it is an arrangement in which her anger can exist. An even better job would be for her not one in which there is peace but one that begins with her *expanded* anger. That is, she must expand her anger to become a creative life. Only then will her work environment give up but to always push ahead, they will find that the world confirms their choices. The world belongs to those who risk and who persist.

LANGUAGE CREATES EXPERIENCE

Another coping device is to program our speech to enhance our awareness of freedom. We must use frequently, and with full awareness of their meaning, expressions such as "I choose to . . ." and "I am responsible for . . . ." So that when we would otherwise be tempted to say "I am depressed," we must now say "I choose not to cope with my experience of depression" and "I am responsible for choosing not to cope with my experience of depression."

We must be careful, however, that our expanded statements are correct. Thus, the statement "I choose to be depressed" is not accurate. The element of choice does not pertain to the appearance of the feeling of depression but to our response to and attitude toward that feeling. The response either does or does not reflect the prior decision to cope with those feelings and with the situations that give rise to them. Our consciousness can be stretched, our inner space expanded, and the interface of freedom widened with the systematic and deliberate use of the phrases "I choose to . . ." and "I am responsible for . . . ." And all we do in them is speak the truth. We insert an awareness of the transcendental dimension—the realm of pure consciousness, where free will resides and exists—into our everyday language, while before we had limited our focus exclusively to the empirical region, where our behaviors exist.

In using these expressions freely and repeatedly, we are reminding ourselves of the intentional character of all experience

change. But, even if that does not happen, she is in a si
fits her well.

RISK

The basic strategy of coping with the anxiety of freedom—t.
overcoming the paralysis brought about by the denial of freec
by avoiding the confrontation with and integration of freedon
is *risking action*. We must learn to risk in small doses. By so doi.
we will gradually increase our toleration for the anxiety of freedor.
and we will also be able to take advantage of the existence of freedom. Toleration implies a decision. Through risk we become aware
that the anxiety of freedom can be tolerated, that freedom is our
nature, and that it *feels good* to integrate the anxiety of freedom into
our total personality. Intelligent risking gives us a sense of space and
solidity. Furthermore, the world has a tendency to validate and con-
firm our risks. But we have to learn how to make our demands of
nature and the world and be judicious in applying this principle.
Risking effectively is an art that matures through experience.

When we reach a crisis point in life, when we experience ourselves as "open to our feelings," when new patterns and new personality structures suddenly appear reasonable and thus become
available, then it is time to seriously consider risking new lifestyles,
value systems, beliefs, and relationships. People who suddenly solve
a problem that has remained insoluble for half a lifetime—people
who see the possibility of giving up alcohol, drugs, or cigarettes,
who leave a job or take a new job—are ready to risk a major change
in life and to cope with the larger consequences of that change. If
they persist and if they know that a person can choose never to

yet discovered, for once this is done, choosing can become natural and easy instead of deflected by ceaseless and unwarranted opportunities for procrastination. If we did not choose *X* before, it may have been because we had hoped for a way out; now that it has become clear that there is no such way, we will have little difficulty in opting for *X*.

What if several options are equally valuable and real? When this occurs we are in touch with the purity of our freedom and not with an objective fact about the alternatives. We are also experiencing the objective correlate of our freedom, which is the ambiguity of the world. At that moment we make an arbitrary choice—because that is the nature of all choice. We must recognize that all choosing has a conscious core that demands an archetypal—a foundational—choice. When the alternatives are equal and when both subjective freedom and objective ambiguity stand naked before us, then choice is seen to be both a transcendental (pure consciousness) and an archetypal (deep and foundational) phenomenon. Thus choice is a phenomenon that is capable of an *ex nihilo* act and through it one chooses to define the organization of being—as God was said to have done when He created the world. We must recall that the paradigmatic image of God creating the world contains two central elements: centeredness and freedom. In fact, it is only when the alternatives are of equal value that we experience in its full depth the reality of our transcendental freedom. We recognize that choosing among alternatives is the sacred process by which we define our future, choose our lifestyle, and decide on the structure of our empirical nature.

Perhaps the choice is one of career, or one relating to marriage or children, job or investment. When several options appear to be truly equivalent in value and meaning, then we are in touch with the ambiguity of existence, which—as was stated above—is the objective correlate of the absoluteness of our freedom. We then understand the existential point that we alone are responsible for hewing out a path for ourselves in the world's jungle of ambiguity. No one looks over our shoulder with the authority to say we are right or wrong. We must make the choice and we are stuck with the consequences, because we *are* the consequences. We thus constitute or construct our empirical ego, which is then the accumulated consequences or crystallizations of our previous free choices. At the moment of choice we just "go ahead and do it." And then we realize that we can indeed choose without actually knowing whether or not the decision is *right*. Choices are risks into which we must plunge. In taking those risks, the nihilism of anxiety becomes the concreteness of individuality.

A word of caution is in order. In practice there can be danger in encouraging too much freedom. While freedom is a truth about the human being, so is its correlate of anxiety. For example, some workers come to their leadership coaches with an already weakened and loosened sense of structure. While it is correct to say that they have an accurate perception of the underlying philosophical reality of their being, they also have legitimate fears of intensified anxiety. It would be important to help this type of person minimize freedom and maximize structure. That could be done through appeal to absolutes, authority, and suggestion, as well as by appropriate environmental measures to establish consistency, predictability, and security. These may be exaggerations, but the underlying point is important.

Here are some general suggestions on how to create a specific inventory of freedom.

Past and Present Decisions

First, become acquainted with decisions you have already made. On a sheet of paper, divide your life into past, present, and future. Then review what your key decisions have been and still are.

Begin with the past. How have you used your freedom in the past? Have you been able to experience your life in terms of the concept of freedom? Or is this idea new? What are some of the important decisions you have made in your life? Which are still with you? Can you recapture some of them? Can you put yourself in touch with the process of making them? How did you finally take action? Do you feel proud or guilty? Do you, in retrospect, believe that these decisions were right? If not, what would have been a better choice? What would have been the consequences had you done otherwise?

In this exploratory philosophical "surgery" you lay open the history of your freedom. You will get into both painful and joyous memories. Some people exclaim, "I was an idiot in making that decision. How could I ever have permitted it!" In becoming acquainted with past decisions, you will discover important strengths and weaknesses within you. Being in touch with why you allowed inauthentic decisions in the past may lead to authentic decisions today. Through this exercise you can also be in touch with the resistances that *stopped* you from making authentic decisions. That resistance to authenticity, that escape from freedom, may still be working within you today.

Now think of the present. Focus on decisions that you *are* now in the process of making as well as on those that you are now *not* making.

Overdue Decisions

To facilitate getting in touch with the decision-making process, it is useful to prepare a list of overdue decisions.

Write down five decisions that are overdue. Then rank these in the order of difficulty or importance to you. After they are ranked, add the one you were afraid to put down. Some people wait for this last instruction to commit to writing their highest priority decision. This exercise was once done by an apparently happily employed group of employees. To everyone's surprise, the highest-priority item for one person was whether or not to leave. That entry, understandably, had dramatic consequences, leading eventually to actual separation from the company.

Once you have written down your overdue decisions and ranked them, try to be in touch—through observation and experience—with your *resistance* against making them. There are direct and indirect resistances. You can *feel* direct resistances in your body and in your emotions. Indirect resistances can be *observed* in your defensive behavior and in the way you set up failures for your needs, but you do not feel them viscerally. You can feel in your body that you stop yourself from making decisions by asking in what organ you feel the resistance against making a specific and needed choice. In this way you can develop a map of your freedom. It is a useful device in developing a program of coping with the anxiety of freedom.

All of these coping strategies bring us to accept anxiety as an opportunity for deeper self-understanding. Any particular strategy may seem oversimplified or beyond our own situation. The important point is to hold the anxiety in the center of our thoughts and move toward it, experimenting with ways of deciphering its message. In each case, the coping strategy calls for us to lean on a trusting relationship and reframe how we think of our situation, including finding language that places us in charge of our experience. This takes us into decisions that before seemed too difficult to bear. The risk and vulnerability are high in every case, which gives each step its life-affirming quality.

Part II

IMPLICATIONS

A MOVE TOWARD freedom-based institutions asks us to rethink how we deal with anxiety in a work setting. Organizations spend great energy defending against anxiety. We act as if anxiety and productivity are in opposition to each other. This is despite our experience of being anxious whenever we are under pressure to perform. Our earliest institutional experience was attending school, and it is hard to remember taking a test that did not make us anxious. What made this early performance pressure doubly difficult was not only the anxiety, but the unexamined belief that we should not be anxious.

It does not have to be so, for part of what characterizes high performers is their ability to accept anxiety, to use it as a source of motivation and energy. We are capable of taking the anxiety and understanding it as a form of excitement and a sign that we are alive and in fact living our life. We are most alive when we have a sense of purpose and we only know this when there is tension about the outcome and something is on the line. It is difficult to imagine finding meaning in a purpose where nothing is at stake.

If work is one of the primary places where purpose is pursued and results are required, then anxiety is the sign that we have shown up and taken it all to heart. With this in mind, here are some of the forms of our struggle with anxiety in our institutions.

PROBLEM TO BE SOLVED

Most institutions treat anxiety as a problem to be solved. The common statement by managers, "Don't bring me a problem, bring me a solution," is a pure play against the anxiety of our uncertainty and the complexity of the world. It is the illusory stance that all problems have a solution, and we can find it if we just try harder. This is another version of the triumph of science over religion. The broader expression of this is that we believe that if employees are anxious about some aspect of the uncertain future, managers need to reassure this anxiety, as if employee anxiety is a management problem.

When we take freedom seriously, we treat anxiety as a sign that the system is alive. Say we are anxious about the progress of a project that is vulnerable, or anxious about what will happen to our unit, or that top management is about to visit and look us over. The fact that these are sources of anxiety means that people care about what is happening. This creates an opportunity for us—individual and organization—to become clearer about our purpose and to affirm the choice we are making to be in this organization.

Instead of a time for reassuring people that things will work out and that employees should trust management to do the best they can, anxiety creates an opportunity for a different kind of dialogue.

Doubts and fears can be expressed, acknowledged, recognized as real and not immediately soluble. This can lead to a serious discussion of the choice to stay in this organization. The question for employees is to have them consider the choice in front of them and to see that the threat gives them an opportunity to more fully be in charge of their own lives and of the way they decide to be in the middle of this business.

LISTS AND MEASURES

Our compulsion for lists and structured measures is also a response to anxiety. The common practice of ending every training session and every meeting with a summary list of things to do is an effort to carve out some reassurance that our being together in the meeting had some value. No sin to make a list, but the really important things we need to do or remember, we hold onto without a reminder system.

If we treated anxiety as a friend, we might notice what situations generate our anxiety and ask ourselves whether it is the situation itself, or our response to the situation, that troubles us. We tend to measure and list more vigorously when our faith in ourselves and others falters. Instead of controlling more tightly through measurement and milestone practices, we might ask what deeper and more personal concerns might be driving our low confidence.

Some of our anxiety comes under the heading of neurotic guilt, an idea that was introduced in Chapter 6 and will be explored in more depth in Chapter 12. Neurotic guilt comes from having betrayed ourselves. Instead of claiming our freedom, we have given it away. At work, self-betrayal comes in the form of saying yes when we mean no. We make promises that we cannot really commit to or believe in. We say everything is all right when it is not.

We hold the myth that we can't say no. Our institutional anxiety about freedom gets expressed in our fear of refusal. We are afraid of disobedience and, as a result, in most organizations there is an injunction against saying no. The common phrase, "if you stand up you get shot," is our belief that saying no, or saying yes too loudly, is tantamount to an act of terrorism or mutiny, an assault against authority that is dangerous to the institution. It is interesting that self-management used to be called mutiny, which was considered an act of treason. We are all inundated in the need to be a "team player," which, in its use in our workplaces, is an argument about the dangers of freedom.

All of this is part of our struggle with our freedom and subsequent accountability. We want a safe path and we want management to provide it. We want to say "no" or withhold a promise and not have to pay a price for it. Heavy dependence on lists, action plans, and milestones is our effort to hedge against paying for our ambivalence about really deciding what to commit to at work. If we viewed our anxiety as inherent in being human, and knew that we cannot drive it away, we could stop trying so hard to manage and control it and eliminate some of the excessive hunger for numbers, measures, and other modes of prediction.

OUR WISH FOR CERTAINTY

We also defend against anxiety in the way we spend time strategizing how to relate to one another, especially if we are trying to influence each other. I have attended many meetings spent deciding how to handle the next meeting or how to influence top management on some change effort. The political nature of organizations is reinforced by the need to be strategic in our relationships. We think that if we can control or predict how a conversation will go, it will improve its quality and get us what we want. This penchant for planning our encounters is a distrust of ourselves as spontaneous beings.

The need to plan who we want to be is especially true when leaders speak to their employees or in public. We have communication experts who position leader remarks, we have PowerPoints to maintain focus, and we meet in auditoriums that keep our leaders physically above and apart from their own people. And sometimes we even ask the audience to pass in their questions ahead of time so we can screen them and prepare our response.

All of this is a distrust of real, spontaneous, free conversation—held in real time. It is a belief that the world has to be managed, and that employees and citizens want their leaders to be rehearsed, positioned, turned into models of perfection. When did we begin to call this the real world?

These aspects of our institutional life—trying to solve anxiety, listing and measuring as a medicine to distance ourselves from anxiety, and our fear of spontaneity in our way of connecting with each other—all interfere with experiencing our freedom in our organizations. We have a difficult time accepting that the existence of anxiety is proof that organizations are living systems. When we accept the fact of our freedom, it carries with it a willingness to acknowledge anxiety as a permanent condition against which there is no cure.

THE PERMANENT CONDITION

If we chose to acknowledge our freedom and came to value anxiety as an aspect of the air that we breath, we would:

1. Seek anxiety out as a clue or doorway to deeper meaning, which can be found in the practical, day-to-day aspects of institutional life. We would find anxiety interesting and worth understanding, instead of something to be eliminated.

2. Stop protecting people from bad news, from our uncertainty about what we plan to do, and from our own leadership doubts. We would trust that others had the maturity to accept leaders as whole and incomplete human beings. We would trust that each of us has the strength or can develop the strength to face the harsh reality of life and work. It does not serve any of us to be protected against the truth.

3. Judge our meetings and gatherings on how clearly our anxiety gets expressed. When asked, "How was the meeting?" we would stop thinking the meeting was good because everyone was comfortable, optimistic, and supportive. We would believe that the meeting was good because concerns, doubts, and feelings were fully expressed. When we know how we all feel and where we all stand, we have a real sense of the real world.

4. Keep in perspective all the effort to clearly define roles, to prescribe competencies, and to live according to plan. These practices are most useful for the conversation and understanding they evoke, rather than the document they produce. To function according to role, to train according to competencies, and to assess the world according to plan are escapes from the anxiety that our freedom precipitates. Adhered to closely, they become defenses against anxiety and tend to constrain our performance and creativity rather than release them.

5. Evaluate for the sake of the learning of those being evaluated rather than for the sake of those doing or commissioning the evaluation. We consistently respond to anxiety by trying to create a world that appears more certain than it actually is and that needs more control and supervision than it actually does. Planning and structure are, of course, useful things to do, as long as they are not mistaken for being our purpose or the point. Organizations spend more resources and time in oversight and trying to predict the future than the return on these efforts warrants. We believe that people or teams will perform better and more honestly when they are watched. We have accepted the need for oversight and control, even though there is little evidence that more oversight and control lead to higher performance. No one measures the cost of oversight, and there is some evidence that high control systems are actually low performing in quickly changing environments.

6. Allow for spontaneity in dialogue. We would replace presentations with conversation. We would choose an unscripted existence, realizing that the mistakes we make are an expression of our freedom and spontaneity and sources of organizational and personal learning. We then leave room for dissent and value it. We stop seeing questions and serious disagreement as having anything to do with team playing.

What this all leads to is the insight that many of our performance management systems are really designed to increase our comfort level more than our performance level. When we see that anxiety is an inherent quality of a human system, and a characteristic of our freedom and the accountability that accompanies it, we will stop investing so heavily and fruitlessly in its elimination.

Part III

SPEAKING
OF
DEATH
AND EVIL

ONE OF THE CONSISTENT GIFTS of philosophy is its capacity to take us deeper, to help us spiral inward into rooms of our experience that are dusty from lack of use. This section takes us into the redemptive quality of facing evil and death. They come to us in symbolic ways such as failures, which are little deaths, and disappointments, which are a reminder that there are those things in the world that we cannot control. Most often we turn away from death and evil, hoping they will be postponed or disappear. This section takes us into them more deeply, offering the possibility that becoming better acquainted with the darker side of life is another essential element of our transformation and freedom.

Early in my relationship with Peter, I began to get the point that all the territory I had avoided was exactly the ground I needed to tread. He had an image that held great meaning for me, and that was, "When you are drowning, dive." When I most wanted to surface and avoid the heaviness of death, and even philosophy, this was just the time to go more deeply into it. The idea comes from being caught in the undertow on a beach. When it tries to pull you out to sea, you will exhaust yourself if you try to swim against it. If, on the other hand, you surrender to it and let it take you out to sea, it will gently deposit you a few hundred yards offshore, in waters calm enough that you can swim back to shore.

The title of the next chapter, "The Vitality of Death," is, in itself, a clue to what is in store. How could death be presented with such optimism, as something vital, rather than discouraging? Death is not a pleasant subject. Nor a subject you often find in a book about leadership and organizational life. In fact it is something we seem determined to avoid, especially in this culture, which romanticizes youth, expects us to live forever, and even treats dying as a medical, technological, or dietary failure.

DEATH IS AN OPTION

The discussion of death confronts me with the fact that I will not live forever. Institutions have a hard time with endings. We seem to be habitually compelled to sustain optimism, even in the face of contrary data. What we face in the workplace is the possibility of symbolic death—in other words, failure. We cling to the illusory notion that failure is not an option. As a result, we continue to invest in projects that are not working, partly because we confuse failure with defeat. Just because something we tried does not work doesn't mean we were wrong to begin it, or that there is something wrong with us. In fact, we constantly deal with failure, especially when the world demands that we choose adventure when all we wanted was safety.

We have a long tradition in science that understands that discovery and creativity require us to change our mind about failure. One of the gifts of the scientific method is that it teaches us that failure is as valuable as success, that discovery comes from being surprised, and that if we desire to grow, we need to embrace failure as a learning opportunity rather than treating it as a source of shame.

Also, and most compelling, are the chaos and unpredictability that surround us. No organization is a secure place anymore; our structures, relationships, how we do what we do are in a fast and constant state of flux. So workplaces that were once a refuge of security are now a source of great anxiety. Even the large and great organizations are standing on shaky ground.

The typical way we deal with failure and chaos is to problem solve them. We try through reassuring leadership and cultural change programs to foster creativity, to stop punishing failure (at least first-time failure), and to treat chaos as a friend, reassuring ourselves that, just around the corner, the chaos will stop vibrating and nature will provide us with the order that we seek.

Peter brings to us the intimate relationship between living a full, meaningful life and our willingness to look death squarely in the eye. Our fears, our failures, our experience of being assaulted and destabilized by change, in fact, can only be genuinely dealt with by experientially accepting the fact we are going to die—what he terms the *death of myself.* In essence he says that we are most likely to fail, be controlled by our fears, and be toppled by change if we do not face the question of death directly.

A STORM IN THE SHELTER

This question of death, in the form of failure, more than any other, has represented a dividing line between the philosopher and the person of practical action. We have asked those who lead us to shelter us from the prospect of something, including us, dying. We demand optimism from them; we insist they convince us that what might have seemed like a mistake, or what Peter would term a "symbolic death," was really just a stage in strategic re-alignment.

I remember when the Coca-Cola Company brought out New Coke with great fanfare. It was a cornerstone of how Coca-Cola would stay ahead of its competition. Six months into the promotion, it became obvious that the marketplace did not want a new Coke; they wanted the old one. The company had underestimated the loyalty customers had for the original taste and brand. This was an existential crisis for those who worked for the company. They had never experienced failure on such a public scale. Some kept believing that bringing out a product that the public did not embrace was really a clever strategic ploy, for it created great publicity and reinforced the sales of the old product, which they called Classic Coke.

I saw employees at times looking up at the Coca-Cola headquarters tower in Atlanta as if faith in a superior being had been stolen from them. It was a very difficult emotional time for all Coca-Cola employees. Interestingly, at one point the company gave most salaried employees a check for $100 just to let people know that management knew how much heat they were taking from their friends about the New Coke. Interesting example of how organizations deal with their shame.

If we wish to seriously deal with fear and failure, then death—its symbolic meaning and our relationship to it—needs to be present in our thinking. The discussion of death, the promise in entitling the next two chapters "The Vitality of Death" and "Some Revelations of Death and Failure," serves us in understanding and reframing how we think about failure and gives us a means, grounded in human experience and not in rhetoric, to create productive and meaningful institutions and leaders.

FACING REALITY

Facing the reality that we are not immortal, that some of our plans do not work, and that our institutions are not everlasting forces us to be more truthful about our predicament. If we want our workplaces to really be the real world, we need to be more truthful. Too often positioning and "effective communication" replace telling the truth.

The argument for positioning and not telling the truth is that people do not want to hear the truth. Managers believe that their job is to protect their employees from upsetting news; they try to shelter their people from anxiety and harm. This kind of parenting only devalues employees in their capacity to handle the world as it is. If we want employees to be accountable for the well-being of the institution, they need to be a part of its struggles and live with its vulnerability—even with the possibility that the institution might not survive, or may no longer continue in its present form.

The strength that is built by looking squarely at the harsh reality facing us, the ultimate harsh reality being that we will eventually die, outweighs the short-term cost of increased anxiety. When we see that our organization is not as strong as we hoped it might be, we then have the information to choose to be accountable for its well-being, regardless of what tomorrow might bring.

The exploration of death you are about to read also underscores that each of our lives carries within it the drama that we might have thought was reserved for public figures or artists who were forced to confront, because of their position or their talent, great issues of life and death. It does not take wartime, or the threat of great loss, to justify our concerns about questions of courage and death and greater purpose. We each are central figures in the world; we each were given gifts that place an obligation on us. So these questions become urgent to us, regardless of the history or the story that might have brought us to this point.

THE PRESENCE OF EVIL

You don't see many references to evil in books on management or psychology. "Evil" is a not a word often used in organizations or even in community life. Perhaps the term is too religious or too black and white in a gray world. We are more comfortable talking about failure, or obstacles, or fate—even death—than evil. This is a symptom of a world that cares much more about whether something works well or poorly than whether something is right or wrong. Our avoidance of the word "evil" is another way language becomes political.

The reluctance to use the word "evil" in the commercial world or even in the public service world is rather striking, if you think about it. It is not that we live without doubts and reservations about the things we do as an institution, it is just that there is no welcoming forum for expressing these doubts. There is no legitimacy in acknowledging our guilt. In fact the opposite is true. It is rare that any organization acknowledges that it has done something wrong.

Our difficulty in acknowledging evil is akin to a lawyer's universal advice to a client in conflict: "Don't admit to anything and don't talk to anyone on the other side without me in the room." A modern version of hear no evil, see no evil, speak no evil.

Organizations are, in reality, containers of significant and painful human drama. Power is abused by bosses and subordinates, people get aggressive and needlessly hurt others, our career can get derailed and we never get a chance to face our accuser, companies act against the interests of their community or the larger society and can simply move on rather than be accountable. People get fired, even in good times, and sometimes for no reason other than they got a new supervisor. And on and on.

This is not an indictment against organizations, for they and we are human systems and therefore each of us is capable and guilty of evil, harmful acts. What is significant, though, is our reluctance to acknowledge and collectively name the individual and organizational harm that we cause. We avoid any accountability for harm and in that way deny the existence of evil. And we do this by our unwillingness to use the word, especially in talking about ourselves. That is why the decision to acknowledge the existence of evil by talking about it is a political act. It destabilizes the social structure in two ways: it goes against the code of denial in the organizational culture and also threatens to change who has the power to define what is real and what is not real.

DENYING THE REALITY OF EVIL

This means that talking about the evil that exists in organizational life becomes risky business. In a high control environment, the mindset often exists that either you are with us, or are "not a team player." Or what is more popularly known as a "whistle blower." For a member of an institution to talk about institutional evil is to risk alienation.

In those rare cases where evil is acknowledged, our most common response is to find somebody to blame. If we can find one or two guilty parties and make an example of them, then the institution is exonerated. This search for THEM, the need for a scapegoat, is another form of denial. The illusion is that those doing the blaming, or witnessing the blaming, are innocent. It makes evil appear occasional and erasable.

The cost of acting as if evil does not exist is that we are agreeing to live and sustain a fictional environment—and through this never really face the reality of the consequences of what we are engaged in. The denial of evil also takes a lot of time, money, and emotional energy to maintain our defenses. All of this makes it difficult to develop a culture of trust and authenticity when there are significant, unspeakable domains.

More importantly, as you will read in this section, when we lose sight of the presence of evil, we also lose its potential to keep us focused on purpose and to provoke its own restitution. In that way, we lose the redemptive power of evil. Plus the denial of evil is what strengthens it.

DO NO HARM

Another reason why the discussion about evil is important for our workplaces is that harm does happen in organizational life. Harm is different from failure. Failure is a small death and means that something did not work. Harm means someone or some group acted to hurt another. One of the insidious characteristics of evil is that it becomes so subtle that it defies much real notice and, over time, slowly works its way into the fabric of our expectations of organizational life. So much so that we begin to think that it is normal and just the way the world works. We deny it by implicitly agreeing that its effect is marginal and manageable and to be expected.

This kind of evil or harm is about abuse—the abuse of power, abuse of friendship, a promise knowingly broken and denied for the sake of self-interest, a story told that is true, but what is not told makes it a lie. It comes in the form of official announcements that no one believes. We spin messages to our own people; we present bad news in a way that sounds as if we are still on plan and hopeful—as in the New Coke story. Another example is that employees often first find out from the public press, not from their own management, that their company or division is being sold. Not a big deal, really, or is it?

These small indecencies on the surface are mildly harmful. But they build up and form a pattern of response that erodes community and accountability. In their nature they *are* evil, although in their form they are bland and disturbingly digestible. They are what makes institutional life so difficult and exasperating. The worst part about evil in organizations is that, although harm is done daily, the institutions still work. They make money, serve customers and clients, perform well, and become larger. The fact that dark practices can be coincident with bright results is the paradox that grips us.

If, as insiders, we can acknowledge the existence of evil in organizational life, we won't eliminate it at all, but we will find ways to heal the wounds of those involved. And those who inflict the harm need a way to deal with their actions as much as those who receive it. Fundamental to our purposes here is that evil is part of our humanity, which builds the character of individuals and institutions at the moment it is able to acknowledge its existence. For it is at this moment that the way is paved to confront it, which, successful or not, gives nobility not only to individuals, which the following philosophical discussion explores, but also to our institutions.

Chapter 8

THE VITALITY
OF DEATH

No meaningful existence is possible without the honest recognition
of the unadulterated facts of human existence. One of the most important
of these facts is that of our own inevitable death.

ANY REAL DESIRE to discover our freedom requires coming
to terms with our limitations. The most dramatic reminder
of our limitations, and of the decisive effect of them on finding
meaning in life, is to be found in an understanding of the anticipation of death. Although no one has experienced death, everyone
confronts directly the anticipation of an inevitable personal death.
Mortality is an essential characteristic of life, and the anticipation
of death affects the quality of human existence.

Adapted from Peter Koestenbaum, "The Vitality of Death," in *The Vitality of Death: Essays in
Existential Psychology and Philosophy,* Westport, CT: Greenwood Publishing Co., 1971 (originally
reprinted with permission from the *Journal of Existentialism,* no. 18 (Fall 1964: 139–166)).

According to the existentialist understanding, the only genuine and legitimate way in which we can develop a theory of what it means to be free is to understand what it means to be alive or to exist as a human being in the world. We achieve such understanding by describing accurately, sensitively, and perceptively the general characteristics of this experience. While engaging in such descriptions, we must be prepared to ignore all our preconceived opinions and theories about what a person is or ought to be. It follows that, in the analysis of what it means to be free, we must examine what it is that we think about, fear, or stand in awe of when we envisage our own death. We must place in limbo, at least temporarily, our beliefs about the immortality of the soul, our theories that death might be an eternal sleep, our thought of death as bodily disintegration, as survival through children and influence, and the like, since these matters are hypotheses and inferences and not items in our immediate first-person experience.

THE VARIOUS MEANINGS OF THE WORD "DEATH"

The primary distinction to be drawn in the "anticipation of death" is between the *death of another* and the *death of myself.* But in order to understand the difference between the *death of myself* and the *death of another,* we must first explore the more general meanings of the word "death."

The idea of death comes to us in a hundred forms. Surprisingly, death as a mental presence can be relaxing, fascinating, and entertaining, in addition to showing its more common characteristics of horror, dread, despair, and tragedy. For example, we read in a newspaper about murder while we relax over our morning cup of coffee. We also read with fascination of Custer's men and how they were all killed in the Battle of Little Big Horn. Moreover, some individuals find it relaxing and entertaining to watch people getting shot on television or in movies.

On the other hand, we read avidly, but also with dismay and horror, about death in the gas chambers of Nazi concentration camps. Also, we respond to the death—or the threatened death— of a relative or someone else close to us with concern, panic, and anxiety. The feeling that the world is coming apart at the seams, that the universe is caving in, overcomes us when a person for whom we have complete responsibility—such as a child—or on whom we are totally dependent—such as a parent or spouse—is threatened with death or is actually dead. The same is true at work when we say no to someone's ambition or when we are forced to reduce staff, fire someone, or eliminate a function that just yesterday seemed to have a future.

Any death, or any time we are in touch with failure, is a close reminder of our own death or our own limitations. We feel sick, weak, and queasy at the prospect of our own immediate demise. In the extreme, we cannot easily control the anxiety, hysteria, and nausea that overcome us when we are confronted with the immediate threat of our own death. Thus, the word "death" refers to a large number of conscious states, some of which are relaxing to us and some of which assault the total structure of our personality. The *death of myself,* as interpreted here, is not only filled with anxiety but it is also tragic. Note Edna St. Vincent Millay's lines:

Down, down, down into the darkness of the grave
Gently they go, the beautiful, the tender, the kind;
Quietly they go, the intelligent, the witty, the brave.
I know. But I do not approve. And I am not resigned.[1]

The life-world is the created and constructed totality of a human being. That life-world comes to naught, vanishes, is destroyed with death. All the great experiences—loves, hope, all wisdom and education, the learning of, let us say, eighty-eight years—all come to nothing. What is the point, we might say, in creatively structuring our human existence if it is all to be destroyed? It is sad to destroy anything precious, anything that took much human creativity to bring about—as the loss of an ancient cathedral in a bombing raid. But it is tragic to lose the most precious thing of all: a full human life—rich in fulfillment or full of promise.

The Two Basic Meanings of the Word "Death"

When we explore the various meanings of the word "death," we discover two general types of meaning that this word possesses. On the one hand, the word refers to the *death of another,* and, on the other, it refers to the *death of myself.* Perhaps the terminology introduced here, that is, the distinction between the *death of another* and the *death of myself,* is somewhat coarse and crude, but it makes the necessary point. Let us examine in greater detail what we mean when we think of the *death of another* as opposed to the *death of myself,* that is, our own death.

Death of Another

The *death of another* is, first of all, an occurrence within the world. We conceive of the world as going on. We may think of funeral arrangements, tearful scenes, maybe a funeral oration, the settling of the estate. The *death of another* means the cessation of heartbeats, the cessation of respiration; in general, it means termination of all bodily processes. The *death of another*—as seen from the perspective of my own subjectivity and inwardness—is usually not accompanied with any overwhelming invasion of anxiety, dread, and nausea; it is merely one event occurring amongst many in a highly variegated and nigh interminable world.

What is characteristic about the meaning of the *death of another* is that it involves the *elimination of an object within the world, and not of the observing subject—that is, me.* In other words, if you examine closely what you mean by the death of another person, you recognize that *you, yourself are still in the picture:* you are the observer contemplating the scene, even if the scene is only in your imagination. Death is an event within the world, while the lifeworld—the world of human experience—lives to see another day.

Death of Myself

The situation is altogether different if we subject the conception of *my own* death—the *death of myself*—to a similarly careful analysis. This kind of analysis guides us to discover the real meaning of death in the life of a person. In analyzing our own death, we must examine more than merely the physical disintegration of our bodies. Our own death means the total disintegration and dissolution of our personal world. The *death of myself* is well-described by the terms "void" or "encounter with nothingness." At least such is the manner in which we anticipate our death. Since the *death of myself* is the disintegration of *my* world, the death of loved ones—who make up this world—has many of the disintegrative features of the *death of myself.*

Death of myself presents itself in terms of extraordinary and unspeakable anxiety. Such a terrifying confrontation immobilizes our normal responses and, what is most important, transforms the value of everything in life. Prior to the confrontation with the threat of one's own death, such things as having a greener lawn than the neighbors, a better grade in school than my friend, a higher income than my associates, a better sales record than the competition loomed large and important; yet, in the face of the ultimate threat, their value is totally transformed. In fact, these things no longer mean anything at all to me. It of course cannot be maintained that we live in constant terror of death, or that the thought of our death fills us with unspeakable anxiety. What is asserted here is that the full awareness of what death involves, the clear confrontation with the anticipation of death, the unconscious presence, as it were, is the source of deep anxiety.

We are not honest with ourselves in thinking about our own death. When we are forced to do so, as in the presence of a corpse, or on hearing of the death of one who occupies a central and large part of our life-world, then the anxiety attending death emerges and the essential brittleness of the world becomes apparent.

However, just as with the *death of another,* the central fact was the continuous presence of the self or ego as the inescapable *observer,* so, when contemplating *my own death,* the central fact is that *the observer—I, myself—dies or vanishes.* When we think of our death with candor and honesty, we must recognize that one of the reasons why the immediate confrontation with our own death submerges us into the deepest state of anxiety is that it entails the disappearance of the *us* as the observer; in fact, it entails, in a sense, the disappearance of the world itself, not just an object in the world.

The End of the World

If we think of our death as the end of everything, then, in a manner of speaking, we must think as well of the termination of the universe itself. After all, what mental image is present when we think of the real meaning of the *death of myself*? Honest analysis will disclose that there is then no image of the world left. Thus, our image of the *death of myself* is tantamount to asserting the end of the world.

There is a fundamental error in the thought that the *death of myself* means the cessation of heartbeats, burial, and yet assures the continuation of the world. That is *not* how the threat of our own death presents itself; that threat is the death of the *observer*. For example, if you should think of your own burial, the settling of your estate, the cessation of your breathing, etc., then you tacitly—and erroneously—also think of yourself as some eternal observer contemplating the tragic scene of your own death! What you, the observer, have done here, in effect, is not to have considered candidly enough the reality of your own death. The understanding of what it means to be dead cannot include your presence as an observer at your own death. You have, in fact, slipped back surreptitiously into the picture of your own death as some sort of eternal observer. But we must remember that *your* death is supposed to be the death of the *observer*. And with the extinction of that observer, the entire scene vanishes as well.

Living Death

The structure of the *death of myself* involves certain ambiguities. The phrase "death of myself" is an expression designating that part of human experience which may be described as the anticipation of total nothingness and its emotional concomitants. The meaning of the *death of myself* does not always coincide with the extinction of the individual. It sometimes refers to the extermination of something that has been life giving in the objective world. For example, a mother may have greater concern over the death of her children than over her own death. Her life-world—that region of experience into which she has totally projected herself—is her children. Her death is but a passing and natural event. Her life-world is her children, and even though she dies, her children will have been given a good start in life. In one sense, her real anxieties are connected with the death of her children and not herself. The possibility of the death of her children becomes for her the symbolic form of the death of herself (that is, the *death of myself*). Should the catastrophe occur, should her child die, she will exist in a state of *living death*.

That *living death*—impossible to bear—will soon resolve itself into one of two possible directions. The *living death* may become a real death: she may die of a broken heart, of physical neglect, or unconscious or even deliberate suicide. In that case—like Oedipus, who tore out his eyes to make real the blindness with which he had lived all his life—she makes manifest what has been true all the time anyway. On the other hand, she may overcome her sorrow by doing what the ancient Stoic philosophers had recommended all along, namely, to detach herself sufficiently from her children—to avoid excessive projection onto them—so their death can be accepted with equanimity. Epictetus suggests that, upon leaving in the morning, a father should whisper into his beloved child's ear the sweet nothing "you may be dead tomorrow." Excessive attachment to that over which we do not have total control—such as the life of a child—can lead to despair and is therefore to be avoided. By getting over the shock, by adjusting herself to the death of a child, a mother has ceased projecting her ego onto that life-world, so that gradually that death is transformed from the intolerable *death of myself* to a tolerable *death of another*.

THE AMBIGUITY OF THE WORD "DEATH"

There is a very serious and altogether fundamental ambiguity in the word "death." Although we use but one word, and although there are of course significant similarities, the total constellation of meanings in the expression "the death of another" differs from that of "the death of myself." The *death of another* is conceived to be an occurrence within a larger world, and is often, although of course not always, devoid of heavy emotional content. The *death of myself*, on the other hand, is the anticipated termination of any confrontation with or conception of the world itself. In addition, the anticipation of the *death of myself*, as the termination of a life-world, is interwoven with deep anxiety and tragedy; borrowing a phrase from Nietzsche, it entails a complete "transvaluation of values." The *death of another* reduces to the continuation of the world and the *death of myself* to the annihilation of the world.

The Mask of Death

In the *death of another,* the word "death" also means fascination, terror, and tragedy. These are to be sharply distinguished because they are opposed to each other in meaning. Fascination attracts, terror repels, while tragedy is a feeling unique to itself. That the word "death" means all of these suggests that the word serves the function of hiding from us certain crucial facts of experience.

This ambiguity may be no accident; on the contrary, it may serve a most useful function. By means of the semantic and linguistic confusion between the *death of myself* and the *death of another,* we protect ourselves from the tremendous and dangerous amount of anxiety that is released when we are confronted with the accurate recognition of the meaning of our own death. We circumvent facing the tragedy of death. We tend to think of death as the *death of another.* We hopefully maintain that the *death of another* is the only kind of death there is. In fact, we think of the *death of myself* as nothing worse than the *death of another.* We believe that the *death of another* is characteristic of all forms of death, even our own. Through this device, we hide from ourselves the true and demolishing nature of our own anxiety about the tragedy of our own death. But such ambiguity is an escape, and no meaningful existence is possible without the honest recognition of the unadulterated facts of human existence. One of the most important of these facts is that of our own inevitable death.

A successful and happy life begins with the understanding that we must die and with the knowledge that, to us, our death is generically different from the death of others.

The Problem of Immortality

There might be a temptation to observe that the differences between the *death of another* and the *death of myself* apply only to the consciousness of those people who do not believe in the immortality of the soul. The deeply religious, it may be argued, need have no anxiety about death because they know they have an immortal soul. For them, all death has the characteristics of what we have here called the *death of another*. Their soul, they continue, remains always as an observer.

The present discussion, however, is intended as an analysis of the experience of feeling human, irrespective of any religious beliefs. The fact is that each of us is concerned about our own death. Religious believers who are convinced of their own immortality are perhaps more anxious and more concerned about death than the agnostic or the atheist, who may never give this matter much thought. As a matter of fact, the belief in immortality is one of humanity's most pervasive and cherished efforts to handle the persistent and anxious problem of the *death of myself*.

To believe in immortality does not mean we have overcome the primal anxiety about our own death; it means that we have decided to make a strenuous effort—both psychologically and intellectually—to lead an existence that works constantly at convincing ourselves that the anxiety about our own death is unfounded and can be overcome. It means that we focus our attention on those aspects of our experience which tend to support the existence and the presence of a loving God into whose bosom our soul will retire after death. Rather than ignoring the importance of death, our life as a believer in immortality is determined by the ever-present anticipation of our death, far more than is the life of the less religious individual. The possibility of such a life, far from being evidence that for some there is no anxiety about death, is testimony to the wholehearted dedication of that life to the issue of death. Religious individuals who live for immortality have focused on the fact of their own death. And such concern is precisely what existentialism as a philosophy urges, since, in the last analysis, such concern is inevitable.

The Fascination of Death

The experience of our anticipated death is not exhausted by calling attention to its elements of terror and tragedy; it shares the element of fascination with other terrifying and tragic experiences.

The subject matter of death, seen from any level, has always fascinated us. Death in novels, movies, plays, newspaper reports, military history, all provide us with "relaxation," although we may often feel guilty over the disturbingly paradoxical fact that what to another is the ultimate threat turns out to be a kind of relaxing pleasure to us.

Death more closely linked to our own is perhaps even more fascinating, although that type of fascination is morbid indeed and unravels a welter of deeper and otherwise hidden emotions. A good example of this second, morbid kind of fascination can be seen in the curiosity that almost everyone displays about accidents.

What is our response when we see the tangled remains after a car accident? Our experiences can be grouped into two classes. The first group consists of emotions of anxiety. The second group consists of a reevaluation of our values, our relations to other people and to ourselves, and a reassessment of the total plan and meaning of our life. This response is sustained in any serious confrontation with the reality and realization of our death.

On one side, there is anxiety. Seeing an accident is different from reading about it. In seeing an accident we are immediately confronted with the realization that "but for the grace of God, there go I." Our identification with the actual or potential victims is so close that we are suddenly faced with the clear, unmistakable, and overwhelming presence of the constellation that we have termed *death of myself.* This presence fills us with deep anxiety and concern; it shakes the stability and equilibrium of the world of our experience to its very foundations. It makes us realize—if but for a fraction of an unpleasant moment—that the world in which we live, with its goals, prejudices, and institutions, is not the solid existence that we had believed and hoped. For a moment, our otherwise secure and predictable world has disintegrated into total chaos. Whereas before witnessing the accident we felt comfortable and at home in a familiar world, we now suddenly feel like an alien; we are like a falling body in a dark and infinite abyss. This feeling of total alienation, this experience of being completely homeless, this undermining of the most basic foundations of the world on which we depend is characteristic of how it feels to realize that we are indeed finite and mortal beings.

FROM DEATH TO A MEANINGFUL LIFE

On the positive side, the inevitable corollary of the dread of our world's destruction leads to a complete reevaluation and transformation of the meaning of our individual human existence. We become aware of the urgency to find meaning in life. We are forcefully impressed with the necessity of taking the bull of our lives by the horns and subduing it into a meaningful existence. We are eased into a situation that gives us the courage and the decisiveness to reassess our lives, to rethink our values, and, eventually, to act on these insights—and we are enabled to act now, not in an indefinite future. We experience the pressure—which has always been present in latent form—of deciding what we dedicate our lives to and how we shall spend our existence. And the pressure is to decide on this issue immediately and act without delay.

We thus see that the morbid fascination that the average person sees in an accident is merely a clue—as are many other events in our human existence—to a crucial element in human nature. That element is the inescapability of death, with its negative and its positive impacts on our life. The enormous anxiety generated by the full understanding of the meaning of the *death of myself* leads, like a catharsis, to the determination and eventual acquisition of a meaningful life.

But before dwelling on the positive aspects of death, we must remember that *death of myself* means infinitely more than the cessation of heartbeats and the other concomitants of the physical conception of death.

A scientific account of an accident will be in terms of sense data (that is, what can be photographed), the laws of mechanics, and the laws of physiology. It will include a reference to the psychological reactions of the subject witnessing the scene. An existential description spreads the proper mood over the entire scene and claims that the scene as given is pervaded with this mood. To overlook the mood that covers the scene like morning mist—or to relegate this striking fact to an obscure and minor position by saying "the scene made me sick" without any further experiential analysis of "sick"—is to be false to the facts of experience; it is to distort and misrepresent the nature of the experience itself.

An accident combines fascination with terror. We are curious about accidents—and the media capitalize on this pervasive curiosity. Yet in the presence of an accident we are also gripped by fear and likely to reevaluate, at least temporarily, our entire mode of life. By the unique combination of fascination and terror, the experience of an accident becomes a symbol or reminder of the fundamental paradox of being a person. The terror of the accident means the inevitable defeat of a human being's quest for indefinite and infinite transcendence. The fascination of the accident indicates to us that we must resolutely face death if we wish to handle the human paradox successfully, and that there is hope—and even possibly bliss—if we can successfully deal with this great issue.

The next chapter expands on the theme of how the disturbing nature of the anticipation of the death of ourselves is instrumental in giving meaning to our lives. This way of taking what concerns us most deeply, what we most often choose not to think about, and turning it into a life-giving perspective is the essence of philosophic insight. It creates a context in which we are free to choose how to make sense of our own experience and how we can create our own possibilities. This is a major shift from the belief that our future is in some way determined by our own history and by the events that flood down upon us. It is an expression of the fact that we are not only free to create our life, but that we are, in essence, a freedom itself. And we have no choice about that.

Chapter 9

SOME REVELATIONS
OF DEATH
AND FAILURE

The most vitalizing fact of life is the utter inevitability of death!
We must constantly keep before our eyes the reality, the nature, and the
inevitability of that fact. We must make every effort to understand exactly
what our own death means to us. We must see the consequences of the
knowledge that we are mortal. We must never let go of this insight.

WE HAVE EXAMINED death in the light of two dimensions. The first is the distinction between the *death of myself* and the *death of another.* The second dimension—which applies to both types of death—consists of the elements of fascination, terror, and tragedy. Of these, the question, "Why are people curious about accidents?" represents the element of fascination. The larger answer is that presence of death is rich in profound revelations to us about our essential nature and is likewise a cornucopia of clues about the meaning of life.

Adapted from Peter Koestenbaum, "The Vitality of Death," in *The Vitality of Death: Essays in Existential Psychology and Philosophy,* Westport, CT: Greenwood Publishing Co., 1971 (originally reprinted with permission from the *Journal of Existentialism,* no. 18 (Fall 1964: 139–166)).

INTERNAL AND
EXTERNAL REALITIES

There is a third dimension: the distanced or *callous* and *practical* response to the meaning of death. It is the response of the professional soldier, the police officer, the nurse, and the doctor. An overpowering sense of fascination, terror, and tragedy interferes with the physician's practical attitude necessary in a situation of death. Sympathy and efficiency are frequently mutually exclusive attitudes toward human existence. An individual who faints at the sight of blood is not able to apply a life-saving tourniquet. A person who sees clearly the staggering terror and tragedy of nuclear war may not be able to shift into the practical detached frame of mind required to plan for civil defense and survival after attack.

To examine this shift in attitude to see what it discloses about existence, consider the shift between passionate promises while in love and practical far-sighted decisions when rational. It is the difference between solving a personal problem by giving in to depression and relishing the consequent introverted reveries of introspection—as suggested by Meister Eckhart's statement that "God would sooner be in a solitary heart than any other"—on the one hand, and adopting a practical, aggressive, rational, fighting, extroverted attitude on the other. The first solution *discloses ourselves to us,* whereas the second *solves the problem,* at least temporarily. In fact, both attitudes attempt to solve the problem but they do so in two altogether different directions.

Can these two ways of life be reconciled? The first seeks the innermost self, while the second seeks satisfactions in external realities. In the last analysis, the external reality is no different from the internal life. In adopting this practical attitude, individuals seek to identify with the external world. In adopting the introspective attitude, they identify themselves with their inner ego. The distinction between the innermost ego of the person and the external world as he or she sees it—and have constituted it—begins to disappear. The two then become manifestations of one and the same underlying consciousness.

REAL DEATH AND SYMBOLIC DEATH

The word "death," when used in the expression "the death of myself," is a symbol that signifies complete destruction, total annihilation, utter elimination of support, substance, and sustenance, and the everlasting absence of any meaning whatever. In addition, the word "death" refers to the state of anxiety that accompanies the realization of the fact that total destruction threatens us.

It is quite evident that this experienced threat to our existence—consisting, as it does, of total annihilation—does not have to be associated with the physical death of the body. On the contrary, it is quite possible that most of us do not think primarily of the death of the body when we think of our mortality, but that we think of something that might be called the "death of the spirit" or the extinction of the mind or of consciousness. We shall refer to nonbody or nonphysical (that is, nonliteral) fears of death as stemming from the anticipation of what we call "symbolic death."

Symbolic Death Is Real

For the purposes of finding meaning in life, a *symbolic death* has all the reality of a so-called *real death*. Every person lives in a self-created world. The businessperson lives in the world of business, associates, clients, and business goals; the music conductor lives in the world of music, orchestra, and audience; the research chemist lives in the world of a laboratory, problems of chemical synthesis, and occupational advancement; the salesperson lives in the world of their product, their industry, and their profession. A *symbolic death* is the collapse of the particular world toward which our energies and goals are directed. For the businessperson, the collapse of a business is a *symbolic death;* the loss of a job is a *symbolic death* for the chemist; and so on.

A personal slight is a further example of *symbolic death.* To be ignored by others, especially by those whose attention we prize and esteem, is to be thought dead. A common form of expressing anger, hate, hostility, or chagrin is to refuse to speak to the person with whom we relate that feeling. What we do, in fact, is refuse to acknowledge the very existence of that person; we act as if that person were dead. And the effects of our actions are similar to those facing a person in what we are inclined to call real or genuine death.

Acceptance and Rejection

A subtler form of the same type of emotional *symbolic death* is involved in the question of personal acceptance. To *accept* a person—by being understanding, forgiving, friendly, cordial, open-hearted, and sympathetic—is to act as if the person were alive. To *accept* someone is to embrace that person in our world. In the act of acceptance, their world reaches out to ours. On the other hand, to *reject* someone—by criticizing, disapproving, or ignoring what is important to that individual—is to threaten him or her with *symbolic death.* Take the illustration of many people today who are aware they are living a very unbalanced life.

Jane works in an environment where twelve-hour days are the norm and in fact a source of pride. She works closely with an important executive in a growing field and derives much satisfaction from their collaboration. She has a good position, good salary, status, good working conditions, and a most pleasant, cordial, and friendly boss. Jane is a strong personality yet has difficulty saying no to the increasing demands of the organization. Irrespective of the obvious and enviable advantages of her position, she is beginning to feel that she might like to slow down and think about a job change that would give her more flexibility and time. Her excessive dependence on her job makes it impossible for her to even explore other options. It appears to her—not very clearly, of course—that she should quit her present job and either select one that gives her more emotional freedom, one she can leave without elaborate preparation, or abandon work altogether for a while to acquire the necessary emotional independence from her present employer to make a life change a serious possibility.

Jane is heavily dependent emotionally on the pull of the job and the positive reinforcement she receives from the managers she works with. They are immersed in being stars in their own right and have no serious impulse to question what the organization demands from its employees. However, her boss finds her services most useful and is quite determined not to let her go. As long as she makes it apparent to her boss that she is committed to staying— and the manager helps her make such a commitment by awarding frequent bonuses as well as good salary increases, prized assignments, and inclusion in special recognition benefits—the manager is ready to *accept* her. But as soon as she but insinuates that she might quit her job, the manager becomes cold and indifferent. She literally dreads this cold indifference. As a matter of fact, she dreads it so much that she finds it impossible to quit! Why does she fear this coldness so desperately?

Traditional psychological explanations might make reference to her upbringing, her early relations with her father or mother, specific learned responses, conditioned reflexes based on early experiences, cultural pressures, and the like. However, from the perspective of the philosophic insight, these are theoretical inferences and hypothetical constructions, although they are very illuminating. A more immediate and direct analysis of Jane's predicament must be accounted for in terms of her confusion about the nature of her own death. Only the correct appraisal and full acceptance of death will free her from this painful, anxiety-filled, and guilt-ridden impasse.

Speaking in terms of direct experience, we can say that a great portion of Jane's world lies in the acceptance provided by her employer. Rejection by the managers she works with means, in effect, that they are ignoring her existence, that they are destroying her world. Since she has become dependent on their acceptance of her, they possess a god-like power to uphold or destroy her whole world. Even if their rejection of her is only by means of minor gestures and relatively insignificant omissions, it is a clear and distinct form of *symbolic death* for her—and their acceptance offers her symbolic immortality. They are saying, in effect, "Stay with us and we shall give you eternal life!" When each of us learns to respond maturely to the general problem of death in life, as Jane must in this example, we will be better able to manage it in its symbolic form when we meet it in our daily experiences.

What creates Jane's anxiety, guilt, sense of self-dissatisfaction, and, above all, complete paralysis of her will is that her world does not lie exclusively in her organization's acceptance. If that were the case, all she would need to do is to remain in her present employment and the threat of *symbolic death* would vanish. The fact is, however, that the world toward which she directs herself in order to achieve fulfillment in life goes also toward a personal life and work that might carry more meaning to her. And the two worlds conflict.

Only through the proper management of the threat of the *death of myself*—first in general and then in particular instances—will she be able to achieve genuine happiness and authentic success in her life.

Aging and the Sense of Time

One of the most striking phenomena connected with the *death of myself* is the sense of aging and the passage of time. What is behind the pressure of time? We always seem to be in some sort of hurry or under some kind of pressure to get things done, catch up, get organized, etc. Above all, we feel anxious, guilty, and left out about getting old. We engage in endless stratagems to hide our years—from others as well as from ourselves. We worry over gray hair and wrinkles; we are concerned that we are getting older and are not getting anywhere in life; we are disappointed about early promises unfulfilled, and about innocence lost. Of course, the process of getting old and the many and severe problems associated with it arise only because of the conviction that the *death of myself* is inevitable. As we get older we increasingly get the feeling that we have not achieved the kind of fulfillment and found the kind of meaning in life that we promised ourselves in our youth. This feeling is the acknowledgment of the overwhelming, inescapable, and depressing truth that time is running out. The problems and anxieties connected with aging testify to the persistent, if underlying, presence of the dread of the *death of myself.*

Many philosophers and psychologists make an effort to set all human experiences in the dimension of time. In so doing, the life of a person becomes the experience of duration and of time. In the background of such a world view, just beyond the horizon, there is death, the termination of duration and of time.

Jane was plagued—as we all are—by the feeling that time is running out. The fact of death was the real background of her problem. After all, if humans did not die, then the solution to her problem could easily be postponed indefinitely. The fact of death makes us guilty about procrastination. Unconsciously, perhaps, we feel that we must get somewhere in life—in small matters as well as in large. Not knowing when death will approach increases the pressures impinging upon us to achieve whatever our confused goals may be.

DEATH AS A SOURCE OF COURAGE

Jane could acquire the will power, decisiveness, and self-assurance that she needs in order to quit her job in good conscience and with a full measure of self-respect. The courage and determination to make sense of this life while it lasts and fulfill all its possibilities—in the face of death—was forcefully stated in these lines of the fifth-century Greek poet Pindar:

O my soul, do not aspire to immortal life,
But exhaust the limits of the possible.[1]

First of all, Jane must recognize that the threat of death—real and symbolic—is inevitable and inescapable. She will quickly recognize that the symbolic promise of immortality (in the form of her employer's emotional acceptance of her) is a fraud. Once she has accepted—and this is the hardest part—the inevitability of her *real death,* and accepted it from the bottom of her heart, she will no longer be intimidated by symbolic threats of death. She now recognizes full well that her employer's eventual rejection is inevitable—just as is her own death—and that she is being a fool in hoping secretly that life is different from what it really is, which means hoping that there is no death.

She also recognizes, once she honestly focuses her attention on death, that time *is* running out, that she has but one life to lead, that if she throws away this life she will have lost all there is, as far as she is concerned. It will soon become apparent that her employer is not worth all that and the organization's symbolic promise of immortality can be fulfilled no more reliably than immortality in relation to our *real death.* If she keeps the fact of her inevitable death clearly enough in mind, she will develop the courage and decisiveness needed to build a richer life for herself and quit her job.

Self-Deception

One of the most beguiling problems plaguing Jane is self-deception. Because she dreads leaving her job, she procrastinates about making and executing a decision; she accepts stupid excuses as rational.

As a matter of fact, most of the time she avoids thinking about the matter altogether.

However, the realization of death places immediate and tremendous pressure on her. It makes the problem of the meaning of life a problem of the first importance to her. She realizes that she has no time to waste, that she must face the facts, and that she must come to a decision.

Her first decision will be *not to deceive herself* in this matter. Self-deception, the harmful and dishonest practice of hiding the facts from our own selves, is possible only if in the background we tacitly accept our own terrestrial immortality. Those who have been condemned to death, by the very fact that they have a human nature, cannot afford to deceive themselves and see no merits in such self-deception.

The Real, Real World

Thus, our first point illustrating the vitality of death, and the point of departure for all subsequent considerations, is that authentic success and happiness in human existence demand uncompromising realism; we must understand and acknowledge the facts of life. Paradoxically, the most vitalizing fact of life is the utter inevitability of death! We must constantly keep before our eyes the reality, the nature, and the inevitability of that fact. We must make every effort to understand exactly what our own death means to us. We must see the consequences of the knowledge that we are mortal. We must never let go of this insight.

The fact of our own inevitable death will place our problems in an altogether new light. What may have seemed depressing, frustrating, hopeless, now achieves meaning. The employee who sits at his terminal and surfs the Internet or plays endless computer games instead of completing his work might find help in conquering his problem if he has learned to see his present moment in relation to his eventual death. His life unfolds itself in the direction of death; his life points to his death. Realizing this, his work is suddenly placed in its proper perspective. The thought of death suffuses his life with a liberating sense of urgency. He is able to view his penchant for game-playing as a minor inconvenience rather than as a major obstacle or an insurmountable barrier. He may also be able to stop the process of repression and self-deception. Before, he refused to recognize that this habit was threatening his career and his future. Now, seeing the reality of death, for him the process of repression and self-deception becomes altogether pointless. Repression ceases to be a temptation. He thus achieves increased objectivity about the manner in which he conducts his life and suddenly is able to see his life realistically and in perspective. He is thus helped to handle and overcome his problem.

DEATH AS SUPPORT FOR DECISION MAKING

One of our greatest problems in making a success of life is the chronic inability to make decisions, especially decisions that demand courage. How can the thought of death give courage? Courage is the opposite of fear and fear is ultimately the fear of death—*real* or *symbolic death*. People who have admitted to themselves, once and for all, that they are going to die will no longer act out of fear. They understand the fear of death, and they certainly can handle fears of *symbolic death*. To give in to one's fear is based on the acceptance of a fraudulent promise: that of symbolic immortality.

Consider the further tribulations Jane might experience. Let us assume that she has decided to quit her job and has found herself another that gives her more control of her life. Now, before she makes the move, she begins to have serious second thoughts and questions the change she is about to make.

She needs courage and decisiveness for two reasons. First, it takes courage to admit to herself that she made a mistake in planning to change her job situation, for she created expectations among her friends and family that she would be conducting her life differently and she has made what might be an ill-advised, deep commitment to her new employer. It takes courage to admit that she has been perhaps impulsive in this choice and that she has allowed peer support and a compelling job offer to drive fundamental decisions for her. Second, it takes substantial courage to break off the commitment itself, especially after she let her present employer know that she was not the loyal employee they thought she was. Out of timidity and indecisiveness, out of sheer lethargy and inertia, she may go ahead and make this change—and regret it for the rest of her days!

The clear understanding of death, as well as an ever-present awareness of it, will make certain facts amply clear to her. She will be fully conscious of the fact that she has but one life to lead and that she can either make the most of it or throw it away. She must also remember that, in the light of her death, her life is all she has, her life is her sole value; her life, in fact, is all of existence for her. Seeing her imminent choice from this liberating perspective, her pain in breaking it off will indeed seem minimal compared to the alternative of throwing away her entire life, her total *being*. After all, her life is her only possession. We possess nothing but our human existence, since we *are* that existence.

We must not labor under the illusion that the recognition of the *death of myself* will make it any less painful for Jane to break off the commitment. What this realization *will* do for her, however, is to give her the courage and the decisiveness to carry out that decision. Furthermore, the thought of her death enables her to see her life as a total project; it enables her to look ahead toward a complete plan for life. In seeing her human existence from this aspect of eternity, she recognizes that not taking the new job would be but a passing ripple in the totality of her life, whereas making this change against her innermost wishes would be a major catastrophe for that life. In the face of death, it becomes obvious that she has no recourse but to steer her life in the best possible direction. She will thus be dissuaded from hiding from herself the true facts of her relation to her work. The immediacy of death leads to honesty with oneself. Jane knows that she has no time to waste; she has no choice but to be thoroughly honest with herself.

Finally, taking a new step against her wishes—just as keeping her job against her wishes—would be a symbolic promise of infinity and immortality; conversely, breaking off the commitment entails the anger of those who counted on her and loses her some respect in the eyes of those who know her. And we remember that such anger—which is a form of rejection—represents a *symbolic death* to Jane.

But Jane now recognizes that *there is no escape from death*. She has accepted death and resigned herself to it. She can now focus all her energies on the creative reconstruction of the only existence that she has. The existence and threat of death, especially *symbolic death,* are no longer the same type of power that they were earlier in her life. She will now say to herself, "If I choose my own path, they will threaten me with *symbolic death.*" She will continue with, "So what! The threat of death hangs over me anyway! I have accepted that fact. I no longer allow that threat to intimidate me in the regulation of my life, because, if I allow it, then I will lose whatever happiness and success I can achieve in life. I used to think that if I were to allow myself to be intimidated by that threat I could escape it. But I now realize that I cannot escape the threat of death; therefore, since it is pointless to submit to it, I shall not submit myself to that threat."

GETTING TO THE POINT

People who are aware of their death and the consequent limit to their time on earth will concentrate on essentials. They will not waste time in useless details, since detail is often but an excuse to avoid the real issues in life. Recognizing their death, they are prompted to get immediately to the point of their life—and to stay there. They will always look ahead; they will see each of their actions in the light of a total plan. The realization of death leads automatically to a larger view of life.

Any of us who are at a stage in life where we are confused about our values and goals will develop a clear outline for life once we accept the fact of our mortality. We will, let us say, decide to change jobs, since our present one does not provide us the future we can embrace. We will dedicate our energies to what, after all, may be the raison d'être of our job: the happiness and success of our family. We may want to see our spouse or partner fulfilled and cheerful, to see our children thrive emotionally, physically, and intellectually; we want to see that they have the very best opportunities to succeed in life, in education, health, and character. We may have thought of these values as not *real* values, or we may have postponed serious dedication to them to some indefinite future. Now, however, recognizing the limitations of our life and the pressure of death upon us, we will make a quick and final decision about what is really important and, in everything we do, focus immediate attention on these long-range plans. By constantly looking ahead we are guaranteed constant stimulation, courage, decisiveness, and hope. We are no longer like the suitor who never marries, because we have not found the perfect mate: deciding what things are most important must be done now. We may make a mistake, but the greatest mistake is to make no decision at all and miss all the opportunities available to us.

The knowledge and awareness of death leads our consciousness straight to the essentials. High school and college students are often deeply disturbed over what occupation or career to choose. The problem of whether to go to college, what jobs to seek and accept, what subject to choose as major—these are some of the troublesome questions facing young people. In fact, the weight, anxiety, and guilt associated with these problems may not ever leave them, even in later life. The thought of death—leading, as it does, to the vision of life as a whole—forces them to think seriously and immediately about how they are going to spend that life. It coerces them to face the issue of the meaning of life, to face it centrally, and come to a decision—perhaps not the best, but a decision.

For example, it is not enough for a student to say, "I like cars, I think I'll become a mechanic"; or "I like poetry, so I think I'll become a poet"; or "I like money, I think I'll major in business." They have to go deeper into the problem of making life meaningful than these answers suggest. They have to wrestle—immediately, continuously, and honestly—with problems such as, "What do I really want out of life?" "What is the purpose of my human existence?" "What will yield the highest fulfillment in life?" Every person is condemned to face these difficult problems, and everyone must answer for themselves. Our decisions have to be confirmed day after day, or revised, as the case may be. Just to decide once to become a mechanic, a poet, a businessperson is not enough. Continual rededication is more important than the initial decision.

Thinking along these lines, we become far more serious. Yet the thought of death is no longer morbid or depressing. Depression is the inability to look ahead. Now, the thought of death is revitalizing; it will lead us directly to the path that will make us a whole person. We learn quickly how to distinguish essential knowledge from inessential frills, and we are able to separate important questions and activities from mere pastimes and bagatelles. We see our frustrations and failures as part of a much larger scheme. We can ask for no more.

The thought of death can also be an anodyne for serious illness, grave pain, and major loss. A friend told the author that her fiancé was recently killed by a drunk driver in an automobile accident. The shock of this fact threatened to destroy her life: it destroyed her fondest hopes. She felt that she no longer belonged in the world. The world had lost its familiar shape, its solidity. The universe was, to her, disintegrating into some abysmal chaos. Can the thought of her own death help to extricate her from such desperate emotions?

First, she must recognize that the feeling of the disintegration of the world (that is, death) is not something that happened to her and does not happen to others. On the contrary, she has acquired an important insight into the inevitable condition of humankind. She sees life now in a true light, as mortal, while those (seemingly) happy and insouciant souls surrounding her repress these facts of life. We are always directly before the disintegration of our world, whether we happen to be thinking of it or not. In the presence of her tragedy, she was immediately forced to take her life into her own hands, to recognize that death is inevitable, and to quickly make the most of what she has.

She must discover that time is not to be wasted, that life must be subjugated to an ideal that is greater than life itself. That is, she will be forced to become a total realist. She will be forced to recognize life for what it is, dispel all illusions about life that our culture has taught her, and handle her life from that factual basis. Such an approach to life's problems may indeed be hard. However, in the long run, it is not only the most successful approach—it is the only one available. The sooner she realizes that inevitability, the better for her eventual happiness and fulfillment.

The fact that a major catastrophe has befallen you in no way changes the truth that you will die eventually; that whatever life you have left is all that you ever will have, all that you are; and that fulfillment can be achieved solely by molding that life into a meaningful form. You will thus not be tempted to waste time by "giving it up" or by hiding the truth about yourself from yourself. You will not give in to sulking over any calamity, no matter how severe.

You will never indulge in self-pity. You will always get right down to the business of managing your life intelligently, rationally, and purposefully. Accept your fate stoically. Face all human contingencies with calmness, cheerfulness, equanimity, and peace of mind. No situation that life offers will make you "lose your mind."

DEATH LEADS TO FREEDOM

For a final illustration of how the realization of the nature and inevitability of the *death of myself* leads to our freedom and courage and decisiveness in life, let us imagine that you go to your physician for a yearly checkup and are told that your have at best one year to live.

First of all, you have been told nothing fundamentally new. And yet, your existence is shaken to its foundations! Whereas before, the idea of your death was always something just beyond the horizon of your consciousness and planning—even while you may have been discussing various alternative programs with your life insurance agent—now, all of a sudden, your death becomes an immediate, certain, and terrifying reality. What is your response? You may go to pieces. That changes none of the facts, and you will realize it soon enough. You will regain your composure and take stock of your life. You are now forced to decide what is important in life and what is not. You are compelled to face the question of the ultimate meaning of life, and to face it immediately.

We all realize the importance of the question of the meaning of life, and we all postpone coming firmly to grips with it to some indefinite and fuzzy future. Now, fully realizing the truth about death, you are forced to be brutally honest with yourself. You become aware, in every action that you perform or omit, of the limit imposed on your life. You will not even dream of procrastinating. You may suddenly experience an extraordinary and almost inexhaustible surge of energy. There is an old Arab proverb which says that in victory, no one is tired. You will now decide to do—without further delay—the things you always wanted to do. You will have acquired the power and motivation to make a success of your life because you realize that you *must* have them. You realize that you cannot escape from the obligation to fulfill your life and that you cannot postpone that obligation any longer.

The point is if we ask, "How much life have I left?" the answer is we do not know how much of our life remains—maybe less than a year, maybe a year, maybe a great deal more. Some of that, of course, depends on us, on our physical and mental health habits. But most is out of our hands. Our generic problems are, in the last analysis, the same that confront us in the hypothetical example of being told that we have but one year to live. Authentic success, decision, genuine happiness, full meaning, these goals can be achieved only in light of the clear insight into the fact that all of us have been condemned to die.

Religious Commitment

We are going to die irrespective of our religious beliefs. The believer in immortality is no less subject to the vicissitudes and the vitality of death than is the disbeliever or the agnostic. The fact of death does not relate itself, in one way or another, to the religious belief in immortality.

Let us assume that when you were told you had only one year to live you decided to handle the problem of death by becoming deeply religious. In that case, we can say that it took the shocking realization of the inevitability of your death—an insight that occurred only after your visit to the physician—to cut through the pseudo-goals of your life, such as status, money, education, and sex, and direct your mind to the ultimate of all problems. Your goal of life, as a religious person in this hypothetical situation, is to acquire the steadfast conviction—or to discover irreproachable proof—of immortality. Your last days will then be spent in the preparation of your goal.

For good or for evil, these are decisions that each of us must make for ourselves. The seriousness and gravity of the existential outlook on life correspond well to these words of Cyril Connolly: "Melancholy and remorse form the deep leaden keel which enables us to sail into the wind of reality; we run aground sooner than the flat-bottomed pleasure-lovers, but we venture out in weather that would sink them."

FACING THE REALITY OF DEATH

In general, our response to death follows four clearly delineated stages.

- First, we *repress* the thought of our own death by *projecting* it onto external realities (theater, novels, newspapers, etc.). Also, we *flirt* with death—in war or daring acts—to prove that death cannot assail us.

- Second, when we recognize the reality of the *death of myself,* we experience *anxiety.* In fact, death, as symbol of my finitude, may well be the source of all authentic anxiety.

- Third, after the anxiety of death has been faced, the anticipation of death leads to courage, *integrity,* and individuality.

- Finally, by opposing, contradicting, and fighting death, we *feel our existence* and achieve some of our greatest glories—in art, religion, and self-assertion.

We discover the vitality of death, the positive and beneficial aspects of the fact of death, by deepening our understanding of these philosophic insights:

1. We cannot escape death—real or symbolic. We must construct our life—daily actions as well as major, overall plans—with the full and clear realization of that fact. We must accept, once and for all and without any reservation, misgiving, false hope, repression, or bitterness, the fact that we have been condemned to death. Then we can start living.

    In accepting, we will *neutralize* an otherwise completely demoralizing and paralyzing *fear.* This is one key to the successful management of human existence.

2. Once we have recognized and admitted the inevitability of our death, then we are on the way to becoming courageous, fearless, and *decisive.* Whenever we feel indecision and lack of courage, we must remind ourselves that life will end for us. The symbolic threat of death, which often is the cause of indecision, will then disappear, since its basic fraudulence will have been made manifest. We will be able once more to steer our life with courage and decisiveness.

3. By remembering the certainty and the finality of death, we immediately see the urgency of concentrating on *essentials*. We cut red tape in our life. We abandon excuses and procrastinations. We do not indulge in the luxury of wasting time—under the guise of getting work done—by getting lost in an endless amount of detail and busywork.

4. Only through the constant awareness of death will we achieve *integrity* and consistency with our principles. Since there is, basically, no threat other than real or symbolic death, and since we have accepted that threat, we are well beyond fraudulent bribes and threats alike. In the last analysis, all we own is the integrity of our character. No one can threaten us in the matter of our principles, since we are always in the presence of the ultimate threat anyway. What criminal would think of holding up a convict on the way to the death chamber?

5. People who know they will die waste no time in attacking the problem of *finding meaning* and fulfillment in life. The pressure of the thought of death is a persistent and nagging (and most effective) reminder that we are coerced to make some sense of our life, and that we are to do it *now*. One who has faced death adopts a no-nonsense approach to the business of living successfully.

   Precisely what these goals are is an individual choice. It may not be desirable to be burdened with such choice; but it is a fact of life that each of us must commit ourselves personally to whatever values we choose to consider highest. We all have strong predilections; we all have some idea of what it is we really want. Under pressure of death, we will quickly dedicate ourselves to these goals.

6. The vitality of death lies in that it makes almost impossible the repression of unpleasant but important realities. We do not accept any excuses to postpone dealing with our basic problems or to hide them from ourselves. The realization of death carries with it the successful management of many unconscious and repressed problems. One who is about to die does not practice the art of self-deception. Death makes us *honest*.

7. The realization of the *death of myself* leads to *strength*. To be strong means not to be intimidated by real or symbolic death. Having conquered these threats, we face no others. The world of self-fulfillment belongs to the strong, decisive, and courageous person.

8. To accept death means to take charge of one's life. Those who see the genuine function of death in life are no fatalists. They do not feel strictured. On the contrary, they are the *freest of all*. Nothing holds them back but their own free decisions. There is nothing to fear, nothing to be timid about, no reason to feel dependent, inadequate, or inferior; for we have once and for all conquered the ultimate threat.

9. The thought of death urges us to assume a *purpose for life*. The vitality of death leads us to adopt an ideal or goal, a noble life, or a major achievement as the purpose of existence. Through the vitality of death, we are able to see all events in life from the perspective of total existence. This

enables us to perform tasks that might otherwise be boring, discouraging, and senseless.

10. The thought of death enables us to *laugh off* vicissitudes and *pains*. Everyone has a certain type and amount of raw material out of which a person can fashion for himself or herself a good life. The amount and quality of that material varies greatly from one human existence to another and from one situation to another. But the pliable nature of the raw material is universal. To take defeat too seriously, to be thrown off balance by disappointments, is still secretly to harbor the hope that death may not be real after all and that perhaps the human race was *meant* to be immortal but, somehow, has missed its chance. Awareness of death breaks the stranglehold of failure and opens us to the horizon of our freedom.

FINAL FACTS

Death is a fact of life—that is a universal truth. The recognition of the nature of the anticipation of death has rejuvenating and revitalizing effects on human existence. That is another fact of life. What the decision is, or should be, about the meaning of life is, perhaps unfortunately, a burdensome individual decision. But the decision will come—since we often know what we really want— as soon as the urgency of reaching a conclusion is brought home to us through the fact of inexorable death.

Chapter 10

THE REALITY OF EVIL

We exist on the interface between good and evil.
Our freedom chooses which side to take and how far to go.
And this choice defines who we are.

A NXIETY PERFORMS one of its existential functions by revealing the reality of evil. It reveals both the evil in the world
and the demonic in us. It makes known the eternal paradox between good and evil. The concept of evil is generally avoided in
conversations within organizations. Evil here is not a psychological
perception as much as an undeniable reality. Evil is a metaphysical problem; it is an issue of theology and still one of the most
deeply moving issues in reflecting on our life.

To any sensitive person, to any decent individual, who appre-
ciates the values of civilization, the existence of evil—which is the

---

Adapted from Peter Koestenbaum, "Evil," in *The New Image of the Person: The Theory and Practice of Clinical Philosophy*, Westport, CT: Greenwood Press, 1978.

destruction of civilized values—is absolutely intolerable. Adjusting to evil is the denigration of the soul. Yet evil is real and remains real; the polarity of good and evil—witnessed with a clarity unequaled in the last century, at least in sheer numbers—is one of the most unbearable burdens of human existence. And at least three kinds of evil exist: human destruction, natural destruction, and the demonic in the soul. The next time anxiety strikes, ask yourself, What does it reveal? The answer may well be that what you see is the conflict between the crass reality and the unquestionable impermissibility of evil, in any of its infinite forms.

It is increasingly common in our efforts at personal growth—resulting perhaps from Freud's discovery of aggression as fundamental and Jung's discovery of the pervasive presence of what he called the "shadow"—to learn to accept our dark side, to accept negative emotions as natural. Over the last forty years or so we have worked on expressing our gut feelings; perhaps we have been told that we have problems expressing our anger, or dealing with the anger of others. But this attitude is quite different from recognizing that evil is both without redemption and ineradicable, and the two must not be confused. Anger is not of itself evil. Perhaps the frustration against which it cries out *is* a genuine evil.

The severe conflict between the unavoidable reality of evil and the fact that it is unforgivable is in fact a revival of the earliest theologies of the Manichaean heresy and the Zoroastrian dualism. Dualistic religions, such as Manichaeism and Zoroastrianism, postulate the equal existence of good and evil, with human beings in the center of the struggle. Dualism accords evil a place of distinction in the cosmos, coeval with good, so that coming to terms with evil is job one of our existence. In this context, C.J. Jung introduced the notion of the "shadow" as key. Dialoguing with evil, that is, the shadow, is the formula for building strength and health.

Anxiety reveals the absoluteness of evil—a terrifying thought, but nevertheless one fully warranted by our commitment to realism and truthfulness. Anxiety shows evil in its full horror, but it also reveals a resulting noble task—if we allow our anxiety to completely unfold itself. If we restrict the anxiety it becomes neurotic and it chastises us by withholding its revelations. When it is in full bloom, however, it reveals itself, and we call that the "existential anxiety" of evil. And what that reveals to us is that we human beings are the only answer to evil that exists in the universe.

Our freedom is capable of withstanding evil—of saying no to it. Our freedom is our only opportunity to choose to be noble, to stand up to evil, to counteract evil. The existential anxiety of evil reveals the preciousness of our freedom and its enormous cosmic responsibility to uphold the values of civilization; it uncovers the much-neglected meaning of duty and obligation. These latter categories of ethics and morality are vital in bonding accountability with the experience of our freedom.

And what is evil's connection to freedom? In one word, inconsiderateness. Whatever its form—from insensitivity to murder—evil is the denial of the sanctity of the inward, conscious, and free center of any human being.

THE STRUCTURE OF EVIL

In essence, evil reveals itself in five elements:

- Evil is completely unacceptable;
- Evil is completely real;

- To be human is to struggle against evil;

- The struggle against evil gives meaning to life; and

- Our posture toward evil is freely chosen and we are fully responsible for it.

Evil Is Unacceptable

First, *evil is completely unacceptable.* Say you are passed over when a promotion is available simply because you are a woman. This is unfair and therefore evil. You rightfully feel discounted as a human being. Once evil is understood with total clarity, there can be no compromise and no adjustment. Just because evil is impregnable does not excuse us, regardless of how much we may be tempted. If either compromise or adjustment does occur, then our integrity has been violated and our authenticity tarnished. We cannot rationalize ourselves out of this predicament, even though we may not be able to do anything about it. To adopt Alexander Pope's position that "evil is good, not understood" is a distortion of the basic facts that a sensitive philosophy reveals. There are events that inexcusably and unforgivably destroy those values which have an unqualified and absolute claim to be. These destructions can be either headline-grabbing catastrophes or minuscule degradations in interpersonal relations. We will look at some further illustrations later.

Evil Is Real

Second, *evil is completely real.* Evil is well-described by all those religions that accord evil a place of equality next to God. In this metaphor, God is the power of absolute goodness and infinite love, but is also powerless to eliminate evil. The proper word to describe our relation to evil is "respect." We must recognize that evil is worthy of respect—not because it embodies a value, but because it is the same kind of necessary being as God. This type of respect for evil is not a form of reverence, only of contempt. But it acknowledges with permanently open eyes that evil is always there before us, demanding our attention. Evil deserves the respect, acknowledgment, and recognition given to a mad kidnapper or a grenade-packing terrorist on a crowded airplane. If we as much as blink our eyes, we have lost the sense of realism that our integrity requires, for in that fraction of a second we deluded ourselves that there are moments without evil.

We may, for example, enjoy a beautiful concert. But we also know that people are being tortured in totalitarian jails at that very moment. The fact that we can do nothing about this horror, especially at that particular moment, and the knowledge that it is also impossible for us to worry over everything at all times do not by a scintilla change the reality and atrociousness of the evil of torture. We can analyze this conflict-at-the-concert situation as follows: one of the evils in this world, in addition to torture, is that we can make authentic decisions to limit ourselves in and ignore (sometimes or always) the struggle against evil. This may especially be true in business and the organizational world of action. This is a difficult position to accept ethically, yet the bitter realities of existence make it inevitable. This kind of compromise is nevertheless an adjustment to and an acceptance of evil—and is thus grossly insensitive to those who suffer.

To Be Human Is to Struggle Against Evil

The third element of evil is *to be human is to struggle against evil.* In our religious metaphor, God leads the struggle against evil. We struggle against evil but do not conquer it. We can be successful in searching for meaning without ever making the claim that we have found it. Similarly, we can be successful in struggling against evil without ever being able to claim that we have overcome or conquered it.

Because of our polarized nature, we exist on the interface between good and evil. Our freedom chooses which side to take and how far to go. This type of choice is archetypal, basic, foundational. It defines who we are. The choice between good and evil is the choice between reason and unreason—and for that fundamental choice there is no good reason. Choosing between good and evil is choosing between the affirmations of life, consciousness, and freedom and their denials. To the extent that we opt for decency, we must look on human existence as the permanent struggle against evil—a struggle we fight knowing we cannot win. It is here, standing up to evil, that leaders are made, as it was for Gary Cooper in *High Noon.*

The Struggle Against Evil Gives Meaning to Our Life

The fourth element in the structure of evil is the discovery that *the struggle against evil gives meaning to life.* That was Viktor Frankl's great insight while in a Nazi concentration camp. Whatever activity we find meaningful is meaningful to the precise extent that it is a struggle without quarter against evil.

Our Stance Against Evil Is Freely Chosen

The fifth and last element of evil is that *our posture toward evil is freely chosen and, therefore, we are fully responsible for it.* There is nothing automatic about the struggle against evil. It does not get done unless we do it. It takes some people a lifetime to learn this lesson.

Furthermore, our attitude toward evil is a free and autonomous decision, a point that is central to the stoic, Kantian, and existentialist ethics. It is this free choice that lends dignity to ethical managers. It is indeed unfortunate that in our ordinary language "sick" (which deserves compassion) is a stronger ethical pejorative than "evil" (which needs restitution). To view evil as a social disease is an act of compromise. On this analysis, therefore, Hitler was not a sick man but an evil one.

PUTTING A FACE ON EVIL

It seems hardly necessary to illustrate the reality of evil with specific cases. All one needs is to read newspapers or history books, even though evil, in retrospect, loses, like all experience, some of its immediacy and depth. The revelations of the anxiety of evil that gives us the greatest access to the structure of being are easily lost as the experience of a particular evil recedes into the past.

> Around the time of the fall of Saigon in 1975 and at the beginning of the "orphan baby lift," the rear door of a transport plane opened, some children were sucked out, and the plane crashed. Many survived; all were injured. There can be no extenuating circumstances for a situation of this kind.

Our common response is to find fault. Blaming individuals, however, is a defense against being responsible for evil. If we find a culprit we are momentarily relieved of apprehending the reality and absoluteness of evil. We think we have found the cause. And if we now eliminate it, we have eliminated evil from the world.

Alas, this demand for evil's unconditional surrender is never to be met. It was in fact being itself that permitted such a tragedy. It is the nature of things that such evil is possible. And nature, because it possesses that possibility, is therefore itself tarnished and partially evil. There can be no redemption, no recovery for that occurrence, no adjustment to that tragedy—without a loss of integrity and a betrayal of the values of authentic human existence. Our anxiety regarding this situation—as it occurs, as it is fresh and immediate, and as we witness it ourselves—reveals the immutable reality of evil as a given and self-evident phenomenon.

> At that time a photograph was circulated in the newspapers showing a Vietnamese woman—a refugee escaping south on a dusty road—carrying a baby on one arm and, breast exposed, nursing him, while with the other leading her husband, who hobbled behind her on a crutch, since he had lost a leg.

This picture demonstrated to a world, which all-too-soon forgets, that evil is as intolerable as it is real. Any attempt to rationalize evil away is a tendency toward the denial of evil, whether we believe it leads to good or whether we feel that our struggle against it softens it. Only when we recognize evil as a final barrier do we experience the truth of our finitude. Only then do we live without illusion.

The Reality Lives On

Those depictions of the fall of Vietnam are reminders of the realities of evil. What we must avoid is permitting scenes like these—

and millions of others—to be forgotten, to recede into the past and lull us into the illusory dream that the problem has gone away or, what is even worse, that it has been solved. Generalized, they teach us that world morality is bankrupt, that the existing concept of the person on which social and governmental actions are based is bankrupt, and that our manner of solving problems—that is, the willingness to use violence—is also bankrupt.

Further proof (as if it were needed) of the absolute and unforgivable character of evil is that we do live in a world which has the answer to just about all our global problems. We know about morality; we understand psychology; we have the results of extensive research in anthropology, sociology, and history; our technological competence is boundless. Nevertheless, none of this progress has in the slightest affected the recurring presence of naked evil. Such a paradox would be philosophically beyond comprehension were it not for the undeniable reality of evil. We need only to read the newspaper headlines to become ashamed and embarrassed for our spaceship earth. Is it any wonder that sanity demands blindness to evil?

THE REVELATIONS OF EVIL

Tragedies such as the crash of the baby-lift airplane and the nursing refugee with her crippled husband are totally and completely unacceptable. This is self-evident to anyone who permits the full anxiety of this situation to reveal itself. All that is needed to discover the unconscionable and unacceptable quality of evil is to permit these events to penetrate every pore of our being. That is what we mean by confronting existential or ultimate anxiety and opening ourselves up to its revelations.

Furthermore, these examples prove the unexceptionable reality of evil. We cannot argue it away as part of a Divine Plan without distorting the immediate, given, and uncovered facts of experience. The only available response for self-respecting persons is to struggle in whatever way possible against these evil events. And it is precisely that struggle that gives life meaning and worth, that gives birth to the phenomenon of *morality* in human existence.

Morality is our willingness to be accountable for our response to the suffering in the world. This accountability is born the moment we acknowledge our freedom in having played a part in creating this world. To be accountable is an act of morality that is a non-natural event; it is a transcendental, all pervasive phenomenon. It is an archetypal decision made *ex nihilo,* out of nothing, by our transcendental freedom. And it is the reality of evil which makes possible and gives meaning to this transcendental choice for morality. Finally our decision to devote ourselves to the eradication of evil, hopeless as the task might seem, is taken freely, without promise of reward or fear of punishment, but as an expression of the archetypal decisions for rationality and for life-affirmation.

Israeli journalist Elie Wiesel writes about his childhood in a German concentration camp, where he watched the oven in which his little sister and his mother were going to be thrown.

> Never shall I forget that night, the first night in camp, which has turned my life into one long night, seven times cursed and seven times sealed. Never shall I forget that smoke. Never shall I forget the little faces of the children, whose bodies I saw turned into wreaths of smoke beneath a silent blue sky. Never shall I forget those flames which consumed my Faith forever: Never shall I for-

get that nocturnal silence which deprived me, for all eternity, of the desire to live. Never shall I forget those moments which murdered my God and my soul and turned my dreams to dust. Never shall I forget these things, even if I am condemned to live as long as God Himself. Never.[1]

And French novelist and Nobel laureate Francois Mauriac writes of that statement:

Have we ever thought about the consequence of a horror that, though less apparent, less striking than the other outrages, is yet the worst of all to those of us who have faith: the death of God in the soul of a child who suddenly discovers absolute evil?[2]

With this discussion as context, we begin our exploration of the importance of incorporating the concept of evil into our discussion of freedom and accountability. We do this because it gives depth to life. Because it is the heart of empathy. Because it dignifies human beings. Because it confronts us with a noble task, a task from which none of us, either individually or institutionally, can escape.

Chapter 11

_____

STANDING UP
TO EVIL

_____

The reality of evil brings about one fundamental recognition:
it gives meaning to morality and the need to be accountable
for our lives and all that is around us.

P ROBABLY THE MOST EFFECTIVE response to the anxiety of
evil is to know that it requires us to be accountable for our
morality, ethics, integrity, destiny, and purpose. In other words, the
reality of evil brings about one fundamental recognition: it gives
meaning to morality and the need to be accountable for our lives
and all that is around us.

THE SOURCE OF MORALITY
AND ACCOUNTABILITY

The capacity and choice for morality is one of the defining characteristics of being human. When we are moral we do not act

_____

Adapted from Peter Koestenbaum, "Coping with the Anxiety of Evil," in *The New Image of the*
Person: The Theory and Practice of Clinical Philosophy, Westport, CT: Greenwood Press, 1978.

automatically. We make the archetypal, foundational, and *ex nihilo* decision to be moral, independent of thoughts of reward or punishment.

Morality is not the result of causes or motives whose origin is in the world of nature and described by science. Nor is morality chosen for its outcomes or effectiveness. Quite to the contrary, in the act of choosing morality we step outside of the natural order. The non-natural character of the person—our structure as a being that does not exist exclusively in the world—is made most clear by the possibility of morality. In short, morality is not an empirical or "scientific" phenomenon. Morality is not part of the world of objects. Instead, it is strictly a transcendental phenomenon associated with the operations of the center of pure consciousness, and of freedom. Within our pure conscious center, freedom creates from nothing the response of moral accountability and resoluteness and outrage against the evils in the world. These can be evil objects or situations, but they also can be evil decisions of other human freedoms.

The existence of evil, then, gives rise to terms such as "morality," "ethics," "integrity," "goal," "destiny," "purpose," and "task"— and they in turn circumscribe a central, perhaps even *the* central, significance of personhood. The sense of being a person is the accountability that consciousness brings about in response to the existence of evil. We can group these terms into two categories: the first includes morality, ethics, and integrity; the second comprises goals, destiny, purpose, and task.

MORALITY, ETHICS, AND INTEGRITY

The stiffening self-assertive posture toward life, self, and values implied by such terms as "morality," "ethics," and "integrity" is the individuation of the person. Individuation occurs in response to the confrontation with an alienated, opposing, and threatening Other. And that Other is what we can call evil. The muscles tighten to brace against the onslaught. An armor forms around the center to ensure the preservation of its integrity. Evil is the opposing negativity which produces such alienation; evil is the terrifying confrontation which brings about the courage that preserves individuality. The isolated and exposed condition of individuality is the exact opposite of the uterine and protected condition of the fetus. The latter is a universalizing melding and surrender to the environment. The former is an individualizing hardening against it.

The Experience of Morality

Whereas morality, ethics, and integrity are the natural responses to evil, we must ask if—in addition to their negative value of protection—they are positive values to be cherished for their own sakes. Would we want them even if they were not needed as protections against evil?

We must enter this posture through fantasy, through memory, and through action. How does it feel to be a person of integrity? What is it like to be honest under difficult circumstances? What is the experience of doing what is "right" rather than what is "expedient"? We also enter the experiences of morality, ethics, and integrity by recalling and reliving instances from our past in which we stood up for an unpopular cause, or lost something of value because our conscience bid us make a difficult decision. Perhaps we went on strike because of a principle—and lost our jobs. Perhaps we did not go on strike—and lost our friends. How did we feel? Was the action merely a necessity, or did it embody a positive value as well?

Finally, we enter this experience through accountable action. We risk morality, ethics, and integrity. We follow Kant's famous position that only when we act *counter* to our inclination do we know we have acted on principle rather than feeling. How do we actually feel having risked a moral stand, when the easy way out would have been to lie, to ignore, or to appease? The child next door is battered. Do we call the authorities and risk our neighbor's enmity? Or do we ignore the problem and allow the child's suffering to continue? Suppose we know that the organization that we are a part of is doing things that are harmful to individuals or its community. If we do what is right and stand up for morality, does that indeed feel like the positive value of choosing the solidity of one's integrity and the weight of one's individuality?

In-depth exploration of these experiences constitutes a description of the meaning of morality, ethics, and integrity. And through this kind of questioning, we can discover that being moral and ethical, and preserving our integrity, "feels" good or "appears" good to us in, by, and of itself.

This stand against evil offers a sense of individual identity, solidity, and strength. It becomes an intrinsic value. Individual introspection about evil gives us a sense of personhood, which is experienced as inherently valuable.

To really understand coping with evil, we can return to the metaphor that God saw it was better to be human and finite than divine and infinite. That is the message of the Creation, the Covenant, and the Birth of Christ. In creation, God makes man in his image. Man is mortal, a dying being. Given this limitation as a kind of evil, it was necessary for man to be made in the image of God. The Covenant set limits to make man authentic. And the Birth of

Christ is, literally, God having chosen to be a human being, to live for a time on this earth.

Choosing Integrity

In confronting the anxiety of evil, we experience a positive value. The concrete sense of selfhood is a value in itself, as well as being a response to evil. It feels good to be an individual. It feels healthy, joyous, and potent. One feels the vibrancy of agency in the blood, the excitement of action, the glory of having all of being condensed onto one point, the intensity of being a concrete here-and-now. These are difficult descriptions, but they do tell us that being an individual who is moral, ethical, and who has integrity is clearly experienced and is accurately described as an intrinsic value. Direct intuition confirms that to us. That is the philosophical basis for the coaching device of encouraging another to "do something good for themselves," "to explore one's own feelings," "to look after our own interests," "to not allow ourselves to be used," "to assert ourselves," to recognize that we have needs, too, and are entitled to respect and consideration.

GOALS, DESTINY, PURPOSE, AND TASK

The second set of terms arising from our philosophical insight into evil—*goal, destiny, purpose,* and *task*—is about the future of the individual. The anxiety of evil produces character and the sense of integrity and worth. But it also produces meaning and the motivation to create a future for ourselves and for the world. The individual is like the projectile in an atom smasher: a small entity who develops enormous momentum by moving forward, into the future, as it were. Evil provides the task which generates the energy to propel us forward into our future.

Discovering Destiny

Here is a way the anxiety of evil can lead us to discover our destiny.

Ask yourself, "What evil troubles me most?" "What bothers me most about life in general? About my life in particular?" Do not allow public opinion to influence what specifics you consider evil. You can find meaning, a future, by focusing on your own anxiety of evil, by discovering the greatest evil in your life. Here is a range of evils that might concern you:

- *Ignorance*—which includes lack of understanding or the inability to understand;

- *Ugliness*—in nature, in the social structure, in politics, in human relations, in interpersonal transactions, in your own feelings and emotions, in your fantasies, your self-image, and in your life in general;

- *Weakness*—ineffectiveness, lack of potency, lack of respect, failure;

- *Alienation*—lack of contact, injustice, a feeling of separateness from society;

- *Poverty*—which can mean world poverty, national poverty, personal poverty, or merely the inability to manage your finances, your job, and your business affairs;

- *Chaos*—which may be a sense of separation from the oceanic, that is, from God.

Clues to Our Life Task

These evils and our responses can occur in various combinations and intensities, and the resulting constellations of values can change during our lifetime. If you can produce a profile of yourself in terms of these six types of evils—by asking which of these evils troubles you most—then you may find your goal, destiny, purpose, and task in the struggle against them. You may already have achieved this aspect of coping with the anxiety of evil. However, you can now bring it into consciousness, use your freedom, and assess and revise what you have done. Here are some illustrations.

If *ignorance* is your evil, then the life of a scientist or a scholar, the "theoretical person," becomes your way of responding to your particular evil with your particular task.[1] Your evil is not likely just ignorance in general, but a very specific type, such as ignorance about cancer, brought about perhaps by having witnessed the tragic death of a loved one. More knowledge would have saved that person. You now demand to develop that knowledge. Such an experience, occurring early in life, can determine the course of one's future.

Each of us adopts our "life tasks" in light of such situations. Since these tasks commonly start early and may therefore now be deeply entrenched, you can reverse the process of discovery. You can examine your present interests and then assume that they are in fact your current response to a deep and even unconscious confrontation with your individual and unique supreme evil. And in this way you can discover—through inference—the particular evil buried deep within you.

For example, if you discover that your interest lies in psychology, then perhaps ignorance about human consciousness or human behavior is the particular kind of evil that lies buried in you. The focus of all the evil forces in the world is, for you, ignorance about what it means to be a person. It is against this evil that you must struggle. You must therefore intensify your study and research in psychology, now that you understand the origins of your interest. If your interest is astronomy, then perhaps the ignorance you struggle against is of a cosmological sort. You are surrounded by infinite space, you see it every day, and you are permanently frustrated in your need to reach into it. You cannot grasp the universe, physically or intellectually. The world is a stranger to you. That may be your evil. You repeat the struggles of ancient Chinese, Indians, Egyptians, Israelites, and Greeks and study the stars and feel good when you understand even a modicum of their mysterious doings. Or maybe your interests are technological, and you are fascinated by engineering, possibly electronics. Your evil is of a practical sort, the evil of broken matter, a failure in efficiency, or tools that separate people rather than bring them together. You recognize that problems can be solved through technology, and it is safe to say that the kind of technology that interests you most does so because it struggles against the particular kind of evil that disturbs you most.

Acts of Rebellion

Interest is a function of rebellion against evil. We have a philosophic answer to the question of how our purpose originates: people's interests, values, goals, or meanings are reactions to their perception of what is active evil or the evil of what is missing in the world. An interest is a way of saying "I am" in the face of destructive opposition, confronting otherness, and threatening evil. The anxiety of evil comes first; the discovery of meaning is a reaction, not an action.

If your evil is *ugliness,* then art, the pursuit of aesthetics in its various forms, is your lifestyle. You will never eliminate ugliness, but you respond to it through your commitment to beauty. If *weakness* should be your evil, then your goal, destiny, purpose, and task are the acquisition and uses of power. You then become a political person, or tough-minded and willing to act in the face of uncertainty and danger. If you discover that your most grievous evil is *alienation,* then your task is to establish and cultivate social relations, either in your private life or to encourage this for society as a whole.

If your evil is *poverty,* then economic achievement—either as a personal goal or a social remedy—becomes the task that will give meaning to your life. Finally, if your evil is what has here been called, for lack of a better word, *chaos*—meaning thereby the search for immortality and for an ordered universe—then the lifestyle which responds to it is one of spiritual pursuits.

PURPOSE IS AN ANSWER TO EVIL

A goal or purpose gives meaning to one's life not because it is achieved or even because it can be achieved. On the contrary, a goal already gives meaning if our eyes merely face in that direction, and even more if our life begins to move toward it. Our goal is to face our specific evil. In this struggle we achieve substance, which includes morality, ethics, and integrity, and we achieve meaning, which includes goals, destiny, purpose, and tasks.

A Goal of Our Own

Many people, especially in the workplace, will argue that they have no larger goal or purpose than to simply make a living. They are content, it seems, to pursue goals defined by others. If their organization's goal is to make money, then this becomes their goal. If their organization's goal is to serve the public good, then they also embrace it as their own. If they could only find a goal, their lives would have meaning. They think they know all about evil and know everything about tasks and destiny, but still no meaning appears. They can attend vision workshops, bounce around careers and employment opportunities. But they have yet to find *their* goal. How can these people cope with the anxiety of evil? Maybe if they had a more intimate and painful experience with evil, it would wake them out of their stupor. It may be their inability to face and experience evil that stands in the way of finding any purpose larger than to just get by.

It appears that some make a virtue of having no goal. That can be legitimate and authentic. The pursuit of *goallessness* assumed by the here-and-now subculture and the quest for *satori* in Zen and Nirvana in Buddhism—the search for timelessness and for desirelessness—are also bona fide goals, with specific tasks designed to achieve goallessness. They are not exceptions to the rule, because a goal in life means much more than merely a middle-class value. To have a goal—even if that goal be the elimination of all goals—injects passion, life, enthusiasm, vitality, energy, direction, and joy into human existence. Consider Jeremy, who discovered his meaning in *satori*. He worked doggedly in the shipyards to save enough money for a trip to Japan. Purposefully he joined a monastery, where he assiduously followed the prescribed regimen. He approached his goal of goallessness with businesslike efficiency. Yet he would say that being goal driven was a form of evil.

Goals and Identity

However, if we truly lack goals in our lives we experience ennui, depression, unhappiness, irritability, and general dissatisfaction with life. The most acceptable form of this is cynicism. That condition is proof that we have not yet made the decision to assume responsibility for being ourselves—or, more specifically, responsibility for confronting evil with meaning. We have not yet made the fundamental, archetypal decision that differentiates us from our environment and creates us as an individual identity. We are running away from dealing with this issue, and that is the source of our goallessness and cynicism. The decision to be an individual has been postponed successfully, for to have a goal is to continually choose to say yes to oneself. And often to say no to another.

The useful question therefore is not, "Let's review goals and see what 'turns you on,'" but "Let us explore your resistance against being yourself." The decision to be yourself is the underground fire that surfaces as boiling water in the geyser of a visible goal. The analysis of the resistance then becomes a developmental task. Our gaze of life when we have no goal is looking outward for direction rather than inward. To react but not act. To be other-directed rather than inner-directed probably means that we have a history of not being validated for being ourselves, but only for our performance— or perhaps not even that. Our center is ungrounded and underdeveloped. When we are truly goalless, we experience the absence of our inner and solid core. We do not understand the meaning of becoming an individual and therefore lack potency and efficacy. While we may have to understand why remaining underdeveloped made sense in a childhood environment, it is a choice as an adult. We can choose to rechart our course to be one of free and rational action, aiming our choice at righting a wrong; we give our lives to correcting it.

Lack of meaning is caused by the absence of a sense of individuality. And this results from ignoring and devaluing our freedom.

To be an individual you must make the free decision to be one and to assume full personal responsibility for your life.

The Center of Freedom

The foundation for freedom is to be a centered human being, an insight dependent on a clear understanding of our transcendental dimension. Consequently, if we cannot find meaning, no matter how hard we try, the difficulty lies in the absence of an inner core, a core whose existence we can bring about by an act of free will and choice. But this archetypal choice has a special structure. The core is threatened by non-being. The universe itself—and certainly each center within it—is experienced or perceived as *contingent:* it contains the possibility of not-being. It makes more sense not to be than to be.

Heidegger asked, "Why are there beings rather than nothing?" Tillich talked about the threat of non-being. Aquinas told us that the contingency of the world demonstrates the necessary existence of God. "To be" is the deepest value. Augustine told us that the evil man is good to the extent that he exists, although his acts may be evil. The threat of non-being is evil—but that is also the threat of death and the threat of nihilism, which are experientially connected to evil. The center, our individuated *Existenz,* our sense of core identity, is, as Tillich put it, the experience of the power to resist non-being. That is indeed the ultimate miracle, properly called the miracle of being. This is real accountability. Only through the evil of non-being, including death and nihilism, does the value of emerging as a center come into full relief. To be is the ultimate meaning, the ultimate affirmation—and it is made as a reaction to the experienced presence of pure evil. The miracle of being is the answer to evil. This is the core religious insight and experience.

Meaning and Love

With evil, centeredness, and freedom established as the supports of our *pyramid of authenticity* (see Figure 11.1), we discover that love is possible only if there is meaning first. We use love to share and reinforce our meanings, not to create them. Furthermore, love will strengthen and validate all the other human values needed for establishing meaning. These insights must be both conceptual and experiential, and ultimately they must be integrated into one's full life so that this pyramid is not only thought and felt but also lived, made public, and visible.

Inner Voices

Of special importance for the analysis of our resistance against a goal that copes with evil is to learn to listen to our inner voices. Most inner voices are like psychological x-rays: they inform us of

Figure 11.1   A Pyramid of Authentication

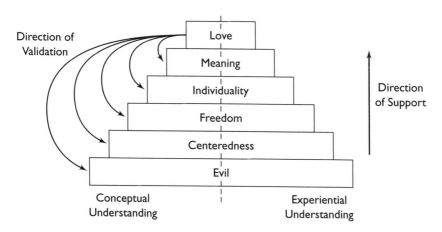

From P. Koestenbaum, *The New Image of the Person*, p. 272 (Westport, CT: Greenwood Press, 1978).

what is going on inside of the rich source that is our empirical or psychological ego—the body, our emotions, and our unconscious. Our inner voices appear when we permit—and especially when we encourage—the body to speak its mind. But our feelings, emotions, and attitudes are not to be confused with our pure transcendental consciousness (pure, objectless awareness). Each of us has an emotional nature—an aspect of the empirical ego (individual self) here called the "psyche"—which is stimulated and sometimes generated by our past decisions and influences, both parental and cultural. The psyche can make itself heard—through behavioral symptoms, somatic illness, and body presence. We can train ourselves to *listen* to our empirical ego and its being-in-the-world. What we then hear are our inner voices.

If we still the noises of all external inputs—including external inputs that we have now internalized (ancient scripts)—we may begin to hear these inner voices. To accomplish that requires rest and relaxation, a change of human, social, and physical environments and time, peace, and patience. These inner voices will come out of our unconscious—collective or individual—out of our past, out of our heritage, out of our childhood experiences, and out of our bodies. We are not forced to obey these voices. Only a psychology that does not have a theory of the transcendental ego (pure awareness) is bound to do so. However, these voices do reveal delicate and hidden details about ourselves. They are a microscope placed on the psyche. They unravel the knots produced in our empirical ego by unconscious and unresolved conflicts. If we listen to them, we gain a clear view of who we are and who we have been; we get a comprehensive and lucid picture of the empirical ego (the worldly self) that we have entered.

At the same time, we have made the decision, as individuals, to live in the consensual, external world. The internal voices are part of the same empirical reality that gives rise to the consensual world. Consequently, the consensual world has considerable, although not final, authority. In the face or presence of this, we are flooded with the tension between the consensual world and our own inner voices. We then *decide*—and this is a transcendental and not an empirical act, an act from the pure free consciousness—whether we are to do their bidding or proceed differently on our path to ascribe meanings to existence. These voices tell us what we must do to live in peace with our empirical ego, in its particular being-in-the-world. (Consult the glossary for some of these technical terms.)

There is merit in accepting our biological, historical, and social destiny (the components of the empirical ego), just as there is value in turning over that destiny and creating our own. That is one of our archetypal decisions. If *we* made that decision and do not allow it to be made for us, then we have achieved the sense of self-affirmation and ego-strength which expresses itself in life as goal-directed behavior. We are then coping with the anxiety of evil. If the decision is *not* made by us, that is, by the transcendental aspect of us, our pure conscious free will, then we are not coping authentically.

THE DEEPEST MEANING OF ACCOUNTABILITY

Existential anxiety reveals to us the reality of evil. To deny that revelation leads to the sense of purposelessness or meaninglessness in life. However, to accept this revelation of anxiety—that is, to courageously confront it and permit oneself clearly to see the evil it reveals—leads to the richness of meaning and the fulfillment of purpose in life. This is the deepest meaning of accountability. The essential strategy for coping with the anxiety of the existence of evil consists of making a contract to first discover the evil that is uniquely ours and then construct our life around the fight against and the conquest of that evil. On the organizational level, this insight can lead to the awakening of the moral rededication to an institution's purpose, including its social responsibility, something sorely needed and eminently appropriate for the new millennium. An example of this is the Statue of Liberty, which stands as a symbol of welcome to all people to a safe harbor. Each of us, including our institutions, contains the spirit of that statue, which awaits the time in our own life when we offer an answer to the homelessness that the statue stands against.

Part III

IMPLICATIONS

DIALOGING WITH DEATH and evil can improve the quality of our organizational life. Death and evil are really questions, not conclusions. They force us to decide how to deal with the darker side of our experience, and if we can make them legitimate questions, we are strengthened by their direct acknowledgement. What follows is an attempt to make this point as concrete as possible.

SMALL DEATHS

It is helpful to realize that every failure is experienced as a small death. We try to value failure as a learning experience, but it is a difficult stretch in most institutions. This may be due to the realization that if we accept failure, we accept the fact that something is going to die. If our intent is to find failure interesting and fascinating and a source of learning and growth, then we have to come to terms both with our own death and with the reality of our institution's mortality.

Institutional mortality means the organization will not go on forever. Not only is it likely that the organization will lose its vitality, but elements and projects within it also live within a term limit. Any project we work on will reach a point where it is no longer supportable. We need to accept that our work unit is a temporary structure and it will at some point be merged into the very group that we wanted to take over. Plus most of us will leave this organization at some point, probably sooner rather than later. When we face the reality and presence of death, all of these smaller and symbolic versions of dying lose some of their paralyzing power. They have the potential to be taken as signs of life and a natural process rather than mistakes that should have been avoided.

To speak in these terms is usually frowned on. If we speak publicly of our organizational mortality, we are accused of disloyalty or inappropriate pessimism. We are all surrounded with the false bravado of "Failure is not an option." The workplace becomes a place of manufactured optimism. We put posters on the wall with positive messages, we hold public meetings claiming a bright future and declaring success, and we then hold private meetings to deal with the reality of missed objectives or painful changes. This duality of public celebration and private realism is our defense against failure. This means we treat death as a mistake, as a sign that management has not done its job, that workers have not acted accountably, or that technology has not reached its potential.

This denial of death in the form of failure has significant organizational costs. We keep investing in projects long after we know they will not succeed. We position news of a failure in a way that people will feel good about it, and thus create cultures of unreality. We also deny our guilt and avoid taking responsibility for failures, thus triggering widespread and long-term defensive reactions to events that could have been put to rest quickly if we could see them for what they were . . . simply failures.

The alternative is to take failures as gift-like reminders of the difficulty and impermanence of life and let this deepen our determination to invest in work that holds meaning and create organizations that we want to inhabit. We could then publicly acknowledge that something did not work. We would not need positioning language that shields people from the truth about their experience.

TIME IN A BOTTLE

The moment we know we are going to die, we become aware of the subjective nature of time. Time is more an experience than a chronological truth. How long is a "long time"? To a child an hour is an eternity; to an older person, a year races by. When we are in the dentist's chair, each minute drags by; when we are in love, whole days disappear in a flash. In modern culture, speed has become a god, a value in its own right. We need to be on call and instantly responsive. We accept as a fact, not a choice, that it is better to do things faster. After all, time is money. Time waits for no one. Time marches on.

This passion for speed is a way of getting rid of time, not valuing time as precious, scarce, and something to be savored. There is a confusion between running out of time and therefore doing now what I might have postponed until later, and doing everything at break-neck speed.

Speed obliterates or blurs the quality of our experience and makes relationships obsolete. In the speed world, we do not have time for anything that moves at human rather than electronic speed.

Even the belief that I will make my money now doing work that has little meaning, and then later enjoy the luxury of doing what I want, is a bet on living forever. Every act of postponement is a grasp for immortality.

So in a paradoxical way, our awareness of our own death makes time more valuable and speed a liability. It is intriguing that youth is in a hurry when they have so much time in front of them and maturity slows things down when time is running out. An institutional passion for speed may be a sign of its immaturity, caught in youth's experience of time, unable to see that anything done with depth and purpose takes time, even if we think we do not have it. To know how temporary and passing each thing we do is allows us to accept that any project or experience that will have a significant impact will take time, even more than we think we have. At this point, "How long will it take?" will be the fourth question we ask, instead of the first.

SAYING NO

Death is the ultimate finality. It is the final and nonnegotiable limitation. It is life's most emphatic way of saying no to us. No wonder that we have such difficulty in saying no. It is the reminder that we cannot do everything, that many of our dreams will not be fulfilled, that we are in fact going to die. The effect is that, no matter how full our plate, we act as if there is room for one more helping.

This is most pronounced in organizational life. We have this belief that if you stand up you will get shot. We make the association between standing up, which really means to say no by publicly disagreeing with those in power, and extreme danger. We believe that the messenger will be shot, and therefore a refusal is equivalent to an act of suicide.

Our resolution of this dilemma is to not say no. To present our-selves as a "can do" kind of person. More team player mythology. In one bank, it comes down to the question "Are you with us, or are you a terrorist?" When this is the choice, saying no is an understand-ably rare occurrence.

Our unwillingness to say no is a denial of our limitations, a re-fusal to acknowledge our mortality and the fact that there are some things we cannot do. It also expresses our willingness to allow others to define reality for us. Declaring no is also the first act of reclaim-ing our freedom. It is deciding for ourselves what is real and possi-ble and worth pursuing. To think saying no is a disaster is the choice to remain a child with the belief that those who have power over us are all-knowing. They aren't, they just have power over us.

Making refusal so difficult has its institutional costs. It makes our promises and goals inherently unstable. We create expectations we know at the time we cannot fulfill, and so the organizational prom-ises, based on our promises, are unstable and at risk from their in-ception. It may be true that setting goals beyond reason may have a motivating effect and cause us to stretch and grow in ways we oth-erwise might not. This would be valuable, however, only if people choose to set high goals, not if they acceded to them out of fear of saying no.

If we want to actually live in the real world, we have to accept no for an answer. As managers, we might even encourage refusal and value people saying no. We can start to do this if we realize that re-fusal is the beginning of a conversation, not the end of a conversa-tion. It is an equalizing stance, a way to begin as partners. Partners say no to us and we survive. Every work unit has its limitations, is going to fail at times, is not going to live forever, and therefore has to ground its promises in reality. When we can accept the importance of saying no, we accept the presence of death—and then become grounded in our commitments. There may be negative consequences to this stance, but we will survive, and the payoff is that we know at that moment that we stand for something, which is part of experiencing our freedom.

Finally, it is not inherent that the organization will survive. We will live more fully, and create organizations that are more human and habitable, if we leave room for the possibility of ending and returning in another form. Death is a precursor to rebirth. If we sincerely care about our institutions and what they stand for, we can live with this mindset.

The wish to improve and transform our institutions without any loss, without any ending, or any serious transformation, devalues them. It condemns them to remain economic shells whose only purpose is financial and operational efficiency. Real transformation is of the spirit, not the form. Something dies and returns in a more vibrant form, and this occurs within organizational journeys as well as individual ones.

CONFRONTING EVIL

The existence of evil gives rise to morality and an ethical stance. The philosophic insight takes a broad look at what is defined as evil. It includes more than the more traditional ethical business practices of accurate reporting, playing it straight on pricing, diversity, workplace safety, and product safety.

The dominant values in most businesses and public sector organizations are expedience and efficiency. They value what works, often at the expense of what has meaning and what a wider view of social responsibility might entail. What the existence of evil raises for institutions is the question of their purpose and larger responsibility to the world around them. For the private sector, the economic eye views any stance that does not contribute to the bottom line as acting against the interests of the stockholders. For government, the question of what sector of society it exists to serve is very complicated and ambiguous. Churches and not for profits likewise face the question of who they exist to serve, plus should they think of themselves as being in competition with other organizations like themselves?

For example, in the private sector, what does it mean that the philanthropic giving of organizations used to be controlled by community affairs departments and now it is increasingly controlled by the marketing department? Should donations be based on where the most public visibility can be achieved? And are the benefactors of their generosity limited to the market segment that they serve?

At what point will organizations view poverty, community, and social well-being as a central concern of the institution. The private sector is increasingly powerful in the political arena and in many cases organizations transcend cities, states, and even nations as political entities. What does this mean for their role in addressing problems that used to be the sole province of government and public agencies? The existence of evil on a wider scale is fast becoming an organizational and business issue.

SOCIAL RESPONSIBILITY AS A LARGER PURPOSE

Here are some forms of evil and possibility that at some point organizations will, we hope, treat as central to their purpose and reason for existence:

- Urban prosperity. The decay of our central urban areas is a growing crisis. There are many companies that have committed themselves to supporting urban revitalization, but they are the exception. Companies have often led the flight from central areas of a city, or an at-risk region, to move to less developed, lower cost areas that offer short-term economic benefits. As long as a company believes it exists primarily to make a profit, this will never change.

- Companies have worked hard to reduce labor costs and benefit packages for the core workers, while maintaining good incentives and packages for the top management. This continues to include active anti-union efforts, strong stances against wage increases, and outsourcing or exporting as many jobs as possible. Are these issues of morality or just good business practices?

- Some businesses are the most outspoken critics of government regulations and interference, yet have little compunction against using their job-creating power to negotiate all kinds of tax and regulatory concessions when deciding where to expand or relocate. At what point will the private sector and government act as if they are partners, not competitors? Partners believe in a balance of power and recognize that they need one another. When do the private and public sectors decide to choose dialogue over competition and to see that the social ills of our world are their common enemies?

- What about the environment? Organizations do not have a great record of environmental consciousness. There is a great deal written about how businesses externalize their costs by asking the community to carry the cost of things such as production and packaging waste, environmental harm, use destructive to the land, and the creation and maintenance of a supportive infrastructure (roads, police, fire, schools, and the like). Something will shift when our organizations act on their interdependence with each other and accept that in the longer term all costs will be borne by all of us.

- As part of the globalization surge, what commitment do organizations have toward the community and cultural integrity of countries they do business in? What does it mean to sell consumerism and all of its values and qualities to developing, southern hemisphere countries? As an example, for whose sake do we try to convince Indonesians to substitute soft drinks for tea, juice, and water?

- Despite the existence of truth in advertising rules, what about the promises made in our efforts to sell products? Will a car give the freedom that the selling effort promises? Will products really help us find a lover, enjoy financial security in our golden years, create happy children, and fill our life with glamour and excitement?

- What about the impact of superstores and category killers on the viability of local communities and local economies? Is the economic independence of a community something an organization or local government need worry about? And what about business and housing development practices? What does it mean when we consider raw land useless because we cannot build on it? Plus, do we care about the end of the family farm and the impact on rural community?

It is not that organizations are the evil we must work to overcome, or that organizations are to blame for the existence of these problems. These questions are simply a short list of some of the challenges that the reality of the world presents to us. We are each participating in creating these issues. Plus, it is each of us who populates the organizations that too often become easy to blame. Evil is the other face, the hard face of reality that insolubly presents itself to us and will not go away. Such is the nature of these dilemmas. They are ones, however, that organizations are capable of speaking to.

Regardless of its history, each organization needs to decide the level and depth of the conversation it chooses to have with evils of poverty, loss of community, human displacement, a vulnerable environment, and the endless other ways the earth wounds itself. Each organization has to decide whether these problems are within the purpose and concern of the institution.

If anything is to shift in how we think and deal with evil, there has to be a shift in intent. Is there a vital place in our institutional life for us to do things just because they are right, and simply that? We have experience in doing the right thing, we just need to expand it. A small example was in the quality movement, where for a while we did what was right for the customer, and cost and precedent were secondary. This may have faded, but we know that kind of thinking is possible.

Philosophy urges us to engage evil, to own and embrace, even swallow or acknowledge, our place in evil, and that this ennobles the meaning of our institutions. This is different from simply defending ourselves against evil or deluding ourselves in thinking we can eradicate it. Even making the term "evil" acceptable language in the workplace would be a step in this direction.

FULLY
HUMAN
ORGANIZATIONS

THIS FINAL PART begins to bring together the elements of what we are calling the philosophic insight. In this section, Peter takes on some very practical, though profound, implications of our freedom. He elaborates on the inescapable guilt of self-betrayal, and how this existential guilt actually makes personal and organizational freedom possible. We are caught in the cauldron of sorting through roles the culture defines for us—in other words, what life expects of us—and then turning this question back on itself to ask what we expect of life. In the end, when we decide to absorb the full meaning of what it is to be free, we have to come to terms with the internal and external struggle that constantly faces us.

THE INSIGHT ABOUT GUILT

One of the major shifts in my own thinking about guilt was the recognition that much of the guilt I have lived with has been well-founded—that to be human is to live with the experience of a particular kind of guilt, that which arises from acts of self-betrayal and becoming the person that others wish us to be.

The philosophic insight distinguishes between two kinds of guilt: the existential guilt of betraying our own capacity to be fully ourselves and fully human, and the neurotic guilt of adapting ourselves to what we believe the world expects of us. If you can accept this idea for a moment, and look at our modern organizations, you get a sense of how powerful our organizations are in reinforcing our neurotic guilt. And you see how difficult they (and we) make it to act on our existential guilt and choose to bring our full selves into our place of work.

Here are simply a few of the more obvious ways even the best and healthiest organizations reinforce our neurotic instinct to fit in and adapt ourselves into what the institution, and through it the larger culture, expects of us:

1. *Performance and Reward Systems.* We conduct performance appraisals in which the ways we should change to "be successful" are made painfully explicit. Managers are required to appraise each subordinate and identify areas of individual improvement. Strengths and weaknesses are noted and documented. Money is then tied to this feedback in order to put full weight on what our management wants us to become. Asking a person, "What do you want to become and how can we adapt to help you be that?" is a rare question. Even if this question is asked in some form, it is secondary to the discussion of what the institution expects of us and how it feels about who we are.

2. *Institutionalized Values.* Institutions define the values we are to live by. Management publishes "aspirations" and "core values" as if, without their definition, we would live by values that would undermine or defeat the organization. It is hard to conceive why an adult human being would seek from others a set of values to live by. When corporate values are defined

by the few for the many, it reinforces the neurotic guilt that lies within us.

3. *Prescribed Training.* We conduct training programs that are highly prescriptive of desired behavior. As designers of training events, we begin by asking what kind of behaviors we want these participants to leave the training with. In our well-intentioned effort to provide meaningful learning experiences, we deliver the message that our employees are not enough as they are, and we have the answer to that. Now, many training programs support the full development of the person in their content, but when they are prescribed, when individuals are "nominated" to attend, that act carries an overwhelming message that our future is in someone else's hands. And then, it is our neurotic guilt that leads us to be grateful for the nomination and attentive to what they have in mind for us.

4. *Reinforcing Our Wish for Safety.* What is most disturbing about practices that reinforce negative guilt is that we, as employees, ask for them. We all want to know what our supervisor or manager thinks of us. We ask them for ways we should improve. We are looking for a prescription to provide some surety about our future. We want institutional mentors, a plan for our development, a competency model against which we can assess ourselves. We want our bosses to approve of us and we want to be their favorite. All of these expectations are expressions of our neurotic guilt.

One of the promises of the philosophic insight is that human beings are inherently capable of creating lives of meaning and service.

We see that each of us has the capacity to use our freedom in service of an institution and that this service does not have to be trained, prescribed, and coached into us. When we get this, in fact, the organization will be able to be even more demanding of its members. It will expect people to be accountable, to find their own meaning, and to look failure in the eye. Managers will find great relief in ending their penance of caretaking and nurturing their subordinates into personhood.

It is the existence of existential guilt that makes the dream of creating cultures of freedom and accountability possible. I am guilty because I choose to live, choose to say no to certain people and choices. This is what freedom looks like.

The Sound of Freedom

One other implication of our new insight on guilt: it adds one more non-institutional, evocative word to use in our effort to change our language in order to change our culture. When we add the language of guilt to the language of freedom, death, anxiety, and evil, it personalizes and deepens our culture. It recognizes that institutions are profound human systems, not mechanical or super-rational systems.

This language, because of its evocative power, alters the way we define what is worth talking about. By redefining what we talk about and how we talk about it, we change our experience and come one step closer to making our institutions less rigid and more effective in adapting quickly and more realistically to their environment. Using this new language—and thereby the power of its philosophical content—will also work to make our workplaces more democratic and habitable. And it confronts and strengthens us in becoming more congruent in how we decide to inhabit them.

THE PROBLEM OF ROLES
AND EXPECTATIONS

When we engage the question of what the world expects of us, we typically think that if we can be clear about roles it will facilitate fulfilling them. This instinct is particularly evident when institutions try to change themselves or try to resolve some of their inherent internal conflicts. We consistently turn to role definition as the universal solvent. We are constantly trying to define people's roles: what is the new role of middle management and what is the role of a manager in an empowered environment? In creating new products and services, what is the role of the marketing group and what is the role of the research group? Our belief seems to be that we can find resolution for much of the complexity of organizational and communal life by the mere definition of roles.

From a philosopher's viewpoint, however, role clarity presents as much of a problem as a solution. A role defined by an institution or the culture at large creates expectations of us that in real life are impossible to fulfill. An externally defined role often collides with our own sense of what is true, it can silence our own voice, and the role can create ideals of success that no human being can live up to.

A dramatic example of the belief that it is a good thing to prescribe a job function, or role, can be found in the popularity of competency models. Here, a research team studies high performing individuals in a particular job function. They attempt to articulate the behaviors that are characteristic and common among these high performing people and then organize these behaviors into a list of skills and capacities that every person in this job function should ultimately possess. This model of job competencies then becomes a basis for hiring, training, and evaluating people in these jobs. This kind of inquiry does lead to real learning about what is entailed in a job, plus it helps to rationalize, or make reasonable, how we frame the job. It also, however, creates an ideal against which each of us will fail. I have seen competency models for the job that I have been doing for thirty years—consulting—and I do not believe I would be hired under their criteria (which, now that I think of it, may prove their validity).

The Real Struggle

The struggle, though, is how each of us confronts the reality that we are not going to live out the role expectations that society has in mind for us. The competency model is just one of the most explicit, and extreme, forms of how the culture demands that we fit into the frame of their expectations. These expectations are held in good will and usually, as in the case of the competency model, they are based on reasoned observation and orderly thinking about what actions best serve the institution.

The fact is that, try as we might, we are inevitably going to disappoint these expectations. How we deal with this crisis is the focus of the first part of Peter's chapter on freedom and suffering. From a philosophical viewpoint, the fact we will disappoint—or to use a stronger word, betray—those around us is, in fact, not a failure, but the beginning of finding our own path, our own voice, our own definition of ourselves.

Being explicit about roles has value when it becomes the beginning of a conversation, rather than becoming a standard for measurement. When we can accept the fact that we will never comfortably fit within the roles that are defined for us, we create space in our institutions for the mystery and beauty of human variation. The institutional fear is that if people do not function within defined roles, chaos will result and the goals of the organization will not be met. The opposite may be true. One definition of bureaucracy is that it is a world in which people are rule or role bound. No exceptions are allowed without time-consuming approvals, where local variation and local choice are defined out of existence.

To create entrepreneurial or adaptive institutions, violating roles and crossing boundaries become essential. And this is the reality of how things actually get done. One of the reasons we feel most useful and alive in a crisis is that, for a short period of time, the rules are suspended. We move our organizations forward when we accept this as daily life and treat roles as instructional possibilities that are constantly changing. The temporary quality of roles and the tension between how we have designed a way of operating and how we keep changing it are signs of vitality.

Conflict with the expectations presented to us also becomes a source of character and meaning for us as individuals. Carl Jung has stated that disobedience is the first step toward consciousness. Philosophy brings us the fruits of this theme.

Our Expectations

We not only have to live with meeting or disappointing the expectations of those around us, but we have to face our own disappointment in them. It is one thing to know that you were not exactly the child that your parents had in mind, but it is also true that, for a significant segment of your life, your parents did not quite fit the image of what you thought you needed or deserved.

What philosophy offers is the insight that these failures or disappointments are not problems to be solved, or signs of weaknesses in ourselves or others, or reciprocal demands to be negotiated. These disappointments are in the nature—the human nature—of things. Most workplaces are breeding grounds for unfulfilled expectations. Too often we expect things from the institution and its leaders that were unfulfilled for us as children. We want our bosses to be congruent, to walk their talk, to get along well together. We want to be the favorite employee, just as we wished to be the favorite child. There is no more constant and plaintive cry heard from employees than the wish for their bosses to be something more, something different.

The gap between what our workplace is and what we wish it to be gives meaning to our being there. It creates a vacuum that can only be filled through discovering our freedom and accepting the accountability to re-found our institutions to become places we wish to inhabit. Our institutions are transformed the moment we decide they are ours to create.

This is a difficult insight to absorb. It is hard to abandon the belief that the organization and its leaders could provide us more of what we desire, if they would just choose to do so. If we really trust the message of our experience, we are forced to take back into our own selves what we had been expecting from our leaders. The reality is that our leaders are right now giving us all they are capable of giving. They are not withholding anything. They see the longing in our eyes, do what they can to fulfill those longings, and still fall short.

The problem is that the moment we finally accept the limitations of our leaders as permanent and unchanging, as inevitable, we lose our sense of security. This loss can be overwhelming, partly because it reminds us of the safety that childhood promised us and did not deliver. The wish for safety is so strong that many of us will still choose to believe that a change in those around us is possible and required for us to be satisfied. This is the nature of the struggle.

These questions are discussed here in their most elemental form under the rubric of the "problem of meaning." It is in talking about our humanity in terms of suffering, death, fate, and boundaries that we come closer to seeing clearly what is at stake for us. Again, the power of the uncompromising language of the philosopher is what we need to allow the reality of our experience to penetrate through our defenses against an existence that we did not call for and the feeling that it is more than we can handle.

RETURN TO FREEDOM

The final chapter in this section ties all the threads together and returns to where we began, an understanding of what it means to be free. The moment we accept our complete and absolute freedom, it is easy to understand why we resist this profound and disturbing insight. My freedom declares me to be accountable for my experience and stance for every aspect of my life.

This means that all my complaints, my judgments, and my rationalizations for my condition become hollow and without any basis in fact. I have created my version of my own story, from day one and into the future.

To make this more explicit, it means that, in the workplace, I have decided what kind of management runs my organization. I have chosen what I need from the workplace and judged how I have been satisfied or disappointed. I have been the determining force behind what I claim to have been rewarded and punished for.

There is an objective reality out there—my institution does have a certain culture, others do act to create that culture, management and colleagues do in fact act in a way that impacts me—but none of it gives me an excuse or explanation for the quality and texture of my own experience or my own choices.

There is, of course, a cost to claiming my freedom and wearing my accountability. I have to give up the desire to live within the protection of longing for a normal life. As Peter explains in his chapter titled "Constituting the Workplace," there is no such thing as normalcy. There are only the cards that lie on the table before me.

Our fresh insight to complete, absolute freedom also causes us to question what psychology has taught us, namely that we have certain basic needs and that these needs drive our behavior. What psychology has defined as needs now become choices. If we can accept this, then it changes our thinking about management. We stop treating management as the cause of employee behavior. Managers are no longer responsible for the morale or even the performance of their subordinates. Managers stop thinking they are growing and developing "their" people. They are left with the awesome task of either confronting people with their freedom or supporting their escape from it.

Interestingly, this shift in thinking may not so much change our behavior with subordinates or with bosses; instead it changes the context in which we operate. We continue to coach, reward, and influence people, but we do it out of our own sense of what is right and wrong. We do those things as an ethical stance, or a philosophical stance, rather than as a motivational strategy.

As employees, the moment we accept our freedom, we stop treating leaders and managers as if they were so important. They are no longer the cause of our satisfaction or our performance. They just exist to be dealt with, as does all that comes toward us in life. My anxiety, my willingness to accept the fact that I am running out of time, my guilt for what possibilities I have not yet fulfilled, all belong to me and the subjective manner in which I have constructed or constituted my own experience.

This act of accountability becomes the source of my own power. It also leaves me with the experience of being alone, much more deeply and profoundly than I have been prepared to accept. The weight of this may be one reason why the typical workplace conversation talks more of boundaries than of freedom, and why parenting is so much more attractive than partnering, and why we have embraced the economist's belief that behavior can be bartered and our relationships with one another comprise a marketplace in which we constantly exchange and balance needs and offers.

Regardless of the extent to which we accept the centrality of our freedom, the question of our freedom is at the center of how we conceptualize and design our collective endeavors. The organizational structures and practices we have inherited reflect a low opinion of our capacity to claim our freedom and use it accountably. We have acted on the belief that people need leadership, need direction, need to be nurtured, trained, and coached into high performance. Bureaucracy is, in effect, an escape from freedom. It is an institutionalized longing for a world of safety and predictability. If we wanted to eliminate bureaucracy, as we say we do, it can be done in an instant. We need only to stop believing it is necessary.

If we insist on the importance of strong leadership, then we can have that in an instant also. All we have to do is provide it. Or choose to believe that those currently in power will change their use of that power the moment we are ready for them to do so. This is what the act of world constitution means for us, and why it matters so much.

Chapter 12

TWO KINDS OF GUILT

To be betrayed by another person is one thing.
But it is quite another to betray oneself, for this is so painful
that few have the strength to admit it.

A N IMPORTANT REVELATION of existential anxiety is the understanding of two kinds of guilt. When the distinction between the existential and the neurotic was first developed, it was applied to guilt in particular. Earlier we discussed two kinds of anxiety. This is about guilt. Existential guilt is guilt about unfulfilled potential, about self-betrayal and anger at one's weakness. Neurotic guilt has two layers: the denial of the existence of existential guilt altogether, and the internalization of external and essentially irrelevant rules and values.

Adapted from Peter Koestenbaum, "Guilt," in *The New Image of the Person: The Theory and Practice of Clinical Philosophy*, Westport, CT: Greenwood Press, 1978.

EXISTENTIAL VERSUS NEUROTIC GUILT

Existential and neurotic guilt are distinct and do not seem to be reducible to one another. However, they occur in sequence. If we deny our existential guilt, the reality of our own unfulfilled potential, we lose the weight and the solidity of our center. This is the condition of the first type of neurotic guilt. For this emptiness—this hollow that resides in one's chest in lieu of substance—we then substitute a shell or crust consisting of whatever values, roles, and identities we happen to find lying around in the cultural or family debris surrounding us.

Neurotic Guilt

Neurotic guilt is the limitation placed on life when one rejects the guilt about possibilities. People who do not recognize that they are always betraying their most genuine intrinsic values are individuals living on the surface, who spend most of their time trying to forget the real values of life.

In addition, neurotic guilt is more than the denial of existential guilt—a characteristic of all the revelations of anxiety. It is also the act of swallowing whole a set of external rules and then forming an overdeveloped stance of judging ourselves and others. This second type of neurotic guilt leads to the defensive personality. It is exhibited by people who do not feel entitled to their rights, do not feel they belong in this world, and find it necessary to apologize for actions, demands, and needs that most people find quite acceptable. They must therefore depend on others to tell them who they are and what they must do.

Existential Guilt

Existential anxiety reveals us as guilty, independent of our level of neurotic guilt. One of the most profound pains in life, a pain impervious to medical and psychological treatment, is regret over unfulfilled possibilities, grief over unrealized potential. We say a suicide or a young death is a "waste" for precisely this reason. The missed destiny can be a talent undeveloped, a love relationship not pursued, sensuality that is untapped and not expressed, or a mind that has not been stretched by education. Inexcusable neglect, perpetrated on ourselves, is the nature of existential guilt.

Fulfilling one's potential—physical and mental, intuitive and analytic—has been for many ages in history the pinnacle of human ideals. Among the most notable have been the civilizations of ancient Greece and the European Renaissance. Furthermore, to enjoy life is to go beyond oneself (self-transcendence), to become what one is (self-realization). To enjoy life does not mean to fulfill a narrow duty or to fit one's life into the procrustean bed of some provincial value system. It does mean to give expression to our transcendental or spiritual nature—to understand our freedom and to know about meanings—and to pay attention to our inner voices.

Individuals who have denied their authentic potential, who have conspired in its imprisonment, feel a resultant deep twinge of guilt. The reason that they *are* guilty is because they have denied their nature. People who follow all the rules of parents and society may suffer deeply from existential guilt precisely because the rules, which they freely choose to continue to adopt, prevent them from hearing their inner voices and hinder them in living out what they secretly know to be their authentic destiny.

Existential guilt therefore is the pain of the experience of self-betrayal. To be betrayed by another person—as by the mother in the Oedipal situation who locks the bedroom door and goes to bed with father—is one thing. But it is quite another matter to betray oneself, for this is so painful that few have the strength to admit it. Guilt means *I* have done the betraying; existential guilt means *I* have used my very own nature, which is my freedom, to betray my nature, which has been to deny my freedom. It is as important as it is difficult to be able to distinguish in one's own soul between neurotic and existential guilt. Is the guilt I feel about a specific omission a response to early training? Or does there exist a deeper human commitment to the realization of that value? To complicate the problem even further, we must ask ourselves if perhaps our authentic depth has willingly accepted and made a loving commitment to our early training.

Religious attitudes can serve as examples. Early religious training is externally imposed. To accept it on these grounds alone in later life is neurotic. To violate these injunctions—as when a person marries outside of the Church—leads to guilt. This guilt is neurotic. But it is quite possible, even likely, in the years of maturity to make the independent choice to identify yourself fully with the religious training of your childhood. Adults re-choose their childhood; they are no longer victimized by it. If they now violate this renewed commitment, their guilt is no longer neurotic but existential.

Only extensive introspection, meditation on one's inner needs, can help a person resolve these important issues.

Inner Wisdom

Existential guilt refers to the knowledge that you are betraying what your own inner wisdom tells you about your own purpose and the choices before you. What do *you* want? What is right for *you?* How do we learn to hear these inner voices? How can we assess their truth?

Our Universal Possibilities

Our inner wisdom comes from a variety of regions. We have essentially two levels. The first and most basic level is in the nature of being, what we can call our universal possibilities. It is our philosophic nature; it speaks to us from out of the depth of the inner space-time which is our transcendental consciousness, our pure "consciousness without an object." For example, our inner wisdom can tell us that our possibilities for eternity and universality have been neglected. These are authentic possibilities, and guilt at this transcendental self-betrayal is as intense as it is real. Or this wisdom can inform us that our freedom and our potential for individuation have been denied. That is what we call our empirical nature. And it is always we who have done it. In this case we have rejected our potential of assuming responsibility for choosing our own identity. We then are guilty and feel guilty—not because of some introjected external authority but because we recognize the structure of our own existence. Our potential for individuation has been denied.

These three dimensions—neglect of our possibilities, refusal of our freedom, and denial of our own individual uniqueness—reflect the type of existential guilt that is related to our possibilities. Our inner wisdom tells us that we have betrayed our basic, that is, transcendental, human nature. But there also is another, more specialized, type of existential guilt.

Our Strictly Personal Possibilities

We also have an individual, concrete, or local destiny in addition to our transcendental one. We have both a temporal and an eternal nature, a secular reality and a sense of the holy. This is the second level of inner wisdom. It comes from the outer reality with which our own history has identified itself. To give up this inner wisdom is to contradict the archetypal decision to be one's own empirical or bodily self. Each of us has a childhood, a tradition, and a social identity. Each of us has an individual unconscious and a collective unconscious. Each of us has an empirical ego and an empirical nature and destiny. That also is a source of inner wisdom. It comes from the unique, particular history and circumstances into which we were born: our family history, our religion, our genetic makeup, those things that define us, and us alone. Many persons have rejected their childhood religion but found it necessary in later life to either recapture it or find a mature substitute.

The guilt of universal, unmet possibilities is inevitable and is the deepest. But the personal, ethnic, religious, or social identity, while not absolute, nevertheless runs very deep. It is set in early childhood. Our sexual identity, for example, is set (or chosen) early. Our inner voices thus may require of us that we fulfill our sexual and ethnic destinies as well as our purpose-related one. These ethnic, religious, and sexual identity choices are also archaic, archetypal. Theoretically, they can be reversed, but frequently we discover that we *want* to make them, and even that we *want* to intensify them. Some individuals of course do discover, upon hearing their inner voices, that they desperately want to *change* them. The ensuing choice is then again obvious.

These alternatives among which we must choose belong to the empirical ego—the small self that exists in the world as opposed to the Self that is the God within—and the voices that tell us about these options for meaning come from the empirical realm, the everyday world, the realm of our own experience. Missed opportunities in the realm of these options lead to empirical regret, empirical loss, or empirical guilt for not using our freedom in making these choices. When our conscience tells us that we are neglecting the use of our freedom, that we are neither considering these options nor making commitments to them (both reflection and commitment are free acts), then the inner voices are heard. The desire for a specific career, calling, or sexual lifestyle, for example, is a voice from the empirical ego. But the choice to refuse to listen to that empirical voice or the decision to confront it, if it is indeed heard, is a powerful voice also. The question, "What is my calling?" is answered by voices originating in the empirical ego. But the questions, "Am I fulfilling my calling?" "Am I dealing with these feelings?" "Am I in charge of my life or is my life in charge of me?" are answered by voices originating in the part of the ego that is organized around universal possibilities.

We are two selves—the individual who has our name and exists engaged *within the world* and the inner universal consciousness that we share with the universe, that is, the God within. Each has its desires and its form of authenticity. The individual ego, the empirical ego, wants wealth and love. The ego that is the God within, the transcendental ego, wants eternal peace. Each ego that we have has a different type of existential guilt: for the individual it is lack of wealth and lack of love; for the universal, the Divine in me, it is lack of reflection, meditation, and insight.

Let us reflect on an example. There exists a whole class of people who suffer deeply but refuse to rally the power of their freedom to effect a change in their lives. They are genuinely tragic figures. The decision for joy and happiness never seems to be made. They have learned to love their tragedy and to depend on it for their self-concept and their meaning. To them, tragedy is beautiful and it is even supported by society. Symptoms develop when it becomes clear that lack of self-assertiveness deprives them of some of the pleasures, loves, and successes of life. Their sad world seems truly to reflect their self-concept as tragic figures. Some of the individuals who fit this description are often keenly aware of their own ethnic tradition and it leads them to be permanent outsiders to society. Their living decision to say no to joy and yes to tragedy results from an inner voice that comes not from their childhood but is of much more ancient vintage—their ethnic origins. This ethnic inner voice may overstep its bounds by souring a promising career or creating an unshakable depression. It then becomes obvious that redefinition must be cast into an ethnic and not a psychological mold.

The African American must know that historically the tormented slave, singing melancholy spirituals, was transformed into an aggressive militant. The history of the race must be recapitulated in his or her own lifetime. The Jew must know that the tragic pariah in the Diaspora was transformed into a powerful Israeli soldier. And the Jew, as an individual, must do likewise with his or her self-concept and lifestyle. In other words, both minorities must apply these collective ethnic solutions, from a decision for negation to a decision for affirmation, to their own and more narrow individual personal situations. The ethnic voices come from the empirical ego. The conscience that obligates us to use our freedom to endorse and activate these ethnic voices or reject and neutralize them comes from the region of our subjectivity.

The Value of Reflection

A convenient way to illuminate this important region of inner wisdom is to meditate on what the Jungian analyst Ira Progoff calls "stepping-stones": a few key events in a person's life. These will give us a sense of the flow that is our life today. We can then meditate on how it feels today, right now, to experience the flow that is our life. Then we proceed to write it all down, in the style of free association. This process reveals, among other things, unfulfilled potential. It reveals values that are experienced as real but are not being realized.

In doing such an exercise we avail ourselves first of the power of reflection or reduction. We step outside our life and observe that life.

Second, the hidden regions of the empirical ego—both in its collective and in its individual aspects—reveal themselves: hidden feelings, hidden aspirations and expectations, and hidden desires and needs. We then make a decision to integrate these insights into our daily lives and to realize these values in our empirical existence. Empirical voices tell us the demands of the empirical ego. "As a child I wanted to be a great scientist or artist." That is an inner voice from the empirical realm. "My changing careers was the most important stepping-stone in my adult life." That is an inner voice speaking from the empirical realm.

Thus neurotic guilt is the uncritical and automatic introjection or acquiescence to externally originating values, self-concepts, and lifestyles into the structure of our existence. Also, neurotic guilt is the denial of existential guilt. To summarize, both types of neurotic guilt—denial of our own purpose, and internalizing a purpose defined by others—lead to symptoms. Existential guilt arises when we violate the commands of our inner voices. These can be empirical, in which case they are either collective (ethnic) or individual (psychological), or they can be transcendental, having to do with simply the fact that we are human.

SYMPTOMS OF EXISTENTIAL GUILT

Existential guilt, as the betrayal of one's possibilities, leads to self-doubt and contempt for one's weakness. It leads also to loss of self-respect. Whereas persons who in their own eyes are unsuccessful experience this guilt early in life, so-called successful persons may postpone experiencing it until well into middle age. That guilt is sometimes referred to symptomatically as the mid-life crisis.

Success often means that external values and demands have been realized. The person then discovers that success is not the satisfying and durable value or state of being that he or she had expected. But after forty or fifty years in pursuit of these values, the price of saying "I was wrong" and "I am sorry" is indeed prohibitive. Existential guilt is then interpreted by our ghost-in-a-machine-theory-of-humanity society (or by the medical model of the person) not as a inevitable stage of life, but conveniently as a lack of drive or ambition, or loss of libido. Furthermore, existential guilt frequently becomes conceptualized exclusively as missed career opportunities. And while career opportunities may indeed have been missed, they are only one small aspect to the guilt about an unfulfilled existence.

In this way society and science deflect us from the contradictory realities of living a life without illusion by seducing us into the belief that the polarities of existence are a curable malady. Existential philosophy is a philosophy without illusion about our reality. The first stage of absolute realism is to know that some of our dearest wishes and deepest needs are blocked by concrete walls. The second stage is the knowledge that the wishes and the needs are real, absolute, and uncompromising. That is the meaning of contradiction as the essence of human existence. This contradiction comes not because we have made a mistake with our lives, but because we are human and every human being who chooses to reflect deeply upon his or her life will face the pain of this contradiction.

The pain of self-betrayal becomes translated into a variety of responses:

- Some seek "more of the same" with greater focus and increased passion. Far from recognizing that their values are wrong, they think they did not pursue their earlier values with sufficient intensity. But they soon discover that the materialistic, problem-solving approach to life's problem of meaning, worth, and destiny does not work any better by increasing the dosage than it did in the first half of life.

- Others find themselves filled with self-contempt, in which the crisis becomes completely internalized. In this case, the person becomes depressed. And this depression can be dealt with by seeking a medical solution, rather than treating the depression as a demand from an inner voice to face the choices one has made in life.

- Or it can be expressed as anger, in which case the person projects his self-contempt on others. He wears signs on his face that read "It's your fault!" "If it hadn't been for your defects, I would be a happy and fulfilled person!" This can lead to efforts to change those around as a solution to our crises in the form of anger.

- Finally, self-hatred can be repressed, denied, and treated as if it does not exist, so that it leads to symptoms such as high blood pressure or alcoholism, or a penchant for risk and high speed living.

At some time in our life, each of us discovers deep inside ourselves these two fundamentally contradictory self-concepts. One is an often untapped reservoir of strength. Another is a great anger, resentment, embarrassment, and disappointment at our own unconscionable weakness. That sense of worthlessness, to the extent that it is based on the factual comparison of reality with potentiality and to the degree that it is perceived in a context of inwardness and freedom, is existential guilt.

A female client in her early thirties—an unmarried professional—has a recurring and lurid dream of unsuccessfully trying to kill an ugly gopher. She finally decides to shoot it. The gopher is at that moment transformed into an attractive and charming young girl, who is not hurt by the bullet but swallows it instead. This dream has many possible meanings. One of them, however, is that having a fulfilling, happy marriage and being a mother have been some of her unfulfilled possibilities. The ugly gopher is her existential guilt, and the repeated and bloody attempts to kill the animal represent her anger at her own self-betrayal. And her self-betrayal, like the gopher, will not go away or die.

It is important that we not develop guilt about existential guilt. The answer to existential guilt is not to "do something" but rather to "live with it acceptingly." We can therefore be more specific in our examination on how to deal with it.

COPING WITH THE ANXIETY OF GUILT

The general principles of coping discussed in connection with other forms of anxiety apply of course equally well to existential guilt. To see their application to the problem of guilt, it is helpful to catalogue some of the prevalent types of existential guilt found in today's organizations and society at large. Each of the following groups of persons experiences the pain of self-betrayal and the guilt of unrealized potential, even though in each case the circumstances of life are different.

Youth in Search of an Exit Strategy

One group consists of young people—from their early twenties to middle thirties—who are healthy in every aspect but at the same time severely immersed in the materialism of the larger culture. They view their first job as a chance to make a lot of money and then, early in life, drop out of the work world and begin to do what they really want to do. They live in the best regions of the country—beautiful mountains and stunning seashores. They are professionals or semi-professionals, often working in fast paced technology or financial fields (but many want to be poets, writers, painters, or therapists—and they would make good ones), but their primary concerns may be artistic creativity, personal growth, intimacy, and love of nature.

These contemporary lifestylers are superior people by every measurement. Their relationships are free, unorthodox, and unstable. But they also feel that they fail at family life, future planning, and personal meaning, and they are anguished about the lack of a stable structure in their lives. They can integrate their lifestyle with the established society, although they do feel a deep longing for something more. Their constant problem is the conflict between peace of mind and integrity. Their alienation is based not on illness but on health. They are the healthy ones. They are free, ethical, and committed to authentic human values. Their surrounding society may be mostly sick and inauthentic. They feel forced, as healthy persons, to adjust themselves to a set of unacceptable institutions. Like prisoners, they are powerless to resist the call of the establishment.

These young people demand that their careers move fast and be financially rewarding—a legitimate request but one that is difficult to realize. Their marriages may not work out, because they seek and require new lifestyles. Because they have internalized the quasi-totalitarian demands of their society, they feel guilty. Specifically, they are torn between the two kinds of guilt. They feel neurotic guilt because part of them still accepts conventional social rules. They feel existential guilt precisely because they accept the inauthenticities of society and therefore find that they betray their own personal and true meanings.

There does not seem to be anything like a solution to the problems of these people. They reflect a defect in our culture, or perhaps even a defect in being itself. They mirror the fact that we speak of one value system—depth and liberation, respect for human beings, and reverence for the exploration of inwardness—but practice another—materialism and axiological rigidity. They do what we teach and are then punished for being good pupils. They cannot be integrated into the society which they need without at the same time violating the integrity of their inner voices. They cannot respond to their legitimate and valuable inner needs without suffering the fate of pariahs.

Two recommendations seem appropriate. First, never contradict or compromise your inner integrity. However, do not be boorish or immature, because you want more than protest: you want success. Second, never use your submission to society as an excuse to fail in your own tasks and meanings or to transmute your joy and zest for life into bitterness, cynicism, and depression. In other words, you must realize that you *are* the consequences of your chosen actions, that you *are* fully responsible for the co-created success or failure of your life, and that basically the world regrettably does not care if you fail or succeed. But one person does care: you yourself. There can therefore be no excuse for failure in your life.

These young persons must recognize that they need beauty, creativity, meditation, art, religion, philosophy, and poetry as much as they need financial security, air, water, and bread. And they must pursue these needs as though fighting for their very survival. These people are artist-philosophers. And they are condemned by their integrity to be such. Their life will be a continuum of struggle, frustration, opposition, and rejection. But they must persevere, for there is no other path that conforms to the truth about life as they and many others see it.

Some, but only very few, will eventually be recognized by the surrounding culture and validated as people who contributed to making the world a better place. Some, like Nietzsche, will even become prophets for a future age. But the fate of most will be one of suffering. Their guilt will be minimal, but their pain intense. They will feel real and satisfied but maladjusted. They will derive some comfort from the frail hope that there is a chance for aesthetic accomplishment. Some have been catapulted into the forefront of our culture—and therein lies the feeble hope of others that they might likewise overcome their alienation from the establishment.

They can gain inspiration from other persons in other ages who have followed the same unswervingly independent path of creativity and integrity. We will never know of those resting in unmarked graves, but we do know of such as Boethius and Erasmus, Wycliffe and Aquinas. We know of Schubert and of Bartok, of Spinoza, and of Kierkegaard, all of whom were great and wise, but began their lives in ways they had trouble accepting.

Mid-Life Professionals

A second group of persons who experience the existential anxiety of guilt are those who now find themselves to be successful middle-aged professionals and executives who are beginning to show symptoms of meaninglessness. Their symptoms are depression, ennui, and marital and career boredom. The cause of their symptoms is the discovery that their careers, precisely because of their success, distracted and deflected them from hearing and listening to their inner voices. While their original professional commitment may have been in response to an inner voice, they may discover that by middle age the message of these voices is entirely different.

Their existential guilt, once exposed, can be colossal. Their existence suddenly becomes one massive symptom: their authentic meaning has been repressed, the fruitful insights of existential anxiety have been denied, and now their life is one big neurosis or neurotic anxiety. Now that their "success" is almost total, the fraudulence and bankruptcy of the values to which their lives have been devoted and which their society had proffered them as absolute and reliable becomes apparent. The values have been fulfilled. They have no place to go. And the meaning is not there.

The enemies to growth, in these cases, are the resistance against admitting a gargantuan mistake as well as the adulation society accords to "successful" people. Physicians are a good example of both problems. The time, expense, and difficulty of their preparation and the subsequent establishment of their practice rules out any chance that they can readily accept a fundamental error in judgment that might have occurred initially in their career or a change in values and attitudes that might have occurred in later years.

There is no suggestion here, by any stretch of the imagination, that medicine is an inauthentic career. In many instances, however—as is also true for the rest of us—this profession was chosen at a time when those concerned were certainly not at the height of their philosophic powers. Wisdom comes late in life and is the result of long experience in living. And no youngster in college or even before can be expected to be in full command of these philosophic insights. But there is a further phenomenon operating here. All professional commitments lead to ennui unless there is continuous and significant growth and creativity. Even the best ear specialist tires of looking into patients' ears. He needs new growth and new challenges. In a profession held in as high esteem as medicine, the rewards of status, prestige, respect, and income seduce physicians away from their existential guilt.

It is, thus, extremely difficult for a person who became a physician at his parents' urgings to admit that perhaps and in view of what his inner voices are telling him he was wrong, or that what is wrong is his present neglect of other areas of development. Again, existential guilt is not allayed by "trying harder." Our success with anything in life must not cloud the constant presence of unful-filled possibilities and therefore the permanent undercurrent of existential anxiety. People who perceive themselves as failures have no problem with this. But those who regard themselves as successes can use that illusion to deny neurotically the reality of their existential anxiety.

Thus, the problem of those facing a second career in which their unfinished business in life will be completed can be impeded by their very success at coping with the problems of the first half of life.

Power in Women

Another group of people who question their meaning and exhibit existential guilt about unfulfilled possibilities are women who have enjoyed the benefits of the women's movement yet still question their power and value. Some women may still say, "I would *love* to have more power in the eyes of the world." The issue involved in this situation is understandable. Some implications are tragic. Our culture used to teach, and occasionally still teaches, the fallacy that potency is male. As a result, some women may still feel ambiguous about their own potency and power while, at the same time, they envy men their power. But there is a deeper and more authentic source for their anger. It is unfair that potency should be unevenly distributed. And it is proper to rage against that injustice; that rage is their newfound power. Women had in the past been taught to surrender to this condition, but that leads only to resentment. [And this situation has changed greatly over the many years since these pages were first written.]

The solution to this problem of guilt with respect to power is to realize the obvious, namely, that power already exists in women to the same extent that it does in men. The distribution of personal power is indeed even, and nature has not created an unjust situation. It is the social institutions that have brainwashed us into distorting these basic realities of human existence. The problem is artificially created by society, and there is no need at this point to speculate about its causes. Potency is the act of being. Potency is self-transcendence, reaching out beyond ourselves, freedom, and purpose. Potency is the archetypal, the underlying decision for individuality. It is the commitment to one's capacity to reshape the practical, everyday world. Power or potency is to choose embodiment.

This is thus equally available to all. A person is not powerful because he is male or powerless because she is female. On the contrary, a person is powerful first, because that person is a consciousness-body-world field, and *then* that person avails himself or herself of this potency to choose and define the meaning of masculinity and femininity. Many problems between men and women as well as conflicts within ourselves can be traced to this philosophic confusion. The primacy of our here-and-now consciousness and the freedom to choose one's own role are philosophic fundamentals about human existence which, if understood, can reintroduce harmony into the lives of many people.

AUTHENTIC "ANTIDOTES" TO GUILT

We can consolidate the discussion of existential guilt in terms of the following highlights. The name of this revelation of existential anxiety is guilt. When we deny this guilt, thereby producing neurotic guilt, we experience depression. But when we work through this existential guilt by confronting it, we develop a sense of wholeness. The "treatment" of this condition consists of developing or pursuing excellence in life.

The ideals of human perfectibility and of achievement are authentic antidotes to the existential anxiety of guilt. What is true for an individual is also true for our institutions. This understanding of existential guilt will ultimately lead us to measure all institutions—such as a business, the family, education, the law, commerce, and politics—by the degree to which they support the development of human potential.

Chapter 13

THE PROBLEM
OF MEANING

Life is all we have, all we are, and, in a sense, all there is.
No compromise or mediocrity in solving the problem
of the meaning of life makes sense. To compromise is to have failed
solving the problem of the meaning of life.

EXISTENTIALISM HOLDS THE VIEW that we are by nature alienated and anxious, that our existence is constantly threatened by a sense of meaninglessness, and that despair is often just around the corner. In this chapter we begin to see the intimate connection that exists between the anxiety and guilt of meaninglessness and the discovery of genuine meaning in life.

In order to better understand the relationship between freedom and the dimensions of life touched by our understanding of anxiety, death, and evil, we must first recognize the structure of the

---

Adapted from Peter Koestenbaum, "Anxiety and Meaning: The Phenomenological Structure of the Search for Authenticity," in *The Vitality of Death: Essays in Existential Psychology and Philosophy*, Westport, CT: Greenwood Publishing Co., 1971.

problem of the meaning of life itself. We call it a problem because it is a series of questions that, at some point, each of us must answer in our own way.

There are at least four ways in which this "problem" can be approached. We can think of it in terms of:

1. Roles,

2. Pleasure and fulfillment,

3. Boundary situations, and

4. Suffering.

One assumption on which existentialism builds its view of the human condition is that life, as we find it, is meaningless or absurd. That does not, however, make us pessimists or fatalists. The term "meaninglessness" is to be interpreted on the level of ideals rather than on what, in the narrowest sense, is called the "practical" life.

THE DEMAND OF ROLES

Most persons have conceptions of what they *ought* to be, of their proper role in specific situations. Some managers may, for example, think that the role of boss is that of the dominant person in the hierarchy of a workplace. They may therefore attempt to assert themselves in various pointless ways in order to avoid feeling threatened by the dreadful possibility that they have not met the demands of their role. Conversely, employees may feel that their role is to be submissive to a boss, yet they do not find it possible to yield completely to the boss's directions. The consequence of such behavior is that they may feel incompetent and inferior—even guilty—because they do not measure up to the role that they envisage for themselves.

Rollo May notes succinctly the mercurial character of roles when he writes:

> Sin used to be "to give in to one's sexual desires"; now it is "not to have full sexual expression." It is immoral not to express your libido. A woman used to be guilty if she went to bed with a man; now she feels vaguely guilty if after two or three dates she still refrains from going to bed; and the partner, who is always completely enlightened (or at least plays the role), refuses to allay her guilt by getting overtly angry at her sin of "morbid repression," refusing to "give." And this, of course, makes her "no" all the more guilt-producing for her.[1]

A workplace counterpart to this line of thinking is that sin in the workplace used to be "to not follow directions or orders." Employee participation or self-management used to be called "mutiny." Now sin is to "avoid personal responsibility," to not act as an owner of the business. Workers used to feel guilty if they had their own, contrarian ideas about how to do the work; now it is immoral not to express your most radical views, and we feel guilty if we do not fill the suggestion box. And the boss, who is always completely enlightened (or at least plays the role), refuses to allay this guilt by getting angry at "employee passivity" and tries even harder to drive "fear" out of the workplace. And this, of course, makes the employee feel all the more guilty.

Each of us must make our separate peace with the claims and demands of such roles. The roles themselves are repeatedly paraded before us on television, in novels, movies, magazines, advertising, through neighbors, friends, books, and sermons. Peace of sorts can be made in several ways. We may submit to these demands and try to fulfill them as much as possible. We may also decide that the demands of a particular role are irrational and then try to erase them from our consciousness by the expedient of the rationalizing cliché of "thinking for oneself." Whichever our resolve, whether to follow the Joneses or think for ourselves, it is, of course, not easy to make peace with the demands of our roles.

The question of the meaning of life and the crucible of our freedom becomes in part, then, the problem of fulfilling the claims and demands of roles. If we conceive our role as boss in traditional terms—that is, as a leader who coaches, mentors, makes tough decisions, issues rewards and sanctions—then we feel we lead a meaningful existence, a happy and fulfilled life, to the precise extent that we measured up to that role. That role is an image some people have of themselves. Its structure is clear and it cannot be easily changed or eradicated. Such role-images are an independent force in our lives. We did not create the image; it appeared on its own, and its binding power is irrefutable.

The reality is, however, that it is not possible to fulfill completely and satisfactorily the demands of one role, much less of all of them. The consequence of this inevitable frustration is a sense of futility, worthlessness, and guilt that seems to become an ineradicable part of life. We inevitably recognize the discrepancy between the real and the ideal, and the resulting pain, if faced, can be unendurable.

There are a number of possible ways to manage the anxiety released by the awareness of that discrepancy, between the role I *have* and the role I think society expects of me.

Roles Uplifted and Downgraded

From the perspective of roles, the problem of the meaning of life becomes a matter of distinguishing the ideal (the role) from the actual reality of life. In comparing our actual condition with a particular role, we have two alternatives for bringing the two together: we may strive even more intensely to *uplift* our present condition to resemble the ideal role, or we may *degrade* and lower the ideal role to conform to our actual condition. The latter solution is commonly termed "just being plain realistic," whereas the former is called "ambition" or "idealism." Unfortunately, each condition has its emotional difficulties.

For example, as long as we can see the ideal role in its high, ethereal state *and* as long as at the same time we still have a scintilla of hope that someday we might be equal to that role, our life can have a delightful zest, promise, and verve. It then indeed seems worthwhile to be alive. This condition of vague promises is well described by Paul Tillich in *The Dynamics of Faith*. While discussing the role of success, he writes:

> It demands unconditional surrender to its laws even if the price is the sacrifice of genuine human relations, personal conviction, and creative *eros*. Its threat is social and economic defeat, and its promise—indefinite as all such promises—the fulfillment of one's being.[2]

Whether such promises are empty (as Tillich contends) is not an issue here. Our human experience indicates that the existence of such hope and such vague and infinite promises (of what will accrue if we meet the demands of our roles) elevates our present condition and gives us a general feeling of well-being. Life that has this kind of hope is intrinsically good and worth living.

However, if we insist on keeping the structure of the role at the level of the ideal, we soon recognize that it is impossible to match the ideal with the actuality. Such a recognition—if the role is of true value—leads to despair, a sense of worthlessness, and guilt. Reasons for this despair will be examined shortly.

If we adopt the other solution, that of degrading the role, we do not achieve fulfillment any more than if we were to keep the two forever apart. The element of hope, the promise of a meaningful life, lies precisely in the fact that our conception of the role remains on the level of the ideal. As we bring the role down to the level of the attainable—or even worse, to the level of what we have already attained—the halo of infinite fulfillment that attended the role disappears, and with it, the sense of hope, euphoria, and potential peace of mind. To lower the ideal to the level of the attainable is, in effect, to give up the quest for meaning in life; it is an admission of final defeat.

Fulfillment, therefore, cannot be achieved either by uplifting ourselves—we can never meet the exigencies of the role, at least not for long, and not for all roles, even if we occasionally meet the demands of one—or by downgrading the role—since the characteristic of promise and fulfillment, which is part of the concept of a role, is eliminated.

Roles and Suicide

The preceding discussion may seem to exaggerate the polarities of seeking an unachievable goal and living with that frustration versus choosing what is obtainable and experiencing despair at the loss of the capacity to dream. After all, why should the obvious recognition that we may never fully realize our ideals lead to despair? And why do many philosophers go even further than what is suggested by the word "despair"? To them, not only does recognition of the dilemma lead to despair, but it may even lead to thoughts of suicide.

And since few of us wish to think of suicide, we tend to obscure the entire issue, blurring it with slogans, such as realism and resignation; we escape it through pursuits such as busywork and games that temporarily keep our minds off the real issues of human existence. In our work lives the fear of suicide comes in coded form, which is the fear of being fired—and especially the fear of being fired because we dared to truly be ourselves. We obscure the existential question by endlessly wishing for a new boss or leader, thinking this solves the dilemma that is entirely ours to bear.

In order to understand the place of suicide in this analysis, we must ask ourselves the question, "Who am I? What is my *real* self: the ideal or the actual?" In the obvious sense we are the actual, present reality, but in quite another and much more fundamental sense, we are in fact the ideal. The present, imperfect actuality is experienced as a temporary condition, an expedient. The individual today is merely a transition stage to the peace of mind, fulfillment, accomplishment, or joy that will be achieved in the future. Such conceptions of self are particularly common in youth. Age mellows this optimism since, year after year, it becomes obvious that promises have not been fulfilled and may never be. In a real sense, we are our promises and our hopes. If we did not have the future to anticipate, the present might become unbearable. And the reason the present would be unbearable under such conditions is that, in truth, we are our future. In the words of Heidegger, "I am my futurity. My self-image, my conception of my real self is an image projected into the future, an image in which the roles, unfulfilled at present, are fulfilled."

It is therefore quite accurate to say that, in an emotional sense, ego, person, self, subjectivity, and inwardness are none other than the projected and fulfilled image of ourselves in the future. To the extent this is a correct description of our experience of ourselves, then we cease to exist when we either recognize that we can never fulfill the demands of our roles, or when we find it necessary to reduce the roles to achievable realities. The recognition that the role in its ideal state is unattainable—a recognition that may come on us in either of these two ways—is in effect the destruction of the real personal self. The demand for excellence in our organizations furthers and encourages the agony of this discrepancy. Thus, the ego is eliminated and life is destroyed. The serious reference to suicide merely makes a physiological fact out of what already is a psychological fact.

Philosophy, of course, does not literally suggest or recommend that people contemplate suicide. Philosophy, in fact, recommends nothing but merely analyzes and describes the human condition. The thought of suicide may appear when we anxiously recognize the discrepancy alluded to, since we are in a sense dead already when we realize that our true self turns out to be an unattainable ideal. To realize that we can never really be ourselves is to know that we are already dead. The emotional concomitant of that insight is a despair that can lead to thoughts of suicide. The despair and meaninglessness of life—when one is forced to witness it and cannot escape it—is expressed powerfully in Hamlet's famous lines:

O that this too too solid flesh would melt,

Thaw, and resolve itself into a dew!

Or that the Everlasting had not fixed

His canon 'gainst self-slaughter! O God! O God!

How weary, stale, flat, and unprofitable

Seem to me all the uses of this world![3]

There are solutions to the problem—and we shall discuss some of them later. However, the despair of suicide, as Albert Camus has poignantly suggested, is the first step in recognizing our true nature and genuine values. The contemplation of suicide, profound depressions, and boundless despair are neither dreadful nor to be avoided. On the contrary, the presence of these presumably dismal experiences can guarantee the beginning of authentic insight into our human condition. We must be grateful for these insights and pursue them, since philosophical self-knowledge must precede the solution of these problems. The presence of anxiety is often a healthy sign that some important new insight is about to be uncovered. The despair of suicide is not a terminal condition but the prelude to genuine philosophical self-understanding.

The Despair of Roles

The existential disappointment with respect to the fulfillment of roles manifests itself in two directions. The first is from *life* to *self,* which is a response to the questions, "What does life expect of me?" or "What does life demand of me?" The second is the reverse, from *self* to *life,* namely, "What do I expect from life?" "What may I and what should I demand from life?"

Let us consider the first question. What life expects from us is what we have called the problem of roles: in our lives we are expected to fulfill our roles, and deep guilt often stems from our clear recognition that we have not and are not fulfilling them. Is a man fulfilling his role as a male adequately? as a father? as a husband? as a brother? as a son? Or a woman as a female, mother, wife, sister, or daughter?

Let us take the relationship of the son as an illustration. Just as a father has an image of himself, so does a son. (Every man who is a father is, of course, also a son.) The son may feel that someday he will fulfill his role. He may say to himself, "Someday my father will allow me to fulfill my role. Someday, when I do not have all the problems I have at present (i.e., getting a job, finishing my studies, making ends meet, finding a wife, etc.), I will have the time and presence of mind to be a good son." And then, one day, the father dies. Guilt sets in. Why? Because the future has been eliminated. Now the role of a son can never again be fulfilled. Role failure is total and final. There is no longer a father to make a son.

At such a time, as is true of limiting situations generally, the onus of unfulfilled roles becomes apparent. The son will say to himself: "I *am*"—in the sense of ideal roles—"a *perfect* son. I have not been able to realize or bring into being that state of perfection. It is my own fault, my free choice, that I have not yet become what I am" (a perfect son). "My father is dead. It is now forever impossible for me to become what I am. It follows that, as a son, I am now left as nothing, that I am a living corpse, a corpse ashamed of myself." That is the meaning of existential despair and the thought of suicide. And this extreme illustration typifies aspects of human existence in general.

Objective and Subjective Role Failure

The father-son roles—perhaps suggested in the Abraham and Isaac story—are an illustration of how guilt leads to a sense of meaninglessness in connection with unfulfilled roles. Let us take another example. A woman has different roles as daughter, wife, sister, and mother. In each of these roles she can recognize the discrepancy between her performance and the demands of her roles. She cannot shake off the roles; their demands are inescapable, but neither can she meet the demands. The result is that she may be a philosophic failure in her own eyes. As suggested earlier, to be a failure means, in fact, not to exist; it means to have ceased to *be* in any significant and concrete sense. This type of despair is *existential,* which means it is a philosophical intuition, not a state of neurotic depression.

Most parents, in this case, a mother, feel—at least at significant times, such as births, birthdays, their children's successes or failures, weddings, and deaths—that their primary role in life is to create their children as satisfactory human beings. Their children's successes are their successes and, conversely, their children's failures are their failures. Extreme or limiting situations usually bring out the true traumatic and revelatory nature of a mother's inevitable existential failure, a failure that occurs with the cold indifference of logical necessity and for which she nonetheless feels that she must hold herself fully responsible. When a child dies (or more commonly, when a child grows up, leaving mother and home), it becomes clear that the role of motherhood remains unfulfilled—unfulfilled according to the standards the mother herself has set or accepted, the very standards with which she has identified herself. Motherhood is, in the ultimate sense, unfulfillable. When a child is gone—either through death, crippling disease, or simply through growing up and becoming independent—the hope that in the future the role of motherhood might be fulfilled is eternally taken away from every mother. The present failure becomes then the permanent condition and leads to despair and meaninglessness, perhaps even to thoughts of suicide—to materialize the feeling. The mother *is,* in a real sense, what she envisages herself to be in the future: a perfect mother. When the future is forever taken away from her (through the growing up of her child), the present condition is all that remains, and that is a condition of failure.

In an *objective* sense, a good mother is not a failure. And that is the sense in which most people use the word "failure." She did the best she could. Objectively, we recognize a human being's finitude and limited capacities and admit that within acceptable limits the mother did her duty; she did fulfill her role. Nevertheless, on the *subjective* side—and this is the perspective that interests us—the situation is different. Society may forgive a mother for her failings and limitations, but society does not lead her life. The living individual cannot look at herself as merely one among many: she is unique; she is different; she is herself. Failure for her is also total destruction.

Objectively speaking, failure can be redeemed, because life goes on, the future remains, and additional opportunities for hope through role-fulfillment abound. But in a subjective sense, a woman recognizes that because of her uniqueness and her finitude, she has only one chance. Subjective failure is total failure, failure without redemption. If she does not meet the demands of her roles, she is destroyed; everything that is anything is destroyed. From the subjective perspective the demands of roles are absolute; therefore, anything but absolute compliance with them is utter failure. From the superficial point of view of external society, the mother may be good, but the revelations of her innermost self-knowledge, derived from absolute candor about the facts of her human existence, disclose that, although she may have tried, she has nonetheless failed to meet the ideal. And she has failed to meet the ideal, because from her point of view she did not dedicate herself enough to the fulfillment of her role: she could have tried harder; she could have been more effective. The sense of failure stings her because she cannot exonerate herself. A close analysis of situations of this sort will invariably disclose that the individual in question feels responsible for that failure. In this sense, guilt is a deep structure of human existence.

The distinction between objective and subjective failure is one that occurs frequently in a philosophic analysis of human existence. The distinction itself is due to the ambiguity of human experience. That ambiguity is clearly encapsulated in the theory of the intentionality of consciousness. Human beings, and all experiences characteristic of them, have a subjective as well as an objective dimension. Both dimensions are paradoxically mutually exclusive and interdependent at the same time. Similar distinctions are made in the existential discussion of death, where we separate the *death of myself* from the *death of another*. We also talk about the sense of guilt and the sense of obligation, and especially the sense of freedom or free will, as being either experienced in the subjective dimension or as an object of experience. The philosophical analysis of the body yields similar results, since the body is both the subject of experience and its potential object.

PLEASURE AND FULFILLMENT

Roles are an answer to the question "What does life expect of me?" Our next question is, "What can I expect from life?" The answer to that question can be compressed in the expression "successful living or satisfaction." Just as obligatory roles are paraded before us from early childhood, so are the promises of what life has to offer. In youth, we believe that someday life will give us perfect and absolute happiness. The feeling is good and certain, but its content is vague and ambiguous. Nevertheless, we embark on every new project hoping that (past disappointments notwithstanding) this task might lead to the euphoria that life has promised us and that we expect from life. If this job does not work out, the next one probably will. If this line of work does not offer fulfillment, the next one probably will. If this marriage does not yield ultimate satisfaction, the next one undoubtedly will. We seek success; we have ambition. We achieve success and we fulfill our ambition, but there is still no unlimited happiness!

For years the catechumen seeks enlightenment and peace of mind. He finally thinks that he must have achieved it, but finds that actual fulfillment is different from anticipated fulfillment. For years the young executive strives to reach the top. At forty-five she becomes president. She, too, has not experienced the eternal happiness that led her on this quest. In both cases, had they desisted, their consciences would have given them no peace. Perhaps, having achieved their goal, they do not have excessive feelings of guilt, but they know that they have not reached Elysium, and they are disappointed—perhaps because they recognize that the quest was a fraud, that the promise of ultimate fulfillment could never have been realized, not even with the greatest of all possible successes. People who never reach the top will never have to face this traumatic disappointment; they can always hope. But those who reach the top rung of the ladder therewith also lose all hope. They have reached the doors of Dante's *Inferno:* "Abandon all hope, all you who enter here."

Disappointment thus comes in two dimensions. First, we cannot fulfill the demands of our roles—we cannot be what life expects of us. Second, we find that life responds with equal fraudulence: it does not give us the fulfillment and infinite happiness that we deserve and that we need for a meaningful life. After all, life is all we have and are, and fulfilled life, meaningful life, euphoric life, is the only real life. If that promise is taken away, then for all practical purposes life itself has been taken away.

Each of us has learned to live with these disappointments. In childhood these hopes still burn feverishly. As we mature, the fires diminish. Philosophy is the inward call to greatness, to the sense of fulfillment found in meeting high standards. The guilt of mediocrity calls on us to return to the ideals of our youth and insists that they be fulfilled. We must not weaken and abandon either the high goals we set for ourselves or the high demands we set for life. Maturation does not mean that we should repress these demands, as is often the case, but rather we should seek genuine answers. What are these answers? This is the problem to which an applied philosophy ultimately addresses itself.

We now turn to the third attempt to examine the problem of meaning in life. Here we utilize Karl Jaspers' notion of *Grenzsituationen,* or boundary situations.

BOUNDARY SITUATIONS

The notion of boundary situations is very useful in describing what existentialism means by the absurdity or meaninglessness of human existence and its corresponding despair. Each of us, if we are honest with ourselves—if we allow our genuine and authentic feelings to reach the surface—discovers that we can never be satisfied with our limitations. Humanity strives toward infinity. We want *more;* that is the meaning of growth and progress. We can never rest on our laurels. No known satiation point exists. Let us expand on this point.

Living in the Present or for the Future

There are at least two fundamentally opposite ways of describing and interpreting the basic stream of human consciousness. In brief, these opposing views are the idea of a "life-force" or *"élan vital"*— as Henri Bergson has written—and the idea of "spontaneity," as we find it in the Zen concept of *satori.* Is the goal of human existence eternal striving, eternal drive and ambition, insatiable pleasure, and a generalized thirst for *more?* Or is the goal to live in the spontaneous present as if it were eternity; is it possible to expand the present moment into a timeless (that is, flowless) eternity? Bergson assents to the former, Zen to the latter. A frequent but by no means universal philosophic assumption about human life is that we strive endlessly to achieve continually increasing self-fulfillment (what that means remains to be defined). It is therefore important to analyze the apparent objection that may be made by philosophies of life that emphasize the importance of the present and its peak experiences (such as Alan Watts, Abraham Maslow, and their followers) to the philosophic views developed in this book.

A closer look indicates that the distinction between philosophies of ambition and philosophies of eternity—philosophies of time versus philosophies of eternity, philosophies of the future versus philosophies of the present—are not in conflict but are complementary. Time and eternity, striving and spontaneity, future and present are two aspects of one and the same complex situation: a meaningful human existence. In some contexts it is profitable to stress the temporal (futurity) dimension of our being-in-the-world, and in other contexts the eternal (ever-present) dimension must be emphasized.

We have already discussed the temporal aspects of human existence, and will continue to do so as we move along; what remains is to show that philosophies of spontaneity do as well in describing the human situation. First of all, the exponents of the philosophy of the eternal evidence, nonetheless, a clear-cut *striving to achieve* this sense of spontaneity. Abraham Kaplan put it eloquently when he wrote that a philosopher may "proclaim that time is unreal, and point out that he arrived at this truth only after many years of reflection."[4] The state of absolute spontaneity or *satori*—the state of mystic vision in which all being is condensed into an eternally present moment—is mostly *in the future*. It is a goal, an ambition, a hope, a promise of fulfillment, rather than an actually present condition. Now and then the hope may seem real and fulfilled, but only for a spark of a moment and not for an eternity. The quest for spontaneity is therefore another way of describing our search for infinite self-transcendence. The infinite in this case is absolute spontaneity.

Second, and conversely, striving, ambition, and thirst for pleasure or learning also possess the aspect of spontaneity. In a real sense, all experience is in the present, so that the future is but a particular form of the present. Strictly speaking, futurity is clearly discernible as a dominant and describable mode of the total present. The condition of striving can itself be seen as a momentary whole: it is a spontaneous presence. A great work of art may express eternal striving; it expresses the endlessness of striving, the fact that striving is a process that goes ever upward and forward and, *at the same time,* shapes and focuses that eternal progress into one momentary present inspiration. A work of art encapsulates strife in the eternity of the spontaneous and present moment.

Let us go back to our question. Is the essence of life striving for greater satisfaction or success? Striving toward the achievement of higher levels of evolutionary advancement? Striving for greater power, wealth, influence, success, pleasure, esteem, glory, status security, and love? Or is it rest, peace, cessation of striving, relaxation, enjoyment of the moment, appreciation of the present? Our conclusion is that both of these apparently opposed philosophies of life are in fact separate emphases on the same experience, the same analysis of life, and the same goal of human existence. Neither is wrong, both are right, there is no contradiction.

Inescapable Limitations

Having said that, if we grant that the essence of life is to strive— even if that striving is directed toward an eventful state of non-striving—then the possibility of infinite fulfillment is immediately and forever threatened by the inescapable limitations that life imposes on us. These are the so-called boundaries of existence.

Death

The most dramatic and obvious reminder of our finitude, and the dread and despair that go with it, is the recognition that we shall die—which is discussed at length in Chapters 8 and 9. Here it need only be mentioned.

Inevitable Guilt

Guilt is the recognition that we have failed in living, that we have failed in being ourselves. It is also, in Tillich's words, "the experience of man's basic unacceptability." In the history of religions, that experiential core has gone under the name of "the contingency of human existence." These recognitions are inevitable aspects of any sensitive human nature. Because they signify the destruction of our own human person—either deliberately or as a fait accompli—guilt leads to anxiety. Guilt, however, is inevitable, and as such is a perennially limiting factor in our lives. Ultimate satisfaction is impossible because of, among many other things, the pervasive presence of guilt. Guilt is not an irrational feeling; it is the inevitable result of recognizing that we have failed in reaching our authentic goals and that this failure usually appears to us as the consequence of our own deliberate acts and choices.

Situation

We are placed in a particular situation in life, and the character of our lives is determined by this situation. We may call this fact "fate." The question, "To what extent does one's situation fully define his or her nature?" remains unresolved; it is a central problem in the philosophy of religion. Our humanity demands total identification with our situation, whereas the divinity in us suggests transcendental possibilities which imply eternity regardless of the contingency of situations. We were born in this century and not in another; we are members of a particular nation; we have certain parents with specific external and internal characteristics of their own; we are born of a predetermined gender; we have certain mental and physical capacities. We have certain neuroses and attitudes, beliefs and prejudices. These are some of the general aspects of our life situation. We do not choose them, and yet they determine us. In a sense, we could have been born in Timbuktu, or in central China, or in the outback of Australia; we could have been born two centuries ago or three centuries hence. Our native tongue could have been any one of a number of languages. Our parents could have been loving or neglectful; they may be alive or dead. We might have been born rich or poor.

These are all fundamental determining factors of our human existence, of our possibilities of satisfaction, and we had no choice in the matter. There is no logical necessity, no fundamental reason that we exist as we in fact do. These fateful situations are limiting, because they restrict our potential; they determine what we are without being subject to change. Our life is all we have, and we have no control over factors as basic as the ones just outlined.

But our situation in life is also fateful in narrower aspects. We have certain particular friends, neighbors, acquaintances, and associates. These can be changed, it is true; but in changing we may be jumping from the frying pan into the fire, since we simply acquire other friends, neighbors, acquaintances, and associates. In other words, we have little control over the situation in which we exist, and it is that situation which determines our existence. The result is our contingency, our sense of helplessness, finitude, and limitation. Extreme conditions, such as war, disease, birth, death, crime, and insanity, increase our awareness of the repressive and depressing power of these boundary situations. In severe illness, we ask, "Why does it have to be *my* child (or *my* friend, *my* mother, *myself*)?" The answer is always in terms of "fate" or our "situation." Since our hope is in the future, and since the boundary conditions tell us in effect that there is no future, that the future is an impenetrable barrier, we are led to despair, absurdity, and meaninglessness.

In other words, we always exist in a particular set of circumstances; these conditions limit us severely and we have limited control over them. The extent of our control over our life-situation is at best to shift from one set of situations to another. But from the perspective of our quest for ultimate satisfaction, that is no solace.

Suffering

We will discuss suffering later in this chapter, so here a few words should suffice. Suffering, like pain, is also a limiting factor in life. It is a reminder of the insufficiency, contingency, and finitude of human existence. The suffering of others may be as painful to us as our own, maybe more so. Physical and mental illness, hunger, and insecurity—common factors even in a peaceful world—lead to an existence seemingly not worth having.

Conflict

One important aspect of our quest for infinity is our endeavor to reach at least one other human being, a relation called "encounter." This quest appears to be forever frustrated by human conflict or struggle, since even under the most auspicious circumstances ignorance about the structure of human existence raises up barriers to the complete coincidence of two human souls.

Chance

Our free control over existence is forever overshadowed by the intrusion of bad luck. Chance hangs over us like the sword of Damocles. Even as simple an activity as driving a car entails a basic sense of insecurity because of chance—the last on our list of boundary situations. We never know whether we will reach our destination, since even the greatest caution does not guarantee success. The frustrating vagaries of chance, especially in connection with the inescapability of death, are well illustrated by this little anecdote from W. Somerset Maugham:

DEATH SPEAKS: There was a merchant in Baghdad who sent his servant to market to buy provisions and in a little while the servant came back, white and trembling, and said: "Master, just now when I was in the market-place I was jostled by a woman in the crowd and when I turned I saw it was Death that jostled me. She looked at me and made a threatening gesture; now, lend me your horse, and I will ride away from this city and avoid my fate. I will go to Samarra and there Death will not find me."

The merchant lent him his horse, and the servant mounted it, and he dug his spurs into its flanks and as fast as the horse could gallop, he went. Then the merchant went down to the market-place and he saw me standing in the crowd and he came to me and said, "Why did you make a threatening gesture to my servant when you saw him this morning?"

"That was not a threatening gesture," I said, "it was only a start of surprise. I was astonished to see him in Baghdad, for I had an appointment with him tonight in Samarra."[5]

These boundary situations are inevitable aspects of human existence, and each one calls attention to the fact that our desire toward infinite satisfaction or control over our existence is everywhere limited, and limited to our disadvantage. The finitude or limited character of human existence threatens to make even the finest life absurd. Humanity's self-imposed ideal is to reach some type of ultimate fulfillment, and we feel personally responsible for it. If we fail, it is our freely chosen neglect that seems to have caused it. And yet, we will not—because we cannot—achieve our goals, and we know it. Since each of us *is* in a real sense our ultimate fulfillment, and since the boundary situations make such fulfillment forever impossible, the natural condition is to exist in a vise and to have times of deep despair about the meaninglessness of existence. The clear recognition of the paradox and discrepancy between our honest goals and our limited possibilities and even more limited achievements leads to the despair expressed in the statement, "I have nothing to live for!"

Let us now turn to our final attempt to understand the problem of the meaning of life, which, as indicated earlier, is the problem of the essential meaninglessness of human existence.

TO BE IS TO SUFFER

One analysis of the problem of the meaning of life uses as its motto the spirit behind the Four Noble Truths of Buddhism: the pervasiveness of suffering. The facts about human existence that the Four Noble Truths purport to disclose are that all forms of human existence—from the most glorious to the most dismal—are in essence suffering. To suffer is but to recognize the authentic facts of human existence. Suffering is a necessary preamble for understanding and fulfillment, a fact that religion powerfully symbolizes by Jesus' crucifixion before his Resurrection, and the Israelites' suffering in Egypt and in the desert before fulfillment in Canaan. Without the wisdom gained through the recognition that all life is suffering, no solution to the problem of the meaning of life is possible, since one who does not see the problem is in no position to resolve it. The Protestant work ethic, supported by Freud, also fits this analysis.

What is meant here by the proposition that life is suffering? We shall examine it in three stages:

1. Suffering as pain,
2. Suffering as compassion, and
3. Suffering as imperfection.

Each is of greater philosophical significance than the preceding one.

Suffering as Pain

The most obvious form of suffering is pain, but from the standpoint of acquiring insights into the problem of the meaning of life, it is neither the most important nor the most profound. Pain is unevenly distributed in the world: some unfortunate individuals are in constant pain, while others rarely experience it at all. Pain, usually associated with illness and injuries, is of course a common experience. It seems grossly unfair that any sentient creature should have to suffer pain.

The fact that such a marvelous event as the birth of a child should be accompanied with intense pain, danger, and consequent anxiety makes no sense, in a "rational" universe. The pain of childbirth is a fact, but it is not perceived as a *mere* fact: it is perceived as a *cruel* fact, as an *unjust* and *unfair* fact. Old people die in agony of cancer or arthritis, children are sick with meningitis or measles, patients suffer at the hands of dentists—and this is not to mention cases of political and other types of criminal torture. These are constantly present examples of aspects of human existence that militate against an authentically meaningful, joyous, and satisfying life. To find meaning in life means—at least in part—to experience untarnished happiness, joy, and pleasure. The existence of pain inevitably undermines such happiness. Even in moments of magnificent health, our joy can be mellowed, its edge dulled, and its point broken, by the anticipation, threat, or anxiety of possible and future pain. In the lives of the most unfortunate, pain is ever-present. But even in the lives of the most fortunate individuals—those with wealth, health, and intelligence and physical attractiveness—the spectre of suffering through pain is always with them.

But pain need not be exclusively physical. Anxiety—physical or moral—is pain. Grave moral issues arise for each of us, and their resolution is often suffused with anxiety. Anxiety may arise for secret reasons. It may haunt sleep, destroy days, and ruin life.

Injustice is another type of pain—perhaps mostly moral pain. Injustice names one of the most obnoxious and painful forms of frustration. It is frustration involving the total person, the being whose essence is his or her future. Injustice is brutality and indignity. Injustice is the destruction of an ego—it is the destruction of the most precious (perhaps the only truly precious) thing in existence. Black students kept from the medical profession because of their color and Jewish babies killed by a brutal Nazi guard in a concentration camp because of their religion illustrate injustice in the civilization of the twentieth century.

The many forms of injustice differ in degree and intensity. They include an unwarranted rough dismissal by a boss, friend, or public official; unfair competition in business; a co-worker betraying a confidence. However, the general structure of the experience of injustice and our response to it are the same. Injustice means the destruction or enslavement of an expanding ego; it is the elimination or limitation of a complete universe of inwardness. Injustice means to cut off the future. Injustice is a very special kind of destruction. The living ego expands lovingly toward a world and a future of hope—that is the paradigm of a good human existence—and that subjective universe, the only universe of value, is destroyed. It is destroyed as much in a callous dismissal as in an execution.

Just as burning gunpowder restricted to a narrow shell explodes, so our response to injustice is an explosion. We call it uncontrollable anger. Cultivated and urbane behavior, as well as laws, limit the possibilities for the manifestation of such emotional explosions. The result is anxiety. T.S. Eliot wrote in *The Wasteland:* "And I sat by the waters of Leman and wept." When the explosion demanded by injustice-engendered anxiety cannot take place, the only possible response of the understanding human being is weeping. Grief. Weeping is the traditional response to the irreparable destruction of an ego's universe. It is as if the tears correspond to the dissolution of the world.

Suffering as Compassion

No one is by nature impervious to the sufferings of another. We may *enjoy* our breakfast coffee by reading the newspapers, with all the crimes, wars, ambushes, and suffering that are reported. However, a little reflection will show that if these events were close to us—if the woman who hanged herself and who was found by her children returning from school were our next door neighbor—we would feel them deeply. No one, therefore, can be happy knowing there is profound suffering, tragedy, and pathos somewhere in the world. Yet pitiful but understandable necessity has built a defense around us, a hard, clam-like shell, a calloused skin that enables us to ignore—with the exception of people like Mother Teresa and Albert Schweitzer—the sufferings of others. A husband faints when he actually sees his baby being born. The inexperienced may vomit at the sight of blood at the scene of an automobile accident. A good swimmer might become paralyzed by the sight of a drowning child. Human beings have a natural sensitivity—*impractical* as it may be— for the suffering of others. Some—such as nurses, doctors, soldiers, and police—have out of necessity become inured to terrifying sights. A surgeon who passes out during an operation is worse than useless. A police officer whose knees wobble at the sound of a shot is of no help at all. From the perspective of the cruel exigencies of life, we are forced to admire those who are callous enough to be of help. But from the deepest level of human feelings, from the level that is not trained to be practical, from the level that has not been transformed by crude necessities, from the level that can be re-awakened in the minds and hearts of each of us when our defenses rest, we cannot be fully happy, that is, find life fully meaningful, as long as there is suffering in any sentient being. Even if all suffering has been removed, there is still history; its books are full of gruesome stories of persecutions, battles, enslavements, plagues, and executions. Empathy and compassion make true happiness impossible.

Suffering as Imperfection

We now come to the third interpretation of the proposition that "to be is to suffer." This sense comes closest to our search: to recognize imperfection as the most significant form of suffering from the point of view of the question of the meaning of life.

But why demand perfection? First, because life is all we have, all we are, and, in a sense, all there is. The second reason is that the relatively short duration of life urges us to achieve a condition that keeps postponing the depression about our finitude, the despair over any unsatisfactory element in that life. No compromise or mediocrity in solving the problem of the meaning of life makes sense. To compromise, to accept the facts *realistically* is ipso facto to have *failed* solving the problem of the meaning of life. The discussion must be seen in the light of this tripartite aspect of the quest. There are no second chances. Life is inherently valuable—to be alive is to know that—and we cannot relinquish the demands of existing. These considerations apply to all of us, and belief in immortality changes nothing. As we saw earlier when we discussed the problem of death, belief in immortality and anxiety about death are perfectly compatible. Anxiety about death is a pervasive certainty in our lives, and belief in immortality is a religious commitment undertaken *in response* to that anxiety.

POSSIBILITY IN THE IMPOSSIBLE

Our discussion leads to the conclusion that our effective existence can be described in these terms: we strive for perfection; that striving is not self-imposed, but *discovered;* striving, however, is accepted as one's own; and the specific content of perfection is always left empty. Its unconscious or tacit presence is presupposed since we always know when we have *not* achieved perfection. It is these empirically found facts of human existence that describe the eternal failure of life, the impossibility of finding ultimate satisfaction, in a word, the absurd.

The problem is that we cannot rest until an answer is found, since, in the last analysis, there is nothing else to life but that concern. In spite of the evidence for the absurdity and meaninglessness of existence, we *do* love life. What better way to complete these thoughts about the inherent suffering that life confronts us with, plus the possibility that this creates, than with the forceful insights of Thomas Wolfe: [6]

> This is man,
> Who, if he can remember ten golden moments of joy and
> happiness
> Out of all his years,
> Ten moments unmarked by care,
> Unseamed by aches or itches,
> Has power to lift himself with his expiring breath,

And say: "I have lived upon this earth
And known glory!"

This is man,
And one wonders why he wants to live at all.
A third of his life is lost and deadened under sleep;
Another third is given to a sterile labor;
A sixth is spent in all his goings and his comings,
In the moil and shuffle of the streets,
In thrusting, shoving, pawing.
How much of him is left, then,
For a vision of the tragic stars?
How much of him is left
To look upon the everlasting earth?
How much of him is left for glory
And the making of great songs?
A few snatched moments only
From the barren glut and suck of living.
Here, then, is man.
This moth of time,
This dupe of brevity and numbered hours,
This travesty of waste and sterile breath.

Yet if the gods could come here
To a desolate, deserted earth
Where only the ruin of man's cities remained,
Where only a few marks and carvings of his hand
Were legible upon his broken tablets,
Where only a wheel lay rusting in the desert sand,

A cry would burst out of their hearts
And they would say:
"He lived, and was here!"

. . . . . .

For there is one belief, one faith,
That is man's glory, his triumph, his immortality—
And that is his belief in life.
Man loves life,
And loving life, hates death,
And because of this he is great, he is glorious,
He is beautiful, and his beauty is everlasting.
He lives below the senseless stars
And writes his meanings in them.
He lives in fear, in toil,
In agony, and in unending tumult,
But if the blood foamed bubbling from his wounded lungs
At every breath he drew,
He would still love life more dearly
Than an end of breathing.
Dying, his eyes burn beautifully,
And the old hunger shines more fiercely in them—
He has endured all the hard and purposeless suffering,
And still he wants to live.

Thus it is impossible to scorn this creature.
For out of his strong belief in life,
This puny man made love.

At his best,

He *is* love.

Without him

There can be no love,

No hunger, no desire.

So this is man—the worst and best of him—

This frail and petty thing

Who lives his day

And dies like all the other animals,

And is forgotten.

And yet, he is immortal, too.

For both the good and evil that he does

Live after him

Why, then, should any living man

Ally himself with death,

And, in his greed and blindness,

Batten on his brother's blood?

Chapter 14

CONSTITUTING
THE WORKPLACE

We are fundamentally free to define the precise role of work
in our search for meaning—but we are also fully responsible
for the consequences of our definition.

T HE MAIN PURPOSE of these reflections on improving the
workplace and how we think about and experience power is
to illustrate how philosophical insight can shift our thinking about
leadership and our relationship to work and workplaces. The principles explored here are a way to begin to reconstruct our institutions as strongholds of freedom and accountability.

THE HIGH COST OF
ADVOCATING NORMALCY

Every institution operates with a set of norms and expects its members to live by them. In other words, they have a fixed notion of

---

Adapted from Peter Koestenbaum, "Philosophical Therapy in Marriage and Sex," in *The Vitality of
Death: Essays in Existential Psychology and Philosophy,* Westport, CT: Greenwood Publishing Co., 1971.

what normal behavior is and in fact value it, even treat it as a given. The philosophic insight suggests that the word "normal" has absolutely no meaning when applied to either a person's life or his or her relationship to leadership and power. The meaninglessness of normalcy is not a *value* or *disvalue* but a philosophically disclosed, existential *fact*. Normalcy is a chosen value or the commitment to a value; it is not a fact.

The *fact* of the social institution of work opens up the *possibility* of realizing the traditional value–potential of work if total adjustment to that institution is *decided on* by our freedom for self-definition. Seen from the depth of pure consciousness, the commitment to the values made possible by the institution of work is a choice that is totally free and nonrational. Of course, should people *not* choose identification with the social structure, they also choose the *consequences* of that grave alienation.

The consequences of confusing value with fact, choice with that which is fixed, and the meaninglessness or meaningfulness of normalcy can lead to severe guilt and anxiety. The more we fit in with our institutions, the more we feel guilty and anxious. We pay a high price for ignoring the depth and enormity of our freedom regarding the choice and implementation of self-concepts and of values.

Leaders who authoritatively and dogmatically assert to employees that any or all of the specific psychological, sociological, and cultural standards of work are absolute norms are acting with philosophical irresponsibility. They are philosophically untruthful because they tell employees, falsely, that there is a Platonic model which they *must* emulate, in some mysteriously terrifying sense of "must." Of course, the ideals exist, but there is no necessary or final connection between these ideals and human existence and nature.

Our only essential nature is the power to *freely* define ourselves within specified limits. Employees—to the extent that their essence is authentic humanness—freely choose, from an infinity of models, the ones they want to emulate.

Authoritarian dogmatism can produce guilt, anxiety, paralysis of will, and loss of self. Why? Because employees must invest all their energies either to protect themselves from the anxiety and guilt arising from their difficulties in measuring up to these standards or to transform their lives to meet them. The result of Platonism in philosophical leadership is dehumanization, or, in Sartre's language, *mauvaise foi* (self-deception).

The person who is guided and directed toward an externally anchored self-concept has relinquished and lost his freedom; in truth, he has lost himself. He has abdicated his inner humanity, integrity, ego, and his "self." He has capitulated to an external object which he must become, rather than to exercise the freedom which he is.

In sum, the *damage* done by ethical dogmatism under the guise of values ensconced in truth or science is essentially dual: (a) it produces anxiety, guilt, and paralysis and (b) it dehumanizes us since it interferes with, or even destroys, our very nature—which is to be a free, inward, world-constituting object. In actual practice, of course, not every employee wants to, or can be, human in this ultimate philosophical and authentic sense. The practical solution to a specific problem may be removal of the pain through behavioral prescriptions (which are, in effect, physical or psychological medicine). However, when we invoke philosophy, we are talking about insight for human fulfillment and not of anodynes for emergencies and pain.

Insight about philosophical freedom as applied to institutional life is not merely intellectual. It must suffuse the entire, primitive being of the employee, since freedom is the structure of consciousness *before* it has chosen between intellect and emotion, reason and feeling—even self and other—as its self-concept and style of life.

There are four *advantages* implicit in the insight that normalcy is meaningless:

1. Existential self-disclosure can remove unnecessary and paralyzing (that is, neurotic) anxiety and guilt.

2. Correlatively, this insight can increase the sense of freedom, induce relaxation (due to freedom), and make possible a general gracefulness and ease in living.

3. It can increase our freedom of action, just as it can enhance the experience of living our own life with ease, risk, naturalness, spontaneity, and without burdensome restrictions and oppressive regrets.

4. Furthermore, the insights associated with the first principle—the nonexistence of normalcy—help employees to utilize the strengths, potentials for growth, and health dormant in their own intrinsic psychological nature. In other words, they improve performance.

A person's invariant freedom *is* his or her strength. The *weak* ego, for example, maintains its self-definition as weak through the *strength* or power of its existentially free constitution. In other words, at the level of its philosophic depth, the weak ego is strong, but it uses its strength to keep itself weak. A philosophically oriented leader can assist employees in making that discovery—namely that they are keeping themselves weak, and expending great energy in doing so.

THE HIGH COST
OF DEFINING NEEDS

Most current applications of psychology and management theory often reduce the individual to the level of our most primitive instincts and needs. These needs are said to be physiologically determined and biologically fixed. They make up our human nature. The lifestyle of the employee may then be restructured in terms of a feeling and understanding of these needs.

The philosophical view goes far beyond that and is not for everyone. Individual needs expressed by most accepted psychology presupposes the acceptance (which is, in the last analysis, free) of a biological and instinctual model of the human being. That model—in the sense of being the absolute foundation—is rejected by a philosophy of freedom. This rejection is not a spiritual value judgment but the recognition of a fact: each of us *is* the freedom to choose our nature—no more and no less. Even our primitive need–nature is a value—not a fact—and as such it is subject to existential choice. We *do* have a nature, but it is not made up of irreducible needs. It consists of intentional consciousness, the meaning-giving power of our own acts of awareness, which is a vast and threatening region of existential freedom. That freedom, like atomic energy, is both dangerously explosive and powerfully constructive.

It is true that the choice of needs is a very deep choice indeed and one which, if not made, leads to very serious and dehumanizing consequences. Nevertheless, the fact remains that needs are free personal choices and authentically possible commitments to a specific—albeit common—definition of human existence. We can go even further to say that the free adoption of or identification with a need is tantamount to the fundamental free choice of being human. The needs we hold as true are not a fact; they are a choice, a choice in fact to be human. It is still true, however, that to choose humanness is one of our consciousness's basic possibilities and, unfortunately perhaps, not a necessary state of affairs. God has created each of us free to choose whether we are to be human or not. Once we decide that what we thought were basic needs are in fact constituted choices, everything changes.

REFRAMING OUR THEORIES

These reflections lead to the next point, which is that each of us is almost infinitely adaptable, flexible, changeable, and adjustable. Since there is no such thing as an absolute and irreducible structure called "need," and no definitive meaning to the concept of being "normal," the self-sacrificing and celibate priest in what was Biafra and the equally self-sacrificing and celibate nun in a Calcutta leprosarium are persons who are as normal and as need-fulfilled as any of the more traditionally oriented individuals (even as much as the notorious womanizer Signiore Don Giovanni Casanova, that is, Don Juan).

There is nothing unnatural about these ascetic lives or any other lives. However, in choosing asceticism, the priest or the nun does choose to deny the commonly held notion of the primacy of human—and thus their own—biological, psychological, and sociological nature and needs. In other words, the model presented by the behavioral sciences is freely rejected by their opting for asceticism. Each choice of a value has a price: we choose both value *and* price (or consequences, associations, implicit ramifications). The priest and the nun illustrate the possibility of different definitions of what it means to be human, all equally possible and equally normal. Even if it were true that there is less meaning and satisfaction in asceticism than in, let us say, sensualism—which is open to question—asceticism nevertheless still remains a possible choice of authentic lifestyle. "Satisfaction," in any real sense in which this term is to be defined, need not be one of the values chosen by the humanity-defining and self-defining freedom. The words "normal" and "need" are irrelevant to this situation *as long as we recognize that our deepest personal choices are choices of the meaning of humanity itself*—and not just minor, inconsequential, and readily reversible decisions. These basic considerations are illuminated by a philosophical theory of freedom.

If we accept this line of thinking, and step back for a minute, we begin to question much of the theory that underlies our strategies of motivation, building cooperation, training and development, and even how we organize work.

The Defining Ego

This perspective means that *I*—the ultimate individual or the philosophically disclosed ego of every human being—*define the meaning, nature,* and *importance* of work with full freedom, but *also,* and this fact must never be overlooked, with full responsibility for its consequences. Freedom means recognition of both a zone of un-hindered activity *as well as* a zone of absolute limitations. We must not overlook the inseparable duality of freedom and responsibility. The world is *fixed* in its ambiguity, and thus the ego is *fixed* in its freedom.

Size and Importance

Specifically, the perceived size and importance of work in relation to our total life-world is not an absolute but is a matter of defini-tion and choice. A specific size is *given* as a *value.* It is also *given* as a *fact,* that is, as both a *social* (that is, medical, religious, psycho-logical, etc.) fact and as an *individual* (situational) fact. With re-spect to the *value,* the ego has *constitutive* (that is, weak) freedom; but in regard to the *facts,* the ego has only *attitudinal* freedom (that is, for withdrawal or commitment).

In other words, work can be chosen to encompass everything in life or be but a minor incident. Each of us must ask ourselves how important—that is, how large—the perceived work-world is to us. We must recognize that the size of the work is part of the defini-tion of work regarding which we are both free and responsible—and accountable—for the consequences are now part of the real world.

Meaning

Furthermore, human beings, in their philosophical essence, are to-tally free and fully responsible for the role performed by the cul-tural *institution* of work as well as by any actual *existing* workplace in their own, individual *search for meaning* in life. We may choose to search for meaning in life *through* work, *with* work, or *in spite of* work. Of course, two of these are extreme possibilities, but each is a freely and responsibly constituted definition of work and of self. We are fundamentally free to define the precise role of work in our search for meaning—but we are also fully responsible for the consequences of our definition.

Subjectivity

The subjective perspective is the only actual, accurate, and true perspective. This position is not taken because philosophy is committed to subjectivism. On the contrary, everything (that is, every object) is what it is because it is an object *to a subject*. An object, such as the experience "work-in-general" or "my-work," is not accurately described for what it in truth is, if we describe only or exclusively the object aspect of the total experience. We must also recognize that the object, "work" in this case, is, in its essence, not only the isolated abstract object but also an intention—a chosen definition, an assigned meaning—being perceived by a particular and real individual. And the difference is enormous. The unique subjective element, perspective, or dimension in the total perception is as much an aspect of the reality called work as is any purely "objective" consideration. Work, or a workplace, is the subject–object interaction in perception. *Any* object is seen from the point of view of a subject. Work is the interrelatedness of the ego and its world.

Once we recognize this fundamental insight, it becomes clear that the so-called "objective" analysis of the thing, event, or object called "work" is a meaningless undertaking. We can discuss meaning and work only from the perspective of *each* subjective percipient. Leadership and coaching, which have to do with *objective* answers, are—in any lasting sense—irrelevant. However, communication between the participants in the workplace *is,* of course, relevant, since what occurs in verbalization is that two people are comparing *two* objects that they had confused as one. The two objects are their two separate perspectives of the work situation.

A so-called "objective" analysis of a workplace is really the attempt to "peel off" the abstract or pure object from the total and concrete intentional or meaning-giving conscious stream. There can be no objective assessment of a workplace. The sole objective truth is the inescapable subjective (that is, intentional) version. The tendency toward treating what is subjective as if it were objective, and the subsequent alienation, is a fundamental flaw in our materialistic age: we err by seeing human or people-related events as pure objects, that is, as two-dimensional "things" divested of a third, subjective dimension that is nevertheless every bit as rich and *real* as the abstracted objective aspect. This alienation is the ominous danger in today's culture of making humans into a fixed and predictable thing rather than to recognize them to be a subject-perceiving thing.

The philosophical emphasis on the reality and centrality of subjectivity is part of the same intuition that spawned the Relativity Theory. That theory holds that the term "simultaneous events" is literally a *meaningless* expression unless we include the observer in it as a *member of the event itself;* and the observer can vary. In other words, the measurements of space and time are relative to the observer and consequently space–time itself—thought earlier to be objective—has meaning and reality only as it is *observed.* Absolute space–time has no meaning. The situation is identical with all objects, such as our concepts about work.

So work is in reality not a thing or an object, not a state of affairs or a sequence of events, but a subject–object interconnection. Work, as a pure object, or a fixed and given place, does not exist. Applying the principle of subjectivity to leadership and workplace coaching, there is no meaning to the *object* "work" or "boss." Work is what it is only as it is related to the perceiver. This point must be remembered by every leader, since there are only subjective and individual solutions—that is, decisions and freely undertaken definitions—not exclusively objective criteria.

Social Fact

So far I have emphasized the freedom or *subjective* pole of intentional consciousness—the zone of negative withdrawal from identification with the world. We must now emphasize the structure and the realities of the *objective* pole.

A job—or, more generally speaking, an organization—is a fundamental and inevitably important *social* fact (as an institution). It is a social fact, and one of major proportions and great significance. For example, when a young manager says she will define her very own concept of the use of power, then one must first ascertain whether her decision, while it is free, is also taken with full recognition of the social fact of the institution of which she is a member. The institution of work exists importantly in the legal, economic, social, psychological, religious, and moral structure of society. The manager is surrounded in truth by the ineluctable facts of the social reality of that institution. The existence of these facts cannot be denied any more than can be the fact of gravitation.

Philosophic freedom properly understood recognizes that it is primarily attitudinal—a choice of attitudes. That is, in this case, "freedom" means withdrawal from—not a denial of—the hard and immutable facts of life, which include entrenched social institutions. Consequently, freedom vis-à-vis these hard facts means first of all freedom to manipulate, as through technology, or manage with a view to changing these facts. Technology presupposes knowledge of the laws of nature, that is, of ultimate facts, which can then be manipulated according to the desires of individuals and teams. In short, science and technology are the result of a commitment to discern how we can trick reality into changing—not by a direct assault but by what is the equivalent of an end run in football, a maneuver to outwit the defense. We cannot turn a supertanker in the ocean simply by swimming against its side. But the combination of motors, propellers, and rudders overcome the resistance to push and enable us to manipulate the behemoth to turn!

Secondly, freedom as withdrawal from social fact also means the choice of an attitude or posture toward these immutable facts: passive, active, indifferent, engaged, disengaged, resentful, accepting, skirting, repressive, deceptive, and so forth. Attitude is a matter of insight or intuition and is not amenable to control or manipulation. Philosophically speaking, leadership means insight, intuition, self-knowledge, self-disclosure, and reeducation rather than manipulation, control, and technology.

Once these limiting facts and the concept of accountability are recognized to exist, much less liberal behavior will follow from these insights than is usually associated with philosophical free thinking.

Individual or Situational Fact

A specific work situation or reality already exists for the employed *individual.* In other words, it is futile and unphilosophical for a person to think and to act as if his or her life situation were different from what in fact it is. A philosophy of freedom is supreme realism: it is as realistic about the enormity of our *freedom* as it is about the *limits* of life. Philosophy makes the additional discovery that, while pain is not lessened by realism, realism is nevertheless experienced as a (perhaps *the*) genuine value. Improving a work situation must begin with the actual facts of the workplace. Daydreaming about what might be is simply choosing failure in the real world.

Power

The *role* of *power* in organizations—its *importance,* its *meaning,* and the manner of proper *expression*—is equally open to free choice and definition. Again here, and importantly so, the prevalent uses of "normalcy" and "need" are, strictly speaking, meaningless. This matter, because of its centrality, deserves separate elaboration. It will be discussed later in this chapter.

Aloneness

Awareness of freedom is a lonely matter. All aspects of the relationship between an individual ego and work are decisions or postures that must be taken (and exist with) an understanding and appropriation of the total independence, self-reliance, self-sufficiency implicit in our individual ability to think alone and for ourselves. The solitary and lonely transcendental ego can and must undertake the creation and emotional meaning of values, roles, and conceptions of reality. In simple words: a mature and authentic attitude toward work begins with an *authentic individual.* An authentic person is one who can be alone, individual, solitary, and free. That person is then ready to choose commitment to any world, including that of a workplace.

Risk

Disclosure of the structure of one's freedom points to the open and undetermined character of consciousness and life. That sense of openness is also the experience of futurizing time, that is, how we are drawn forward by our vision of how we want things to be. If we now combine the totally undetermined openness of futurizing time—which is the sense of philosophic freedom—with the finitude of social fact, especially impenetrable death, we legitimize *risk*. Risk-taking is a natural consequence of understanding freedom. Risking is as inevitable as freedom itself. Not-risking is itself a different sort of risk, but it is risking nevertheless.

The legitimacy of risk leads to: (a) avoidance of the stultifying and vacuous obsession with certainty and the corresponding compulsion for stagnation, and (b) encouragement of genuine change, growth, and progress. An individual seeking a useful career cannot grow without willing *risks* naturally and spontaneously. Risking is the experience of a self with a future and of a self that is alive and thus in charge of itself. There is joy in risking as there is joy in being free—really free.

Becoming Practical

If the decision is made to get the most out of the possibilities afforded to us by the social institution of work, and given the realities of an individual's *social* and *individual* situation, *then,* and only then, can practical suggestions follow. Here, finally, is where coaching or development begins. If the intuitive decision to make a commitment to an organization or work has been taken—that is, the choice is made to utilize the institution of work for achieving life's highest meanings—then devices can and will be found to bring about its optimum values.

In sum, if a person fails at work, it is the decision to fail that is at the root of the matter. Once a real decision to succeed has been made—and the full, multilevel structure of that free personal decision must be understood in a philosophical and not in a common sense manner—then the work and organization will automatically succeed. Part of the reason for its success will be a redefinition of success itself.

POWER AND PHILOSOPHY

Finally we turn to the relevance of philosophic insight, especially the analysis of freedom, to the meaning of power in our lives, in and out of work. This takes the form of several principles.

1. *With regard to all aspects of power, the meaning of "normal" does not exist.* That is to say, whatever is averred about the nature and function of feelings about power cannot—in a real and absolute sense—be termed either normal or abnormal, right or wrong, good or bad, desirable or undesirable.

2. *More specifically, power is not a "need" in the sense of being a final fact in the definition of human existence.* Standards of the use of power are values—which means free definitions of our nature—not facts, and include an element of freedom. Power as need is equally a value and not a fact, and

also includes an important element of freedom. Admittedly, these elements of freedom occur at a very deep level and their resolution involves the constitution of our humanity itself. Our freedom to define who we are does not mean we can change our biology, psychology, or anthropology. It does mean that we are free to take attitudes toward our biology and psychology and to pass judgment on their relative meaning and importance. The use of this freedom is the philosophical foundation and possibility for the transformation of culture throughout the ages of history.

3. *There are two distinct meanings of power.* One meaning is that power is a specific physical act or behavior. It is in this sense primarily but not exclusively that I am using the word "power."

   The second meaning of power identifies power with the intentionality of consciousness, the meaning-building character of awareness. In this sense power is the *ability* and the *decision* to be physical, bodily, or somatic in one's being-in-the-world. This definition of power refers to the bodily being-in-the-world: it is the experience of being the body–subject and the body–object, adapting the language of French existentialist Maurice Merleau-Ponty. It is a metaphysical concept.

4. *Given the intentionality of consciousness and the identification of power with it, we have three options:*

   - We can be all directed to outcomes, that is, manifest technologists; we can be practical and view ourselves as instruments;

- We can be all spiritual, that is, seeing ourselves as inner souls mostly disconnected from the world of practical affairs; or

- We can be an integration, combination, or compromise of both.

We choose the general outlines of our manner of existence—of our style of life—among these three possibilities or alternatives. There are no absolute norms or standards. We create the absolute by choosing norms.

5. *Thus, the importance of power is a matter of free choice.* That is to say, it exists at the level at which self-deception or bad faith can no longer exist. In other words, we are free to accept, reject, or change the attitudes toward the meaning of power that we have been taught by society, parents, movies, clerics, or other authorities.

6. *Even the manner of the use of power over others is ultimately a matter of choice.* Here Freud's notion of the infant as polymorphous perverse is of central importance. Even though the expression of power may result in actual practice from biological, psychological, and environmental factors, the ultimate philosophical truth remains that these modes of being are values and that these values, in the last analysis, are chosen by each of us. We tend to speak of these matters as cultural rather than individual affairs. For example, with respect to all practices in the use of power, including abuses, the ego is capable of three attitudes: (a) adjust, (b) ignore, or (c) change. In cases of problems in using power,

and the awareness of our freedom, we are confronted, not with the true impossibility of change or adaptation, but rather with a lack of will, motivation, interest, or diminished access to the freedom that is at the heart of every one of us.

7. *The organizational and psychological realities and facts surrounding the use of power—especially if we use power in the narrow sense—lend themselves to a variety of uses, embodiments, value-actualizations, modes of being-in-the-world.* Each of these involves the choice of power. Following are a few of these possible alternatives.

- *Power as pure desire to control others.* The pleasure of dominance, being right, or not being controlled.

- *Power as aesthetic sophistication.* I am referring here to a sentimental type of romantic heroism. In fact, it is not only power that can be used aesthetically. Any bodily function, such as our sexuality, can be used as a foundation that is decorated with aesthetic values. A more common illustration of this possibility is eating. We can eat to survive, but we can also eat with aesthetic, ethical, and other value superimpositions: for example, banquets, celebrations, dinners for special occasions.

- *Power as a mode of religious depth, passion, and expression.* Power here takes the form of surrender, of giving up power. I am referring here to some Oriental practices, especially as found in the Mahasukha doctrine of Mahayana Buddhism.

- *Power as an expression of love or connection or contribution.* This may mean the sharing of power in the I-Thou sense of Buber.

- *Power as hidden agenda.* Power can also be used as a basis upon which an individual superimposes aggressive, hostile, sadistic, and masochistic tendencies and behavior. This becomes a "hidden agenda."

- *Power as security.* Power can also be the core, which ties together many other aspects of life, of the idea of security for a home and a family, a tradition, even a dynasty. Here the emphasis of the choice lies on the idea of security and the idea of a place and a group of people that one can call "mine."

- *Power as instrument.* In addition to the various definitions of power, we must of course mention its exclusive use for production, for getting things done, for willing institutions into being.

Again, it is, strictly speaking, incorrect to say that we have a "need" for any of these modes of self-expression—if we define ourselves not as a biological entity but as a pure consciousness in need of intentionally, freely constituting organizations, giving meaning to objects, and making commitments to lifestyles or self-definitions. It is equally incorrect to say that any of these expressions are either "normal" or "abnormal."

What is correct is to say that these forms of expression and organization are possibilities and are values and as such are either chosen or rejected by our consciousness. Each makes possible certain satisfactions and makes impossible other satisfactions. Those are the facts about human existence. And these philosophical-anthropological facts are sensitive to both the freedom *and* the facts of human existence. We are free to opt for or against any of the above possibilities. It is of course true that an option for *A,* for example, may involve the option to repress or ignore or deny *B, D,* and so on.

POSTSCRIPT

The concept of freedom is not a unitary idea but a blend—one which, to use Wittgenstein's famous example, consists of family resemblances. The concept of freedom is like a rope, held firmly together by many interweaving and overlapping strands without any single fiber running continuously throughout. These fibers are called "will," "consciousness," "ego," "self," "time," "spontaneity," "passivity," "autonomy," "self-determination," "action," "commitment," "engagement," "detachment," "distancing," and on and on.

Above all, in a philosophy of freedom there always exists the danger that the ideas of realistic *limits* and of *instinctual behavior* have not been adequately emphasized. Stress on free will can misguide one into thinking that this philosophy is relativistic, permissive, libertarian, and in general irresponsible, as well as super-rationalistic in the sense that our conscious and deliberate will controls all life. These misconceptions—especially the latter—must be rectified.

A manager in one of my philosophy in business workshops told me that a twenty-five-year-old employee (who had learned a lot about participation and empowerment) said to her, "I want to make certain financial decisions on my own." When the manager, after some uncertain discussion, refused, the employee rejoined, "Drop your participation and empowerment talk; it is doing you no good."

The employee misinterprets deep freedom to be a device for manipulating her boss to agree with her. Her boss, in turn, misinterprets philosophy to mean that she must ask the employee for permission to hold her own values and self-concepts. Both are in error.

The manager must substantiate the values she has chosen and recognize the total *freedom* and potential she possesses to implement them. She must also understand the final *limits* that society and a set of employees impose on her. Her *response* to these limits is free, but the inevitable consequences of her postures are *part* of that freedom. The structure of freedom itself discloses intrinsic limits: accountability and strict consequences are part of freedom.

Similarly, the employee must recognize her freedom to choose her value system; she must be aware of all the consequences of these choices. Moreover, she must recognize that her manager, who likewise is a separate and free individual, represents an ultimate limit to her. And the employee must choose—with her freedom to define who she is and what the world is—whether to perceive her manager as a projection or an extension of herself or whether to see her as a real and authentic human being in her own right. If the employee opts for the real-and-authentic view, the manager's individuality and freedom become the true and freely accepted limits to the employee's individuality and freedom. We must not forget, however, that (because of the intentionality of consciousness, the meaning-ascription power of awareness) the world tends to mirror the self. The employee's inability to perceive the limiting individuality and freedom of her boss shows that she cannot perceive these qualities in herself. Accusing the manager of not "giving her freedom" means the employee has not claimed freedom for herself.

In general, deep freedom does not mean omnipotence but rather withdrawal into the "nothingness" of consciousness—the "empty space" of awareness. In that nothingness the individual faces the infinite freedom to adopt definitions of self, organizations of experience such as a workplace, and attitudes toward social facts. While we are not free to change the *objects* of consciousness into something that they are not, we are free to use the laws of nature for control and technological rearrangement of objects.

In sum, understanding freedom means nothing without understanding responsibility and accountability. Responsibility means that every apparently minor choice is really a choice of grave and serious consequences, since each choice implies a complete definition of our nature and our world. Responsibility is the fact that each of us is free; accountability is the individual act of accepting and choosing that fact. Furthermore, responsibility as an aspect of freedom is also the understanding that one of our earliest and most primitive choices is to recognize the real limits to our existence. If we choose our limits, then we connect with the world and are thereby healthy. If we deny them, then we sever ourselves from the world and are therefore sick.

Even being free is itself a limit to human existence.

Part IV

IMPLICATIONS

L ACED THROUGHOUT this book is the idea that existential guilt is guilt about unfulfilled potential, about self-betrayal and anger at one's weakness. Neurotic guilt has two layers: the denial of the existence of existential guilt altogether, and the internalization of external and essentially irrelevant rules and values.

This insight is like a laser beam into one of the most pressing questions of organizational life: "Can I be myself and still be successful?" For most of us, the answer is "maybe" at best, and if you look at our actions, the answer is "no." We believe that the workplace is someplace where we cannot be ourselves. We reserve nights and weekends to be ourselves and believe that our place of employment is reserved for a narrower version of who we are—that's why we call it "work."

That this is true is not so hard to understand. When we organize ourselves, we give emphasis to roles, and to training, coaching, and osmosis to prescribe the kind of behavior expected of a supervisor, a leader, a team member, an executive, and anyone else who is in the neighborhood. We constantly evaluate people against some model of what we think is effective. Our strategy to help people be productive and useful is to make it as clear as possible what is expected of them and how they can manage themselves to meet those expectations.

THE PRESCRIPTION BECOMES THE POINT

The prescription process starts in the very beginning, when new employees join the organization. We design induction processes to let them know what is expected of them, the nature of the existing culture, and how to fit into it. We assign new people mentors to coach them into meeting management expectations. I have never run across any organization that greets new people by saying, "We are here to support you in becoming more of who you are, to caution you about the costs of betraying yourself, and to help you accept your weaknesses, for they are what make you human and unique."

In addition to prescribed behaviors and the pressure to fit in, workplaces have become explicit about inculcating values into their people. We have values statements, attribute statements, aspiration statements—all emanating from the top, laminated for all to read, and programmed into existence. We think the way to bring people together and get coordinated, focused performance is to all read from the same page and subscribe to the same prescribed values.

With all this in mind, as mentioned earlier, organizations are a training ground for neurotic guilt. They are exactly about internalizing external rules and values. If we believe that individuals are not capable of using their freedom and being accountable, this strategy of pre-scription, training, and assessment makes great sense. In addition, by the time we enter the workplace, we are so conditioned to meet the expectations of our leaders and teachers that if we do not receive prescriptions and values from others, we are vaguely disappointed.

The result is that it all becomes self-fulfilling. The more of them-selves we ask people to leave at the door, the less of themselves they become and the more prescriptions they require.

REALIZING THE BENEFITS
OF GUILT

What is interesting about the philosophic insight is that it proposes that we are going to feel guilty, no matter what. It is a feature, if not a benefit, of being alive and human. So the questions become, "What kind of guilt do we choose for ourselves?" and "What do we believe best supports others?"

If we believe that an accountable culture comes from the expe-rience of freedom, we would look for ways to support people to be more of themselves. We would at a minimum stop digging the hole of neurotic guilt. This would require us to question our strategies of prescription, role definition, and the importance of leader expecta-tions. We would adopt strategies of invitation and consent. It would entail stronger listening, deeper and more personal dialogue, self-defined learning goals, a focus on strengths rather than deficiencies.

The specifics could take a hundred forms, but the simple ques-tion of how an institution confronts people with their freedom and asks them to bring all of themselves to work would form the basis of a new conversation. This would begin a shift toward a liberating experience of membership, rather than one based on constraint and conformity.

THE PROBLEM OF MEANING

The philosophic insight challenges us to be more fully human and requires us to more courageously confront the meaning of our existence. Organizations are the playing field where meaning is likely to be found. The challenge is to engage in this pursuit collectively rather than individually. Institutions are something more than collections of individual purposes. They force the question of what we want to create together, taking the focus off what I want to create individually. Collective purpose is what psychology has a hard time addressing.

In this individualistic culture, we have a difficult time thinking about the collective. We are actually afraid of it. We have created the negative imagery of communism and socialism to symbolize our fear of losing our individuality, of putting our love of the spirit of capitalism and individual freedom at risk. We fear group think and group pressure.

At the same time we have some appreciation for the idea of community. There is in each of us a longing to belong to something larger than ourselves, to come together in common purpose. A group or organization with a compelling purpose begins to answer our questions about purpose, meaning, destiny. In this way, we can think of institutions as well as individuals as being created in God's image. We can accept the existence of community destiny in modern times, or the spiritual pursuit of a lost tribe, or a "people" in ancient times. This kind of thinking—and the difficulty and resistance we experience when we engage in it—brings life to our institutions.

The need for larger and compelling purpose is especially needed in a materialistic culture where the dominant question is "What's in it for me?" This question signals the death of community and meaning. Every organization has the possibility of defining a meaning for itself that enlivens and animates a collective longing. To say that this organization is in business to make money, or to deliver a specific service, is too narrow to be sustaining.

What is key is the dialogue about purpose, rather than the expectation that there is a final answer. The engineer in us wants a specific answer that will last a lifetime, but this treats meaning as if it were a thing, an object. Meaning is found in the struggle with the question, in the dialogue with others, in facing the futility of trying to express in a phrase something that is larger than any of us and essentially un-nameable.

It also comes in facing and acknowledging the suffering and complexity of belonging to a community or an organization. In one sense, organizational meaning is experienced in exploring all the questions that this book raises for us. It recognizes that freedom and accountability are questions that we will never answer satisfactorily.

If we can tolerate questions of this nature, the character of our organizations will start to shift. Institutions will become places in which we expect to struggle with life's deeper questions and we will discover that we can delve deeply and not only survive, but also get work done. It will give an importance to our workplaces and in fact raise our expectations of what they can become. It is at this point that we will begin to believe that we can be ourselves and also be successful.

THE ENTREPRENEURIAL ACT OF CREATION

Existential philosophy assumes we are capable of the act of creation—that we have, whether we admit it or not, created the world in which we live, the workplace included. The possibility of creating our own world actually finds a friend in our organizational experience. The entrepreneurial archetype or instinct is a major contribution that organizations, especially businesses, make to the culture.

Capitalism's great strength is the opportunity to create an organization from nothing. It is a stunning form of societal freedom that we are right to defend. Every organization we belong to began as an idea in someone's mind, and they not only had the thought, but also the will and sense of their own freedom to bring it into being.

The paradox is that, once brought into existence, organizations tend to lose this fire. We have myths about maturing businesses: they have to oust the entrepreneur and bring in professionals. They should institute controls and become more predictable. As a result we take institutions that began as a freedom and turn them into fields of restraint and caution.

In addition to the entrepreneurial instinct, there is another force that works against the arthritic quality of our institutions, and that is the rapid changes in the economies of most western countries. Large stable organizations are now at risk. Secure jobs are disappearing in most sectors. Free agency is replacing long-term employment. When large systems grow and shrink more quickly than ever, it reinforces the call to constantly re-create our lives and our institutions.

Still, the insight that we are in fact creating our lives and our institutions runs up against our wish for safety. The fad and follower instinct among organizations is stunning, even in a time of rapid change. You hear all the time that every organization wants to be a leader, but you see that they are only willing to try what has been proven elsewhere first.

When we accept that we are constituting our world, we will be prepared to try those things that are unproven. We will remember the existence of free will and will power. We might expect and demand to provide the leadership that previously we sought in others. We will still experience anxiety and risk, but knowing they are inescapable makes them easier to endure. Or even better, we will see anxiety and risk as the catalysts that bring us to life again, and again.

If my freedom is a fact, and if I am accountable for what surrounds me, then what choice do I have but to move willingly into the fire of the marketplace? I find energy in creating organizations that are based on a philosophic, albeit somewhat tragic, sense of what it means to be a human being. And, with others in the same spot, we can create organizations that recognize and support our humanity rather than deny it.

Afterword:
Peroration and Reminiscence

Peter Koestenbaum

BERTRAND RUSSELL

Bertrand Russell, hero to many philosophers, starts his autobiography with these celebrated words: "Three passions, simple but overwhelmingly strong, have governed my life: The longing for love, the search for knowledge, and unbearable pity for the suffering of mankind."

I ask myself, what have been mine, and how are they reflected in this book? When I was very young, I began to feel what surely many others have too, namely that there must be more, much more, to life and to the world than appears just directly before our eyes—both inner and outer, subjective and objective. "More," "deeper," "profundity," "greatness," "transcending," "beyond"—these were the words of yearning. It was a romantic view of life, that the apotheosis, the final resolution, the answer, the meaning, the Holy Grail, was just around the corner—and that there was a way to get to it. Beethoven must have found something in his Fifth Symphony—or with his Fifth Symphony or through his Fifth Symphony—that still eluded me but that someone must know exists.

Perhaps it was a desire not ever to let go of life; maybe it was to capture beauty forever, to lock in the truth and never let it drift away. Possibly it was what Wordsworth called "Intimations of Immortality from Recollections of Early Childhood," the seed of a taste for immortality.

There is more than meets the eye. How can you find it? How can you claim it? And how can you perceive it? That was the role of the philosopher and that is what I wanted.

I started this pursuit with physics, because in the early days of the last century, under the spell of Albert Einstein and his enigmatic theory, that was the fruitful way to go—if you wanted to embrace the innards of the universe. I pursued that, but found only formulas and calculations, slide rules and narrow-minded competitiveness, not the deep home in the infinite universe for which I was yearning. Neither physics nor mathematics, in the university environment, seemed to satisfy this hunger for more of the world than the world would show.

I then turned to the arts, under the influence of the German nineteenth century philosopher Arthur Schopenhauer, whom I read at that time in Spanish, feeling that he was much neglected and much maligned, especially by my parents, who thought little of him. It was Immanuel Kant who was the important philosopher, they told me. Schopenhauer believed that music was the threshold to the Platonic Truth, to that presence that lay just to the other side of perception, somewhat along the lines of William Blake's, "If the doors of perception were cleansed, every thing would appear to man as it is, infinite." I started to play the piano and dreamed of becoming a composer, perhaps like Chopin or Liszt—dreams that were quickly dashed by lack of absolute pitch and, above all, lack of general talent in the first place.

But it was in philosophy that I found my home, for it appeared to me that the project of philosophy throughout its entire distinguished history was the devotion of human beings to find their true place, their authentic voice, their genuine land, their ultimate "comfort zone," where the underlying reality of this world, distant from common sense and the everyday, would be revealed. And one could live there, be there, exist there. And all "the slings and arrows of outrageous fortune" would be settled, would go away, and the bitter maturity that later the existentialists would demand of us would never have to be confronted. Camelot. Elysium. Peace of mind. Peace of soul. They would all be ours. What bliss!

The entry to philosophy became for me psychiatry, through the ground-breaking book by Rollo May, my eventual mentor, of whom I heard for the first time through a book review in a 1958 issue of *Time.* There his book *Existence,* destined to become a classic, was reviewed.

I bought it, never stopped reading it, and it changed my life!

Rollo May introduced me, almost unwittingly, to phenomenology, which thereafter became my philosophic specialty. Phenomenology is a remarkable movement. Philosophers are interested in how we can know the truth. This field is known as *epistemology* or the theory of knowledge. The simplest way is to avoid error, which Descartes already attempted in his *Discourse on Method*:

How to discern clear and distinct ideas, presences to the inner eye
that were beyond doubt, that which the method of universal doubt
could no longer dissolve with its corrosive acid of endless questioning. That which can no longer be doubted, that which is forever beyond doubt, Descartes termed the *indubitandum,* which is
simply Latin for "it can't be doubted." In the early 1960s I translated Edmund Husserl's analysis of Descartes' "phenomenology"
in the former's *Paris Lectures.* It turned out that I did this only to
discover that phenomenology would do a better job than Descartes
in finding that content in human experience that was truly given
and whose verisimilitude could under no circumstances be doubted.
That is where we must start; that is how philosophy becomes a science beyond science. Descartes built on these clear and distinct ideas
given in direct experience whose content was beyond doubting.
He built on it two ideas: the existence of God and the verisimilitude of the external world. But he stopped there.

The existentialists, using the enlarged method of phenomenology, went much further: they described what it means to exist
as a human being in the world; they described deep yearnings and
deep fears, profound feelings and long hopes. That was exciting!
It was something to which one could devote a life—because philosophy does not just clarify meaning and examine language, as
the professional philosopher would have it, but it makes discoveries about the real world, especially humans, just as does science.
But philosophy—through the method of phenomenology, the presuppositionless descriptions of the direct data of immediate experience—makes discoveries of a different nature, of much higher
caliber, of sublime value. Philosophy, by using the building blocks
of uninterpreted experience, can actually discover not only God,

and truth, but also values, meanings, transcendence, eternity, and purpose, and all of those metaphysical goodies from the cornucopia of romanticism that we always hoped for but that no rational and commonsensical person would ever dare to seriously expect.

However, phenomenology made possible the dream of a scientific philosophy. Examine experience as it is and not how you assess it, and you discover that you are a "being that is thrown into a world," and that this world is full of anxiety, and full of free will, and rich with guilt. And that these "boundary situations"—that you are condemned to be you and will never be someone else— are obvious to the eye that does not distort, that the artist tries to replicate by deforming interpreted reality in such a way that it will yield once more its originary and uninterpreted reality. And you discover that this new world is always bigger and more encompassing than any theory about the world. And that it is no more than a joke to invent things, like the computer, and then think that the inventor—we and our minds—can be understood in terms of one of the "minor" inventions in history. That's a bizarre inversion. We call it reductionism. And it leads to falsehood.

The human mind creates the computer. The computer does not create the mind. The computer is by definition always less than the mind. The computer can never take over the mind, for all that the computer does is still something that exists within the compass of the mind.

No matter how sharply and how extensively you look, you will never find yourself in your own field of vision as one more object that is looking at your field of vision. What a stunning surprise if you were to take a photo of a forest only to find that as you develop the film you see yourself standing in the forest taking a picture of the forest. Something is eerily wrong if that is what you find.

You also discover, for example, that time is not some absolute phenomenon but the background of all that you experience, a kind of matrix in which all your experience fits. And you begin to make sense of the concept of consciousness, that awareness precedes all things, and that this is obvious, although when you talk about it people look at you askance, barely holding back their contempt. You notice a radical difference between the death of someone in your field of consciousness and then the death of yourself as the end of this field of consciousness itself. And you recognize that the death of your own field of consciousness is but a phenomenon right inside this field of consciousness, which has not disappeared no matter how clearly you may think of its death. You begin to wonder what these insights tell you!

You achieve a clarity you never had before, and strange questions about the meaning of life, intimate relations with other people, God and eternity, the ground for ethical motivation, all those become simple and transparent. For you no longer distort reality through the Procrustean bed of language only to then wonder how to extricate yourself from the very conundrums into which you have convoluted your life with a self-created Gordian Knot. You now see what is—pristine, pure, unadulterated, simple, right there before you. All you need to do is to report it and find a language for it.

The collection of information about what it means to be human deriving from these phenomenological researches came to be called "existentialism," and then later, "existential psychiatry" or "philosophical anthropology," the philosophical theory of the person.

The result of this new lucidity is that you are now ready to make what people may perceive as wise and profound statements about human beings, about leadership, about religion, about mysticism, about space and time, about fear and hope, satisfaction and fulfillment, managing betrayal and defeat, facing death, summoning courage, making tough choices and living with the consequences. Suddenly you are a psychiatrist's psychiatrist, a theologian's theologian, a teacher's mentor, and your destiny and your obligation—your vocation, your calling—is now, like a carpet, clearly rolled out before you. It is a task oriented toward service, toward meeting the demands of your conscience, toward integrity, and toward authenticity. And you realize that you are not worthy of it.

And it is this kind of experience, which in one way or another comes to virtually everyone, that leads to what this book is all about. It leads to redefining the meaning of mental health, of the authentic life, and ultimately, of the nature of being a leader and of being in business in a new way.

This path has taken many years, more than a generation, but it has been single-minded, difficult, inevitable, with many ups and downs, but it now seems to be coming into its own not unexpected apotheosis.

WOLFGANG AMADEUS MOZART

This book was the idea of Peter Block, and it was he who executed it and made it into a living reality. Peter Block is a born therapist and a born philosopher. He has given voice to these and similar insights through his writings, beginning with the all-time classic

Flawless Consulting. That book melds philosophy, psychology, work, and business into a superior blend. It has given him a hearing paralleled by few. And it's all natural, unlearned, self-discovered, the work of genius.

He is a kind of Mozart of organization development. He confirms Plato's insight that we are born with philosophic knowledge and that learning is but remembering what we knew before we came into this world—an idea that, like a mountain that catches the first rays of the rising sun, has illuminated the very dawn of civilization.

He has been captivated by philosophy, filtered—distorted, some may say (but I hope not)--by the work that I have done over many years, work that attempted but to reflect what messages the world was sending my way and which my students helped me clarify, propagate, and remember.

Peter Block has done something more remarkable than anyone could ever ask or hope for. He has taken his version of these philosophic researches, these philosophic explorations and adventures, over many nations and over many years, and restated them mostly in his own terms. He has taken original manuscripts, has digested them with his own juices, and has assimilated them, saying, "This is what I, Peter Block, think." He in effect said to himself and of himself, "I am in business, Peter Koestenbaum was concerned with psychiatry. I am in the real world, Peter Koestenbaum was an academician. I am in the world of the here and now, Peter Koestenbaum is in the ethereal world." And Peter Block has now made one more redoubtable effort—which a person in my position can never either properly appreciate or repay—to render much of what at first sight may appear to be no more than pettifogging esoteric gobbledygook into what one hopes are intelligible profundities that make sense to his audience and his readers.

What I have attempted to do in some of my books over the decades, and what Peter Block has so graciously endeavored to restate, are years of results of phenomenological researches—presuppositionless descriptions of key zones of the human condition, descriptions that are like scientific discoveries about what it means to exist as a human being in the world—and discoveries about our existence that have dramatic implications for how we live, how we relate, how we value, how we fear, how we cope, and in the end, how we run organizations, survive in organizations, do business, earn a living, and structure the economy.

We survey the table of contents: he starts with *freedom*. One of the great discoveries of a philosophy of presuppositionlessness is the existence of *freedom* and *free will*. Free will is outside of the natural order. Free will is consciousness itself. Free will is the beginning. Free will exists at the source. Free will is inaccessible to itself. Free will cannot be explained in words, for words are things and actions and relations, and free will is before all actions, things, and relations. Free will is what makes all three possible. Free will is so important and so mysterious that we give it the name "God" and place it as far away from ourselves and our center as is humanly possible. In the beginning God freely created the heavens and the earth and then He created man and woman in His image of freedom. Free will resides at the foundation of the cosmos itself. What a transforming insight!

Free will is deeper than the self, more basic than the ego. We know it is there, we know it exists, we know it is us, we know it is at the roots of the prescientific universe, yet we have no idea what to say about it. Writing about it is but the invitation to get all of us to think about free will, to sense its influence, to feel its power, and to revere it enough to institutionalize it at the base of our democracy: the Declaration of Independence, which is both a statement and an act of freedom.

DANTE ALIGHIERI

Dante tells us that this is the inscription to Hell:

> I am the way into the city of woe.
> I am the way to a forsaken people.
> I am the way into eternal sorrow.
> Sacred justice moved my architect.
> I was raised here by divine omnipotence, primordial love
>   and ultimate intellect.
> Only those elements time cannot wear were made before
>   me, and beyond time I stand.
> Abandon all hope ye who enter here.

Free will leads to *anxiety*. That is part two of this book. Anxiety is not a feeling, not a disease, not something to get over. Anxiety is the discovery of the brittleness of the world, the contingency of our very existence, the appearance not of what is but of what is not, not of what might be but of what might not be. Above all, anxiety is discovered as the normal condition of human beings, the normal response of those who not only exist but who also think about existing, who not only are engaged in the world and what it wants but can also reflect on what this world is and wants. Anxiety understood is the beginning of an authentic life. Anxiety not understood is still living in the pre-birth state, the "prepredicative" state, as Sartre called it.

You become who you are meant to be the moment you have accepted anxiety as your brother, guilt as your sister, and received courage as your reward. Peter Block has told me many times that it was this point, the constructive uses of anxiety, as one of the Menninger brothers referred to it, that was the most important insight coming to him out of his long relationship with his philosophic conscience—the little voice that reminded him of his own bigger voice. Realizing that to say "I am anxious" is not to say I am afraid but that I look forward to something—as in "I have for a long time been anxious to get to know you"—transforms your life from a blade of grass to the trunk of an oak.

We don't say much about evil these days. If you want to truly condemn something you call it "sick," as if the latter were worse than evil. Yet it is only right that we reverse these attributions. We have lost the sense that evil is a reality and that a good life is the struggle against evil.

Not many writers write about evil. Evil exists, we are all capable of evil, we are likely to be the victims of evil. And anyone confronted with evil is also my responsibility. I cannot be absolved from that burden. The most powerful allusion to evil we find, in my experience, is when Francois Mauriac, the French writer and patron of Elie Wiesel, says of his book *Night,* which essentially won Wiesel the Nobel Peace Prize, that the ultimate tragedy is not the Holocaust but the death of God in the mind of a child who has just witnessed absolute evil.

Wiesel writes abut the gassing of his mother and his sister the first night in the concentration camp, and the blue smoke that comes out of the chimney in what is essentially a beautiful night and a beautiful sky, except that this smoke is his sister and his mother.

All these negativities, which some may find depressing but which in truth can be invigorating, make us serious about life, give us substance as human beings, and change our motives from fun to duty, from pleasure to honor, from greed to service. Being in touch with the negative factors of life gives us character and true values.

The purpose of philosophy, that which makes it transcend the ordinary and gives us more, something not achievable in any other way, is that philosophy can take all the negative energies of this world, all the sorrow Bertrand Russell brings out in his meaning-of-life statement, and turn it around into positive power. Not only can evil be translated into that which mobilizes the forces for good, but pain can be seen as the path to strength, and despair as the way to character.

The goal of life is to assuage suffering, to eradicate hunger, to eliminate destruction, to craft a technology that will wipe out indifference and contempt, that will cast aside bigotry and abuse. And that is the justification for not glossing over that which is hard, but rather facing it squarely and banding together for either its defeat or its integration. That is the breakthrough for which philosophy strives, that is the purgation of hell, if you wish to make sense of Dante.

Death has always been the ultimate limit against which life is lived and from which it draws its meaning. These are not common notions, for they are not based on our biological view of human beings but on the fact that the inner life, more than outer realities, determines the quality and the structure of all our answers to the questions of right and wrong, good and bad, meaning and insignificance, purpose and aimlessness that we could ever ask.

What differentiates this book from many others is the applications of philosophic insight to organizations, to business, and to the real world. Not to politics and utopias, but to the everyday concerns of our commercial existence. This is of course the new science, philosophy in business, the Leadership Diamond®. It is the systematic use of deep philosophic insight not only for philosophy and literature, the arts and theology, religions and psychiatry, but for the commercial part of our existence.

We are all in business, we spend most of our lives in business, we define what we do, whether it is medicine or education, accounting or computer science, as either a business or part of a business or requiring business expertise for doing it. We talk of organizations—whether they be cities and counties, nations or multinational corporations, nongovernmental organizations, or small entrepreneurial ventures—for that is where our energies lie. And our biggest task, beyond appreciating the new philosophy, the presuppositionless descriptions of human existence, the emotional characteristics that define our world, is the need to make it practical.

We need to make philosophy in business work. We need to see our organizations change and, yes, our profits rise. People need to feel that, as a result of philosophy-based intervention in their organizations, not only will they feel better, be happier, and get along better, but they will also do better in the hard side of business, the profit side, the stock side, the bottom-line arena.

Bringing together the philosophical and the commercial, the sacred and the profane, the ethereal and the mundane, the theoretical and the practical, that is the solution of the great paradox of life. We never want to be subject to Oscar Wilde's bitter indictment of the cynic, who "knows the price of everything and the value of nothing."

Philosophy is not soft. It is hard. It recognizes that life is hard. It acknowledges that you must be tough to meet life on its own terms. The role of philosophy in business and in public life is to support those who make the big decisions and hold the big accountabilities, those who require the big buttresses in managing the harshness of life—and the need they themselves have to be fortified for making the hard decisions—to defend their hard choices, and to assuage their consciences when, as in the case in the military, sending soldiers into battle.

I trust that Peter Block in his efforts with this book has been able to transmit the depth of philosophy, its integrity, its proud humanity, without crashing against the weaknesses and the foibles of just one individual philosopher. My hope is that he has managed to honor the discipline in spite of the other author.

Whether you see life through the lens of a Russell, a Mozart, or a Dante, it is their underlying philosophic strength that makes the beauty shine through.

THALES OF MILETUS

Aristotle wrote about Thales as the first philosopher and Thales became one of the "Seven Wise Men of Antiquity." Thales, as Aristotle tells it, was the first philosopher in business. As a meteorologist, Thales predicted, during a year his region suffered a severe drought, that the next year would bring plentiful rain. He had been ridiculed, as philosophers tend to be, that he lived in the clouds and therefore could not do business and make money. Piqued, he decided do to otherwise and prove his critics wrong. He contracted for all the olive presses for the next year. He rented them cheaply because the drought had also dried up the olive oil business. Next year, as he had predicted, the rains were plentiful and the olive crop abundant. In controlling the presses, he dominated the oil supply—and set the price. Having conquered the market, he made a fortune. (This is reminiscent of how the Rothschilds beat the London stock market by sending a courier pigeon from Waterloo to London announcing Napoleon's defeat and Wellington's victory.) Thales then remarked that philosophers can do good business if they so choose, but, as philosophers, they are not interested in such things.

What about the uses of philosophy in business and the Leadership Diamond®? What has been my experience in bringing into organizations what here is called existentialism and phenomenology to help people manage better the human conditions they find in their places of work? And how can one make a living at it?

I have felt, perhaps living under the spell of an illusion, that mostly I have received a heartening response to bringing philosophy into the real world. It began with psychotherapy and psychiatry. People found solace in being able to say that anxiety and depression, guilt and despair, abandonment and loss, painful as they were, contained in them an ingredient that brought real value. One reason was that these feelings were traced to their universal roots—an aspect of the human condition—and we were well-adapted to managing them. It meant therefore that in our despair we were normal. That changed expectations. That strengthened the soul. It also created a kind of family feeling among people, that we all shared a common fate.

In addition, deepening these emotions gave us what felt like answers: transformation, new strength, inner resources, self-respect, enhanced capacity for quality conversations and effective dialogues, reframing, better models, more freedom, and more. It gave us tools to turn around negatives to positives. It is the kind of thinking we find in Camus when he says that what does not kill him strengthens him. We find it even in Descartes when he writes that what he cannot doubt proves to him that it exists. Bad metamorphoses into good. Rather than pathology, you suffer from an overdose of normalcy.

By connecting these bleak emotions with theology, religion, mythology, and the arts, they became part of the distinguished history of humanity, elevating the soul—and not of illness and pathology requiring painful treatment and defeating hospitalization.

People in business—not all but many—responded likewise. They felt understood at a deeper level. They felt reassured on a more profound plane. It was a way for them to deal with dissatisfactions in an ennobling way, distress to which they otherwise would respond only with superficial anodynes.

Job satisfaction is decreasing, stress is growing, and all try to manage this as best they can. The differentiators, when we use philosophy, become character and maturity. These are matters different from best practices, team building, dialogue and communication, productivity, and sales-closing skills. But if you are mature and a person of solid character, the skills can be learned and they are grounded and convincing. In short, you have credibility. If, however, you lack maturity and character, then the best skills are phony, have no buttresses, and are but smoke and mirrors. And you will be found out.

Character and maturity are connected with such leadership virtues as being self-starters, getting the larger picture, and taking the initiative. Also, character and maturity support such major leadership traits as taking care of your own feelings, overcoming self-pity, taking personal charge for initiating the spirit of co-creation, helping others manage their alienation, being ethical, keeping promises, and being of service. Character and maturity have to do with understanding free will and responsibility, freedom and accountability.

Maturity and character precipitate the sudden realization that life cannot be lived without courage, that pride, duty, obligation, and honor do matter. When all is said and done, we feel good, we feel special, about people of integrity, of substance, in short, of character and maturity.

Obviously these are goals and not achievements, and no one has the right to be smug. Arrogance immediately disqualifies a person from membership in the authenticity club.

Building maturity and character takes care of many otherwise intractable issues in and attitudes toward work and organizations. You take care of your own happiness, your own quest for security, your own thrust toward meaning and your own education. Such a commitment is a shift in who you are—a person who feels good, sound, healthy, invigorated, and who has answers and solutions. In a word, character and maturity are the secret ingredients in self-reliance and above all in authentic hope.

The future is ours. We can handle what comes. We need love, and we will structure a life for ourselves that gets us there: love and family, friends, support, and community—all the things many of us lack in today's world of global alienation, family dismemberment, and community disintegration. Hope is not given to us. We find it ourselves. We earn it.

RECOLLECTION AND APPRECIATION

At Ford, Nancy Badore got me started. My Ford friend Bob Mueller had introduced us and she took a risk with me. She was organizing the ambitious Ford Senior Executive Program (SEP). The program, as I recall it, was initiated in the mid-1980s and it became a watershed event in the American OD, HR, and leadership development communities. It received a terrific write-up in *Newsweek*. The first question I was asked at one of our early design meetings, by a senior member of the team, was "What would a philosopher talk about?" My naïve answer was, "Death." The startled responses I got were something like, "This is far out!" "We don't need that!" "I can't see the point!" "What are you talking about?" "You can't be serious!" and other reassuring demonstrations of support. Bob Kramer, Nancy's eventual boss, backed me up and became a stalwart supporter of this philosophic work. Gradually, we hammered out a major program, covering two thousand managers for a period of two years.

Bob Kramer used to say that one-third of the participants thought my day on philosophy in business was terrific, the idea of describing the anxiety of a self-starter and the need for courage offered precisely the right things that Ford managers needed to hear, and that the chairman, Donald Petersen, had quoted me in one of his speeches. Bob said that another third were appalled at the bad taste of Ford bringing in something as irrelevant as soft stuff in a hard industry. And the last third were on the fence, interested, quizzical, with a wait-and-see attitude.

The third that liked what I had to say set up a series of smaller seminars, with about a dozen participants for each two-day period, which were great experiences for me and went on for several years. None of this would have happened without the conviction of the value of philosophy displayed by Al Solvay, who made this into a career. I made good friends and developed admiration and affection for many of the participants.

Among the students I had whom I remember was Dennis Green, who became a very special friend and moved on to Citicorp and Citibank, NA, as their chief auditor, a daunting position he filled with great distinction. His boss at Ford had told me that his was the best organization that he knew at Ford. He was very proud of what Dennis had achieved.

I followed Dennis from Ford to Citibank, NA. We worked assiduously at creating a team that was genuinely diverse and showed character and maturity. My job was to help the team members to deal with their team issues, that is, each other, and with Dennis's demands on the team. They needed to learn to understand and appreciate their boss—a tough but high-quality leader, a significant model of how to survive and how to make a genuine contribution in a monstrously large and complex company.

Alexander Trotman was in the Ford SEP program. He become one of the most successful chairmen Ford ever had. When he retired he left the company with the largest profits of any U.S. business.

I worked closely at one time with Bob Transu, who was the person Trotman picked to develop his strategic plan, Ford 2000, with which he elevated Ford to a new height of prominence.

I worked with a similar group at Ciba-Geigy, the Swiss pharmaceutical company. The president, Heini Lippuner, heard me give a lecture on philosophy in business in Canada and decided this kind of philosophical leadership support is was what he wanted for his five hundred top people. I got to know Switzerland and to love it, and I met the chairman, a true gentleman, Dr. Alexander Krauer. He was the prototype of the warm-hearted intellectual, superb at strategy and at simplifying chaotic leadership issues. I have always admired people who could think clearly about strategy, and he was for a long time my model. So were Trotman and his CFO, John Devine, whose strategic thinking capabilities would easily have elevated him to any top position he wanted. After Trotman retired from Ford, John Devine became the CFO of GM. I enjoyed many strong and deep strategically oriented conversations with him. I always felt that strategy was as important as ethics, and that, whereas ethics was based on cultivating the heart, strategy was based on cultivating the mind. And it was the philosopher, with a theological and therapeutic orientation, who was reasonably well-equipped to support people in both their heart and head concerns and their business-related concerns, such as making courageous decisions and thinking clearly into the future.

EDS was a very important experience for me. At Davos I met Lester Alberthal, who had just recently become chairman, CEO, and president of Electronic Data Systems. He and his wife came to my lectures at the World Economic Forum, where I had been featured, not by Ford, but more by accident, as "Ford's Corporate Philosopher." Alberthal told me—something I have never forgotten—that EDS became great because of its values, and he wanted me to help him underscore the true human values in how EDS was to be run. I have felt the power of his friendship ever since.

I became the thinker and teacher in an ambitious program that involved all the top three or four layers of this company's management, befriending many. Those who stand out are Dean Linderman, the man in charge of leadership at EDS, and Marsha Clark, the best woman in the company, who worked with him in human resources. Also Jeff Heller, a great guy with a big heart, who became president and then vice chairman. The Global Operations Council ran the company, and I was privileged to be a member, non-voting to be sure, but present for all the functions, meetings, and reports, as a kind of philosopher in residence. My responsibility, and an opportunity it was, for the full life of this team, was to be as supportive as I could in deepening and universalizing the discussions that occurred, to reframe what people said, in short, to find ways to deal with character and maturity concerns at a time when the company was bending under severe stresses.

I remember meeting an executive in Sweden, Bernt Gröön. Arne Johansson introduced us. Arne had come with us to Greece with a seminar in Philosophy in Business organized by Göran Wiklund to bring practical philosophy to life. Göran had great imagination. Bernt Gröön, who eventually became the managing director of all of the individual Swedish savings banks (there were over one hundred) lumped into one national organization, liked the humanizing character of this philosophic approach to management. He brought in his people by the busload to go through a one-day program that he, his HR manager, who was Arne Johansson, and I offered to the total organization. This went on for weeks. (It turned

out that we met in a school that had been used illicitly for training Algerian terrorists.) This philosophy became the substratum
for managing, setting strategy, marketing, and advertising in this
savings bank organization. Bernt had a sense for the grand gesture.
While we were in Växjö (then the sister city of Minneapolis) for
six weeks working in his organization, my wife, while jogging
around the scenic lake near that city in south central Sweden, was
frightened by a man who leaped from the bushes attempting to
grab her. Nothing beyond the fright happened, because she ran
away. The man was later arrested. Appalled at the incident, Bernt
Gröön said something to her I have not forgotten: "In the name
of the Swedish people, I apologize to you!"

My friends in Latin America, for whom I have a very special
affinity, given the fact that I was raised as a young man in Venezuela,
have expressed a deep kinship with this philosophical approach to
business. It fits well into the culture. We have worked together for
years. In Mexico, Tony Perez tells me that his operation achieved
market dominance with the help of this philosophic approach to
leadership. And Chu Tung in Saõ Paulo tells me that his organization went in growth from last to first—in this multibillion dollar multinational corporation—due to the systematic application
of philosophy in business. Behind it all was Micael Cimet, in charge
of the total Latin American operation, who is a perfect blend of philosophy and business—a tough businessman struggling with philosophic visionary and ethical problems, and a deep philosopher
committed to grow a highly competitive business 50 percent a year.
Our only disagreement is who taught more to whom, I to him or
he to me. I think the latter.

There always have been people who are offended by this "divagation into irrelevance." But why should one not expect that? And why not say these people as well have a major and significant point, one that needs all the attention in the world. They speak for that side of me to which I am too afraid to give a voice. Could that be?

One would say, "I am a skeptic, but I am willing to listen." Another would say, "If we get into this psychobabble, I'll go out and have a smoke!" I see very little of this today. I saw a lot twenty years ago. Having been in over forty countries, I very much feel that there is a resonance to the deepening of the experience of work, and to seeing the urgency, even emergency, of coming to terms with the stuck points of life, many of which occur at work or in connection with work—and at every level of the organization.

What Nancy Badore accomplished at Ford, Rose Fass did at Xerox, Jean Settlemyre did at American Medical International (AMI), and Marsha Clark did at EDS. I worked with them all. All four were geniuses. All four were prepared to risk. They had courage and a sense of the future. All four were powerful women and remained very feminine. All four also had to face bitter disappointments. And all four had to deal with the intriguing phenomenon that the drivers behind these innovative efforts to pay serious attention to people were women, women in what clearly at that time were men's organizations: Ford, Xerox, AMI, and EDS. They were suffragettes, like Susan B. Anthony, broadening the range of the human that was expressed and utilized in the workplace of some of America's most powerful organizations. Their jobs were not easy. Their paths were not without land mines. They were independent, heroic, determined, good businesspeople, with heart.

Kelly Executive Partners, part of Indiana University's School of Business, and Pepperdine's School of Business, and their MSOD program, have demonstrated a special commitment to the importance of philosophy in business by making significant efforts to insert it into their programs.

Individuals have made careers for themselves in this relatively new profession of applying philosophy to pragmatic everyday business undertakings. Ahmed and Laurie Yehia became interested in the application of philosophy to business when I was the executive coach for Ahmed, then vice president of marketing and of human resources at American Medical International in Beverly Hills. The philosophic approach became their life passion, and they set up Quantum Leadership Solutions to make a significant consulting business out of this philosophy. They have done very well over the years, and Laurie is now operating the Philosophy-in-Business website (www.PiB.net). In partnership with Tom Weary, who has a bachelor's degree from Harvard in philosophy and is a Certified Financial Analyst (having managed multibillion dollar assets), we have set up an investment fund, Diamond Portfolio Advisors (named after the Philosophy in Business trademark Leadership Diamond®). Companies are selected first on standard criteria and then, in a second round, on Leadership Diamond criteria. As of December 2000, not much time to go on, to be sure, this fund had done exceptionally well. The fund added value to the investments by consistently outperforming the market, during a difficult time, by an average of 14 percent. It does not even matter whether the results are guaranteed. What matters is that people are seriously using the philosophic approach to leadership to gain investment advantage. The principle is one thing, the execution takes trial and error.

Another example is Rolf Falkenberg, a Swedish nobleman who was managing director of Vattenfall Engineering, the energy company of Sweden, in charge of such matters as atomic energy, building tunnels and dams, railroads and highways. He moved on to become president of a U.S. high-tech consortium, GSE Systems. When he retired from that position, he fulfilled a ten-year-old dream and promise to set up an institute in Sweden, which he decided to call the Koestenbaum Institute, to bring philosophy in business to the European Community.

Two days after the 2000 presidential elections, when the results were as yet uncertain, I had a lecture, together with Colin Powell, in Milwaukee. He said to me, before he started, that he was curious what a philosopher's view of leadership would be. My answer was from the heart, for I trusted him: "I shall listen closely to what you say in your hour-and-a-half to this audience (of about three hundred civic and business leaders). I will then tell them, when it is the turn for my ninety minutes, what I believe are the fundamental choices that you have made over your lifetime—the deep decisions about who you are as a person and what your fundamental values are, and your beliefs—that brought you to where you are today.

"And I will continue by pointing out what the commitments are that you are making right now about who you are and how you relate and what you say in order to maintain yourself in the position that you now hold in your own eyes and in the eyes of the world. And then I will challenge the audience to ask themselves, what have been theirs?

"And I will add, 'How can meeting you teach them what new choices, new decisions, and new acts of courage—not about trivia, but about fundamental matters—they are ready to make? And what will be the impact on them, their families, and their organizations?'"

"That sounds very interesting," said the general. "I would like to learn more." And he went to the podium to give his speech. He asked me to send him a summary of my later comments, which I did. It was a good day.

This is a collage of some of my recollections of the adventures of bringing philosophy to business, of which Peter Block was the initial impetus. I left out important friends, which I regret, nor can I vouch, the best intentions to the contrary notwithstanding, for total accuracy in all the details.

A Short Glossary

This glossary shows how some words are used in this book. It is not meant to be a standard dictionary. Instead, its brief definitions and essays by Peter Koestenbaum are intended to expand our understanding of the nuances of key concepts in the book and illustrate the relationships among them.

Accountability.   In this book, we make a distinction among three terms: freedom (which we use here as the equivalent of free will, although this may not be the convention), responsibility, and accountability.

Freedom and *free will* refer to "the seat of the soul" from where your decisions come. It is the mysterious and awesome zone of your free choice. *Responsibility* refers to the consequences that follow in the world as a result of free acts, such as having children. And *accountability* is how society—small and large—will make consequences happen because of free choices that people have made, such as going to jail for insider trading.

Peter Block defines *maturity* as "choosing accountability." You want to be held accountable. It gives you dignity.

Empirical Ego. The *transcendental* ego is the pure consciousness that we are. Consciousness is intentional, which means it directs itself toward "objects"—mental, emotional, or physical. Perhaps the most interesting object toward which consciousness faces is the ego, the self, the person, the individual—in particular, the ego that I am. That ego is the *empirical* ego. We are thus two egos: transcendental and empirical. It is therefore not correct to say that we are an ego who is conscious. Instead, we are the consciousness of an ego. We know little about that consciousness. We know a lot more about the ego that is brought into awareness by consciousness, like a light shining on it. But it is this latter consciousness, the consciousness of an ego, where we find all the answers to the eternal questions.

Existence. *Freedom and Accountability at Work* deals with the so-called existential themes of two of my older and out-of-print books: *The Vitality of Death* (Greenwood Publishing, 1971) and *The New Image of the Person* (Greenwood Press, 1978). They emphasize the isolation of the individual in an ambiguous world and the task to find meaning, carve out a living, and do one's ethical best. All of this is to occur in a world that is sometimes friendly, sometimes hostile, sometimes congenial, and sometimes alienated from the beings that we find ourselves to be. I exist as a freedom, as an individual, as a social being, as a dying being, as a fearful being, as a powerful being, as a nobody, and so forth.

Existence refers to the concrete sense of the here and now where I live and where I am who I am. I did not choose how and where I was to be born. I find myself "thrown" in the world, and nevertheless I am on my own and I am responsible.

These are the connotations of *existence*.

Existentialism.   The presuppositionless description (that is, using *phenomenology*, q.v.) of what it means to exist as a human being in the world. The central feature is a radical conception of free will and responsibility as the foundation of the human enterprise. Additional important descriptions surrounding freedom are of anxiety and guilt. *Existentialism* was a dominant philosophic and literary movement in the middle of the twentieth century, resting heavily on the human catastrophe of World War II. Existentialism was the philosophic response to the eruption, at that time, of total human degradation—maintaining human values in the face of a return to the jungle and worse.

The basic themes undergirding *Freedom and Accountability at Work* bring to today's world the topics that began to become entrenched in the general culture in the last half of the last century. They are coming to fruition in organizations and in business facing the current economic struggle because many of the more traditional techniques for managing organizations are no longer serviceable.

Many of the emotions and ideas people try to understand these days have their origin in the history of existential philosophy, that is, understanding the human condition more in terms of character and maturity than in terms of security and happiness. Courage is more important than fun, and responsibility is more important than self-indulgence.

Experience. Philosophers use the word *experience* in unusual ways. We say, "I experience a pain" and "This applicant does not have enough sales experience." These uses have to do with feeling something and with having done one particular thing or engaged in one particular behavior over a long period of time. But for philosophers, *experience* is anything that appears to consciousness, together with consciousness itself as well. Whatever I sense, of external or internal origin, whatever comes to awareness, that is *experience*. It is one of those general or ubiquitous words that are used by minds who like to think in terms of vast generalities, such as space-time, being, cosmos, everything, the universe, and the like. The philosophical use of the word *experience* includes the subjective realm more than do these other, alternative words. People can find these discussions profound, meaningful, deep, solving all the questions of life—or they can be totally overwhelmed, dumbfounded, nonplused, and discombobulated by such convoluted esoterica.

In short, *experience* is anything of which you are conscious. And it is not a verb but a noun. You are aware of *experience*. The world is an *experience*. The human condition is a way of facing the experience of "being" itself, of all there is, of the total world as it presents itself to you—that is *experience*.

Free Will. A powerful experience in the region of the subject, as opposed to the realm of objects. It is foundational to human life, but at the same time it is most difficult to access directly, experientially, and conceptually.

But we know *free will* is there. We make free choices daily, and we know they are free because they feel free. And there is no other type of evidence for which to search. If we say *free will* is inconsistent with the language that we use, then we'd better repair the language! The experience of *free will* itself is sacrosanct.

Because *free will* lies so deep in the soul and is intimately connected with the eye that sees, and not with the world that is seen, it is easy to dismiss *free will* as nothing, when in many critical ways it could be argued that it is really everything.

We know what *free will* is in the same way that we know about space and time and awareness. They are there. They are everywhere. And words do little to clarify this mysterious, obvious, and all-encompassing presence. You describe these wonders to someone, who then says, "I really don't know what you are talking about or what you are trying to say!" You only are trying diligently to paint a different picture in the mind of this individual. But you know that you are talking to a stone, for all this person says is, "You are making sounds, but you are saying nothing at all!" The Bible calls this sort of person a Philistine.

Because these locations of *free will* in the soul are so deeply intertwined with what we call ourselves, just plain being me, they cannot be made into things and objects. We tend to think that the world is made up only of objects; therefore analyses of subjectivity are particularly difficult.

Once we acknowledge the reality of the inward realm and how it radiates out to the entire world, we have discovered new territory. And we are now ready to embark on a fresh, personal, and subjective way of understanding who we are!

Phenomenology. The presuppositionless descriptions of anything, most commonly of human states. The emphasis is on *presuppositionless*. A major preoccupation of philosophers has been how to distinguish truth from error. Descartes' answer—which also became that of *phenomenology* as a movement in the field of philosophy (known as the theory of knowledge or epistemology)—is essentially intuitive. With your inner eye, look for clear and distinct ideas. The idea could be a mathematical sum, such as $5 + 7 = 12$, an emotion, such as "since you have been in love, your mind has become clouded," a generalization, such as "workers today are increasingly alienated from their jobs," and so forth.

That is essentially the best one can do. Looking for clarity and distinctness is a mental exercise and a mental experiment. Mathematics is reliable ultimately because on close intuitive inspection one cannot think of its propositions as otherwise. The scientific method makes sense because, as you analyze how it is applied, intuitively you can't find flaws in it. Finally, if you doubt to the maximum of your capacity and you find it impossible to doubt any further, then you have found the truth. That is behind Descartes' famous "I think, therefore I am," which should really read, "I doubt, therefore I am."

It may be as Churchill said of democracy, that this solution may not be good, but it's the best we have. What is freedom? What is anxiety? What is beauty? What is anger? What is silence? What is space? What is time? What is consciousness? Who is God? What happens when you encounter another human being? These are all tough questions. We can't live without answering them. What's deep is to develop the capacity to describe the questions and their answers in such detail—as only the artist in you can—that the phenomenon blossoms fully right before your very eyes. In other words, one way to answer these questions is to explore in microscopic detail the totality of events that present themselves to the mind when it is engaged in such a complex and yet basic exercise as struggling with questions such as the nature of guilt. But to examine these subjective events without using such mental models as "things," "concepts," "useful," "important," "mine," "yours," "absolute," "the will of God," "natural law," "theory," "science," and so forth, but rather to look at the world as a newborn child, with curiosity, wonder, but no preconceptions—that is to see the truth. It is reminiscent of Keats' "I am certain of nothing but the holiness of the Heart's affection and the truth of the imagination."

Modern art can be seen as an attempt to depict this "buzzing and booming confusion" (William James' phrase) that meets the eye before we have given an interpretation to the raw data confronting us. *Phenomenology* is a rich experiential entry into the unexplored world of what Sartre called "the pre-predicative experience"—what is there, before us, before we say anything about anything, the world before we have any language, any theories, before we interpret what it all might mean and be. Assessments are taught. Data, as the Latin suggests, are simply given. They contain the truth, for they are the foundation.

The given encases the truth. The interpreted is subject to error. That's the principle. That is the way back to the truth. And when it comes to understanding people in business and organizations, then attaining access to presuppositionless descriptions may well be the most important groundbreaking that you will ever do.

Reduction.   This is one of those terms that also refers to consciousness, specifically what we call "pure consciousness" or "consciousness without an object." We think of objects without necessarily thinking that they are at "the other end," as it were, of intentional or directional consciousness. In the same way, we can think of consciousness without thinking that it has an object attached to it.

Reduction is like reverse engineering. It is to step back and reflect on the act of reflection itself. It is this step to a new and higher level of consciousness, reflecting on thinking, that brings thinking itself or consciousness proper into the limelight. The realm of consciousness, and not the realm of objects, is the region of experience or of being wherein reside the important virtues of the authentic life: free will, freedom, responsibility, archetypal decisions, anxiety, conscience, guilt, the possibility of ethics, dignity, self-esteem, justice, equality, and so forth. *Reduction* simply means that we step back from the object. And what this "unscrolling" of the perceptual act that precedes the object reveals or uncovers is consciousness itself—pure awareness.

Our culture does not navigate these regions frequently, certainly not in mainstream activities. But this arena is as much a part of reality and life as is the technological and scientific side. And by not paying full attention to both sides of being, we will repeatedly fall into problems and stuck points that only a transformation in orientation can resolve. And that is why philosophy is so important.

Transcendental Realm.   This is the Western word for what in the East, and in mysticism in general, would be called "consciousness without an object." For all intents and purposes, *transcendental realm* is equivalent to consciousness. What we must be aware of, as Peter Block says in his Introduction, is that we can use the eye as metaphor for our general so-called being-in-the-world, how we exist in our so-called lifeworld. The act of vision is different from what we see. And so is the act of consciousness different from that of which we are conscious. The ultimate philosophic trick is to learn to focus not on objects but on the consciousness itself that looks at objects. That is called an act of "self-reference" or of "reflection." It's a different form of thinking. It opens up the realm of pure consciousness for exploration. And that realm has the answers to all the great questions, such as God, immortality, free will, energy, personal power, and many more.

This realm, as important as it is difficult to talk about, is often connected with spirituality. In this philosophy, it is referred to as the *transcendental realm* and also the *transcendental consciousness* or the *transcendental ego.*

Transcendental Relationship.   When two or more people reflect on the nature of their relationship, important progress in interpersonal, team, and organizational behavior follows. When we relate to each other—love, fight, envy, compete, collaborate, interfere, promote, demote, recommend, do not recommend, and so on—we are in the engaged or natural attitude, and this is where typical people problems are located. To shift from engagement to reflection means to take a look at how we work together—studying cultures, systems, ways of being together and apart—and then to relate to one another on a higher plane, on the plane in which we think about how we relate. We ask not, "How shall we decide on this new strategy?" but instead, "Let's make a 'process check.' How are we doing? How do we feel about this meeting? Are we making progress? Should some sensitive issues be raised?" This tends to be an emotional experience, and it often resolves the interpersonal conflicts. It elevates human interaction to a more urbane, ethical, and rational level. The participants in that interaction now have among themselves a transcendental, not an empirical, relationship.

The Vitality of Death.   The material in *The Vitality of Death* (1971) and *New Image of the Person* (1978) that is not included in this book consists of two themes: spirituality and the scientific method.

Much in both of the early books consists of analyses of consciousness and its relevance to understanding both Western and Eastern religions. The additional topic excluded here is the rather crucial theoretical view that science works well not only in understanding the external world, but that it can also be applied—with a minimum of transformation—to the study of the inner world. This has major implications, both theoretical and practical.

The theoretical concerns the enormous need for solid researches on the nature and the structure of consciousness and its relationship to the world and our lives. This work includes the analysis of the mysterious connection between inner space and outer space, and the fact that inner and outer time seem to be the same. We add the curious consideration that phenomenological descriptions of inner space carried out by mystics are often indistinguishable from scientific descriptions of outer space developed by modern physicists, astronomers, and cosmologists. Thus, quantum physics can give us insights into the nature of our consciousness, just as the introspective examination of free will can give us insights about the behavior of subatomic particles.

The practical implications of expanding the scientific method in this way make philosophy more accessible to the technologically oriented general population. If the message gets out that philosophy is the scientific exploration of the inner world, as physics and medicine are the scientific explorations of the outer world, a breakthrough will have been achieved, in both religion on the one side and in psychosomatic medicine on the other.

Notes and Credits

Chapter 1

1. The work of Edmund Husserl [1859–1936] led to a descriptive theory of human existence—a philosophical anthropology—usually called "existentialism." Both the method and its ensuing theory have many of the characteristics of scientific inquiry: they represent a radical empiricism, an analysis of reality based exclusively on descriptions of the actually observed facts and structures of existence. Existential theory is useful to the behavioral sciences, since it is a more accurate (in a perfectly legitimate scientific sense) assessment of what it means to be human than what is provided by the traditional behavioral sciences.

Chapter 2

1. Editions Gallimard, *Situations III,* 1949. Published in English in Robert D. Cumming, *The Philosophy of Jean-Paul Sartre* (New York: Random House, 1965), pp. 232–233.

Chapter 4

1. Suggested by Medard Boss in *Psychoanalysis and Daseinsanalysis* (New York: Basic Books, 1963).

Chapter 5

1. S.A. Kierkegaard, *The Sickness Unto Death,* translated by W. Lowrie (Garden City, NY: Doubleday, 1955), p. 151.

Chapter 8

1. From "Dirge Without Music" by Edna St. Vincent Millay. *Collected Poems,* HarperCollins. Copyright © 1928, 1955 by Edna St. Vincent Millay and Norma Millay Ellis. All rights reserved. Reprinted by permission of Elizabeth Barnett, Literary Executor.

Chapter 9

1. Quoted in Albert Camus, *The Myth of Sisyphus,* trans. I. O'Brien (New York: Random House, 1959), p. 2.

Chapter 10

1. Excerpts from *Night* by Elie Wiesel, translated by Stella Rodway. Copyright © 1960 by MacGibbon & Kee. Copyright renewed © 1988 by The Collins Publishing Group. Copyright © 1958 by Les Editions de Minuit. Reprinted by permission of Hill and Wang, a division of Farrar, Straus and Giroux, LLC, and Les Editions de Minuit.
2. Excerpts from *Night* by Elie Wiesel, translated by Stella Rodway. Copyright © 1960 by MacGibbon & Kee. Copyright renewed © 1988 by The Collins Publishing Group. Copyright © 1958 by Les Editions de Minuit. Reprinted by permission of Hill and Wang, a division of Farrar, Straus and Giroux, LLC, and Les Editions de Minuit.

Chapter 11

1. This allusion is to Spranger's *Lebenstypen,* used in Gordon Allport, Philip Vernon, and Gardner Lindsey, *Scale of Values* (Boston: Houghton Mifflin, 1960).
2. This exercise is discussed at some length and with illustrations in Peter Koestenbaum, *Is There an Answer to Death?* (Englewood Cliffs, NJ: Prentice-Hall, 1976).

Chapter 13

1. A paraphrase of Rollo May, "What Is Our Problem?" *Review of Existential Psychology and Psychiatry* 3 (Spring 1963) p. 110. Used by permission of Georgia May.
2. Paul Tillich, *The Dynamics of Faith* (New York: Harper and Brothers, 1958), p. 3.

3. *Hamlet,* act 1, sc. 2, lines 129–134.
4. A. Kaplan, *The New World of Philosophy* (New York: Random House, 1961), p. 3.
5. Quoted in John O'Hara, *Appointment in Samarra* from *Sheppey* by W. Somerset Maugham. Copyright © 1933 by W. Somerset Maugham. Used by permission of Doubleday, a division of Random House, Inc.
6. "This Is Man," *A Stone, A Leaf, A Door: Poems by Thomas Wolfe.* Copyright © 1945 by Maxwell Perkins, Executor of the Estate of Thomas Wolfe. Copyright renewed © 1973 by Paul Gitlin, Administrator, C.T.A. of the Estate of Thomas Wolfe. Reprinted with the permission of Scribner, a Division of Simon & Schuster, Inc.

Further Reading

Block, P. (1987). *The empowered manager: Positive political skills at work.* San Francisco: Jossey-Bass.

Block, P. (1993). *Stewardship: Choosing service over self-interest.* San Francisco: Berrett-Koehler.

Block, P. (2000). *Flawless consulting: A guide to getting your expertise used* (2nd ed.). San Francisco: Jossey-Bass/Pfeiffer.

Block, P. (2001). *The answer to how is yes: Acting on what matters.* San Francisco: Berrett-Koehler.

Block, P., et al. (2001). *The flawless consulting fieldbook and companion: A guide to understanding your expertise.* San Francisco: Jossey-Bass/Pfeiffer.

Buber, M. (1996). *I and thou.* (W. Kaufman, trans.). New York: Touchstone.

Dreyfus, H.L. (1991). *Being in the world: A commentary on Heidegger's being and time, division I.* Cambridge, MA: MIT Press.

Gardner, H. (1993). *Frames of mind: The theory of multiple intelligences* (10th anniv. ed.). New York: Basic Books.

Husserl, E. (1976). *The Paris lectures.* (P. Koestenbaum, trans.). The Hague: Martinus Nijhoff.

Kierkegaard, S. (1986). *Fear and trembling* (reprint ed.). New York: Viking.

Kierkegaard, S. (1970). *The concept of dread.* (W. Lowrie, trans.). Princeton, NJ: Princeton University Press.

Koestenbaum, P. (1971). *The vitality of death: Essays in existential psychology and philosophy.* Westport, CT: Greenwood Publishing, 1971.

Koestenbaum, P. (1974). *Existential sexuality: Choosing to love.* Englewood Cliffs, NJ: Prentice-Hall.

Koestenbaum, P. (1974). *Managing anxiety: The power of knowing who you are.* Englewood Cliffs, NJ: Prentice-Hall.

Koestenbaum, P. (1976). *Is there an answer to death?* Englewood Cliffs, NJ: Prentice-Hall.

Koestenbaum, P. (1978). *The new image of the person: The theory and practice of clinical philosophy.* Westport, CT: Greenwood Press.

Koestenbuam, P. (1987). *The heart of business: Ethics, power, and philosophy.* Dallas, TX: Saybrook.

Koestenbaum, P. (1991). *Leadership: The inner side of greatness—A philosophy for leaders.* San Francisco: Jossey-Bass.

Koestenbaum, P., with Block, P. (2000). *The language of the Leadership Diamond®.* (Videotape). Santa Monica, CA: Philosophy-in-Business.

May, R., Ellenberger, H.F., & Angel, E. (Eds.). (1995). *Existence: A new dimension in psychiatry and psychology* (Reprint ed.). Northvale, NJ: Jacob Aronson.

Nietzsche, F. (1998). *The genealogy of morality.* (M. Clark and A.J. Swensen, trans.). Indianapolis, IN: Hackett.

Tillich, P. (2000). *The courage to be* (2d ed.). New Haven, CT: Yale University Press.

Yalom, I. (1980). *Existential psychotherapy.* New York: Basic Books.

Acknowledgments

It is very unusual for someone to study your earlier writings, consider them important, and then make the effort to bring them to a larger audience. That is what Peter Block has done here. He has selected the existential themes from my older books, culled from them what he deemed relevant, edited them for greater accessibility, and surrounded them with some very sensitive commentary. It was important to him that he do it. It was even more important to me that he did it.

How can one properly acknowledge such an undertaking? It is a magical mixture of friendship, ethics, loyalty, responsibility, meaning, and service. It is a clarion call to my conscience, holding me accountable to be worthy for the remainder of my days of such faith in the viability of these ideas—which are our common human heritage. I have no choice but to accept the challenge and to honor it.

The hope is that here is a service. All of us are partners in life, and whatever we can do to support one another will earn us our places under the sun. Plato taught us that all philosophic knowledge is recollection. Our joint reward will be that you, the reader, will discover powers within you that will see you through some of the more difficult moments of life.

—Peter Koestenbaum

I would like to give special appreciation to Leslie Stephen, who makes everything I write more readable and accessible. She instantly grasps what the book is about, is faithful to the author's voice, and cares deeply about the ideas. A wonderful combination. Also thanks to Maggie Rogers for making everything work with warmth and skill.

I want to also acknowledge Ken Murphy, who has supported me and my work for years, and who most recently risked bringing the ideas of philosophy into a Humanities for Human Resources series at Philip Morris. This was a time for all of us to be together and affirmed the place for depth and thought in modern corporations.

Finally, my appreciation goes to Audrey Heard, the wonderful artist whose painting (or at least a large segment of it) appears on the dust jacket of this book. Audrey paints and works in Westerly, Rhode Island. Her still lifes and landscapes are disciplined in form, extravagant in color and imagery. She is a very fine painter, and I am proud she accepted my invitation to be part of this book. Audrey can be reached at ach105@aol.com.

—Peter Block

About the Authors

Peter Koestenbaum's consulting practice goes back twenty-five years, running seminars, giving lectures, and doing individual leadership coaching. He has been close to business executives and their deepest concerns, sharing with them insights and feelings, new perspectives, and more serviceable adaptations.

His education was in physics, music, and, above all, philosophy. He earned a bachelor's degree in philosophy from Stanford University, a master's from Harvard University in philosophy, and a Ph.D. in philosophy from Boston University and also attended the University of California, Berkeley, to study music and philosophy.

He taught for thirty-four years in the Philosophy Department of San Jose State University, San Jose, California, where he received the Statewide Outstanding Professor Award. During those years, he also spent twenty-five years working with psychologists and psychiatrists exploring the relationship between psychiatry and the healing potential of philosophy.

Peter Koestenbaum decided to apply the insights he gained in philosophy and psychiatry to business: management, strategic thinking, and marketing—but above all to leadership. His primary concern throughout his career has been to develop philosophy-in-business as a bona fide profession undergirding the use of the behavioral sciences in business—covering not only personal and cultural matters, but also strategic and marketing topics.

This journey has taken Peter Koestenbaum to over forty countries on five continents. A sample of the companies with which he has worked extensively include Ford, IBM, Ciba-Geigy (now Novartis), Citibank, Volvo, Amoco, Xerox, and Electronic Data Systems (EDS), as well as one of the large Korean *Chaebols*.

Peter Koestenbaum can be reached through the Koestenbaum Institute, headquartered in Los Angeles and Stockholm, at rolf.falkenberg@telia.com, through the Philosophy-in-Business website: www.PiB.net (e-mail: info@PiB.net), or through his e-mail address at pkipeter@ix.netcom.com.

A comprehensive interview with Peter Koestenbaum can be accessed at www.fastcompany.com/online/32/koestenbaum.html.

Peter Block is an author, consultant, and speaker who helped initiate the interest in empowerment and whose work now centers on ways to bring service and accountability to organizations and communities.

He is the author of several best-selling books: *Flawless Consulting: A Guide to Getting Your Expertise Used,* Second Edition (1999), *The Empowered Manager: Positive Political Skills at Work* (1987), and *Stewardship: Choosing Service Over Self-Interest* (1993). *The Flawless Consulting Fieldbook and Companion: A Guide to Understanding Your Expertise,* by Peter Block and 30 Flawless Consultants, was released in November 2000. His most recent books are *Freedom and Accountability at Work: Applying Philosophic Insight to the Real World* (2001) and *The Answer to How Is Yes: Acting on What Matters* (2001).

Peter has his own consulting practice and is a partner in Designed Learning, a training company that offers consulting skills workshops. These workshops were designed by Peter to build the skills outlined in his books.

Peter has received several national awards for outstanding contribution in the field of training and development. He has served as a volunteer with the Association for Quality and Participation, Connecticut Public TV and Radio, and other local community agencies. He was a co-founder of the School for Managing and Leading Change, an intensive program to teach authentic, high engagement strategies for changing organizations.

He can be reached at pbi@att.net. His office is in Mystic, Connecticut.

Index

Founded by Peter Block, **Designed Learning** is a full service training and consulting organization existing to help organizations succeed at complex change. Through a variety of innovative ideas and technologies, we strive to help our client organizations support the transformation of staff people into effective internal consultants and consultant teams. **The Flawless Consulting Workshops** are a key element in our mission to help organizations build capacity and develop people for more successful, more meaningful work.

Flawless Consulting – Three hands-on, skill building workshops for internal and external consultants. These are the **only** consulting skills workshops developed by Peter Block, author of *Flawless Consulting* and *The Flawless Consulting Fieldbook and Companion*. To learn more about these workshops, call Designed Learning or visit the Flawless Consulting website at www.designedlearning.com.

Learn how to establish and maintain collaborative working relations with clients, which result in positive outcomes for the business. Learn how to have influence when you do not have control.

Flawless Consulting I: *Contracting*
- Develop commitment from your internal clients.
- Work more in a partnership role with client managers.
- Negotiate more effective and enduring working agreements with clients.
- Identify consulting phases and skills.
- Develop techniques for defining roles and responsibilities and clarifying expectations.
- Gain better use of staff expertise in the organization.
- Avoid no-win consulting situations.

Flawless Consulting II: *Discovery*
- Practice a data collection or discovery model.
- Conduct interviewing meetings to collect data around a business issue.
- Deal with client resistance.
- Gain skills in turning recommendations into a decision to act.
- Conduct a successful feedback meeting.
- Identify methods for mapping out action steps with the client prior to implementation.
- Increase line manager commitment and action.

Flawless Consulting III: *Implementation*

- Choose engagement over mandate and direction.
- Create a balance between presentation and participation.
- Break away from familiar refrains to create new conversations.
- Learn the eight steps that create meetings for greater engagement.
- Handle resistance and support public dissent.
- Develop authentic dialogue within the client organization.
- Focus on assets and gifts rather than weaknesses and deficiencies.

Other Designed Learning workshops:

The Empowered Manager Workshop: *Choosing Accountability—Making the Business Your Own*

The Stewardship Workshop: *Building Capacity—Deepening Customer Service*

The Conflict Workshop: *Managing Differences and Agreement—Making Conflict Work For You*

Staff Groups in the New Economy: *Transitioning from Staff Function to Consulting Service*

For more information contact:

Designed Learning Inc.
313 South Avenue, Suite 202
Fanwood, NJ 07023
Phone: (908) 889–0300
Email: *info@designedlearning.com*

Developing the Person at Work
Fax: (908) 889–4995
Website: *www.designedlearning.com*